GENDER AND THE WELFARE STATE

Care, Work and Welfare in
Europe and the USA

Mary Daly
and
Katherine Rake

polity

First published in 2003 by Polity Press in association with Blackwell Publishing Ltd

Editorial office:
Polity Press
65 Bridge Street
Cambridge CB2 1UR, UK

Marketing and production:
Blackwell Publishing Ltd
108 Cowley Road
Oxford OX4 1JF, UK

Distributed in the USA by
Blackwell Publishing Inc.
350 Main Street
Malden, MA 02148, USA

Library of Congress Cataloging-in-Publication Data

Daly, Mary.
Gender and the welfare state: care, work and welfare in Europe and the USA / Mary Daly and Katherine Rake.
p. cm.
Includes bibliographical references and index. ISBN 0-7456-2231-3 (alk. paper)—ISBN 0-7456-2232-1 (pbk.: alk. paper)
1. Family policy—Cross-cultural studies. 2. Women—Government policy—Cross-cultural studies. 3. Welfare state—Cross-cultural studies. 4. Social policy—Cross-cultural studies. I. Rake, Katherine. II. Title.
HV697 .D335 2003
361.6'5—dc21
2002015369

Typeset in 10.5 on 12pt. Sabon
by Kolam Information Services Pvt. Ltd, Pondicherry, India
Printed and bound in Great Britain by TJ International, Padstow, Cornwall

For further information on Polity, visit our website: www.polity.co.uk

Contents

List of Tables

List of Figures

Acknowledgements

Both authors would like to acknowledge the benefits of their stay in Summer 2000 at the Minda de Gunzberg Center for European Studies at Harvard University. We are particularly grateful to Professor Peter Hall in this context. We would also like to express our appreciation to Professors David Piachaud, Jane Lewis and Fiona Williams for their comments on an earlier draft of the text. The research assistance of Sara Clavero and Kikuka Kobatake is also gratefully acknowledged. Katherine Rake would like to acknowledge the support of STICERD throughout this project.

Introduction

Gender is one of the most fundamental cleavages in contemporary social life. While there is no denying that the last twenty years have seen major changes, inequalities between women and men persist in the public sphere, just as divisions continue in private life. Yet gender relations are at the centre of social reform, even though proposals for change are not always framed in these terms. For example, the reconciliation of work and family life, which is arguably one of the most important pressures underlying the redesign of social policies, is centrally concerned with the roles and relations of women and men. To know the significance and prospects of these and other reforms, it is essential to understand existing arrangements. We especially need a fuller sense of how the welfare state exists in women's and men's lives. We know intuitively that the welfare state is one of the most important social institutions, but, while considerable attention has been paid to how social policies affect financial well-being, there is too little coverage of how the welfare state influences the organization of everyday life.

Against this backdrop, this book focuses on gender differences and inequalities, especially in terms of how they are shaped by the welfare state across countries. The book is framed around one major question: how do welfare states affect gender relations? This question is elaborated theoretically and investigated empirically by an analysis that focuses on patterns internal to a number of countries as well as variations across them. Theoretically, the central question directs attention to societal processes, privileging the role of the welfare state in the construction of gender relations in society by virtue of how it affects care, work and welfare. Understood as both shaping of and shaped by gender relations, the role of the welfare state as it affects resource levels, the division of roles, and power relations between women and men is of especial interest. The book is informed by three core convictions about the welfare state and how it relates to gender. First, one cannot acquire a comprehensive understanding of the welfare state without recognizing that norms and values concerning gender relations are a part of all welfare policies and practices. Second, gender relations are, in part anyway, products of public arrangements for welfare. Third, welfare states directly or indirectly affect gender relations by virtue of how they impact on the nature and distribution of resources, social roles and power relations. We treat of these and other issues in a comparative manner, studying the following eight countries: France, Germany, Ireland, Italy, the Netherlands, Sweden, the UK and USA. The juxtaposition of these country cases will be used to reveal similarities and differences among countries that have been carefully chosen to reveal the causal fabric of the relationship between gender and the welfare state.

The welfare state is broadly conceived in this book in terms of the content of social policy and the processes set in train by it. While state programmes and services have been well studied from a gender perspective, research has rarely considered how welfare states affect social and economic processes and bring about certain (gendered) outcomes. To examine and explain the impact of the welfare state on gender relations, it is necessary to move beyond formal rules and written policy to take account of the processes that are brought about by policy. For example, putting in place a cash payment for those caring for young children activates a series of decisions on the part of individual parents about the way they live their lives and, at a broader level, affects the nature of other policy on caring, the view of care that prevails in society, and the construction of other groups' claims to benefits. The most widely studied aspect of the welfare state is income redistribution. We too focus on this, but augment the discussion by adopting a broader understanding of the agency of welfare policies. We argue that the conditions attaching to benefits and services can fundamentally affect (and reflect) the relative power of women and men. This aspect of the welfare state's activity is to be seen in how it affects patterns of control and relations of authority. One could on the basis of this conceive of the welfare state as a regime of power. As well as thinking in terms of power relations, we are interested in how the welfare state is embedded in society. This spells a concern with the interaction between the welfare state, the family and the market. Hence we bring to the foreground what in other work is considered as context or setting. This is especially the case in relation to the family.

If the welfare state is one focus of interest, gender relations is the other. This term has to be used with care; the more familiar term 'gender' tends now to lack a specific set of references because it is used in a very general way. Apart from its descriptive currency, 'gender' can refer to a set of structural properties in society or to a form of agency. 'Gender relations', as we use the term, incorporates both of these meanings. It embeds women and men in the relationships within which they live their lives and, secondly, emphasizes dynamic processes. Our view of gender relations incorporates an interest in the specific situation of women as well as sets of differences and inequalities between women and men. In the pages that follow, we elaborate a threefold concept of gender relations to encompass resources, roles and power. Hence we consider that the relationship between gender and the welfare state comprises material, normative and behavioural elements associated with relations of power. It will be obvious that we are attributing to the welfare state a much broader influence than is usually the case. Inspired by feminist work, we anticipate that the welfare state reaches deep into people's lives. One of the ways it does this is by affecting the options open to women and men and the conditions under which they assume their respective roles at different stages of their life course, especially in regard to relative power relations. It will be obvious that our notion of gender relations crosses spheres and that we are trying to bring together the public and the private. Qualitative aspects are as important as quantitative aspects.

This set of interests poses the challenge of identifying the interconnections between gender relations and the welfare state. To bring such interconnections to life, we have chosen three lenses that are at once primary spheres of life and fundamentally defining of the quality of social life. These three lenses are care, work and welfare. The welfare state's activities are to be observed in these three domains as regards how people organize for care, work and welfare, and indeed how these are organized for them by the welfare state and other social institutions. What is attractive about care, work and welfare is that each has a purchase at both micro level – being the main axes around which people organize their everyday lives – and macro level – as key societal needs and functions. Care will be observed in terms of the conditions under which the activity of caring for children and the elderly is carried out. Work opens up an analysis of the presence and situation of women and men in the labour market as well as divisions between paid and unpaid work. Welfare leads to an analysis of the distribution of resources along gender lines (for both families and individuals).

The primary literature to which we address ourselves in this book is the feminist scholarship on the welfare state and gender relations. We draw upon the strengths of this literature. Such strengths historically lay in an interest in theorizing, especially in regard to patriarchy and relations of power between women and men. Interactions in the 'private' sphere were seen as conditioned by, and reflective of, a broader set of power relations. A second strength was the elaboration of everyday processes of social life, bringing out the importance of the seemingly ordinary. Within the context of welfare state scholarship, this meant an exploration of how welfare was realized in practice, women's contribution to it, and the consequences for women's lives. A focus on the micro level led the scholarship to an appreciation of social relations. That is, it demonstrated how gender roles were subject to constant negotiation and renegotiation.

Recent scholarship has developed in a way that has tended to overlook these strengths. We attribute this, in part anyway, to the fact that, rather than following its own organic process of development, feminist scholarship has taken its impetus from developments in conventional welfare state scholarship. Theorizing has been downplayed, and individuals and other social actors have tended to be disembedded from their social setting in an analysis that focuses on key structural characteristics of welfare states. Furthermore, power relations between women and men as they are to be seen in the functioning of the welfare state have been neglected. Too little attention is devoted to how welfare state services and benefits are empowering or disempowering of women and men. The methodological approach has also altered. In comparative welfare state studies, for example, much endeavour has been oriented to building typologies. This is an approach that tends to underplay complexity and overemphasize consistency and comparability. In addition, constructing typologies runs the risk of conceptualizing the welfare state in such a way that the actual functions and operation of social policies are lost from view. Our methodology, by contrast, is attuned to the significance of the welfare state in people's lives.

A comparative approach is integral to our method. Such an approach serves a number of functions. It is, as Castles (1989: 9) points out, a way of locating and exploring a phenomenon as yet insufficiently understood. This work, therefore, aims to investigate the forms taken by the relationship between gender and the welfare state under different national conditions. In detailing gender differences and divisions in the spheres of care, work and welfare across eight countries, the text responds to the lack of sustained empirical investigation in much of the existing work. A comparative approach also helps to order the search for explanation, because it interweaves an analysis of both generality and specificity. A prime interest on our part is to try and identify whether there are general forms of the relationship between the welfare state and gender. Empirically, the book is guided also by a consideration of what is distinctive about each country in the light of comparative similarities.

In opting for a comparative approach, this book is in line with the trend in welfare state scholarship that has for a decade or more been strongly cross-national. It is timely to raise questions about the nature and quality of the comparative research that has been carried out. This has tended to be polarized into two types. On the one hand there are the 'many country' works that, in an effort to manage a large number of cases, usually focus on a few narrow measures of welfare state activity. This kind of approach leads to work that generalizes very widely – for example, about the nature of the link between the welfare state and particular political and economic structures. At the other pole is research focused on a small number of countries, treating each country as a case study. A problem for comparative social science is that there has been too little work that falls between these two extremes. Against this background, this study explores a middle comparative way between the highly quantitative (many countries, few variables) and the highly qualitative (few countries, many variables) approaches.

Eight countries are investigated, chosen for their diversity and to control for key aspects of variation in regard to the welfare state and gender relations. The countries are France, Germany, Ireland, Italy, the Netherlands, Sweden, the UK and USA. These represent a broad range of welfare states, including at least one exemplar from the now standard differentiation made by the literature between the Nordic, continental, liberal and Mediterranean welfare state models (Esping-Andersen 1990; Leibfried 1990; Ferrera 1996). Sweden represents the Nordic 'welfare society' approach. The Swedish state is highly interventionist, and places a strong emphasis on gender equality. To explore the diverse set of features of the continental European welfare state type, we have chosen to study France, Germany and the Netherlands. Across these three countries, welfare is very closely tied to work, a linkage that tends to marginalize care. A heavy reliance on social insurance rewards a typically male pattern of lifetime employment tying benefit entitlement closely to labour market status. Significant variation nevertheless exists between the three, most notably in terms of support of women's employment opportunities. Although there are very significant differences among them, Ireland, the UK and the USA resemble each other to the extent that they share a liberal approach to social policy, with income transfer systems that are oriented above all to the prevention of poverty. Welfare therefore has a public character (although less so in the USA), but care is primarily a matter of private relations. Our other country, Italy, represents another 'mixed' model. In a general context of limited welfare state intervention, work and welfare are partly matters for the state and the public authorities, but care is almost totally a private good, located first and foremost in the family.

In the chapters that follow, we work systematically through a set of evidence about the relationship between the welfare state and gender in these countries. Information is assembled from a wide variety of sources. We have always sought the most up-to-date information and could be judged to have succeeded in this, given that most of it is recent. In addition, we undertake many new analyses, especially availing ourselves of the Luxembourg Income Study (LIS) data base to identify the financial situation of women and men in different countries and the role played by the welfare state in income redistribution and poverty alleviation.[1] While we rely considerably on quantitative information, we seek to draw out also the qualitative dimensions. Care, work and welfare are not for us quantitative in nature, but rather qualitative, especially in terms of the patterns of relations and behaviour to which they give rise.

The book is organized into eight chapters. The first two introduce the research by setting out some of the most relevant work on the topic and, in the light of this, elaborating our own framework. The first chapter reviews how the key topics have been approached by existing work. It organizes the discussion in terms of the main problematic of the book rather than, for example, undertaking a general literature review. Hence it considers how the welfare state and its relationship to gender have been conceptualized in work to date. The insights of the comparative literature are also outlined. Because of the tendency in existing work to treat the welfare state as a set of properties rather than an agent or force for change in society, we devote some attention in this chapter to work that has a more dynamic focus. This leads us to consider approaches that are organized around, on the one hand, the life course and, on the other, the making of claims.

Having considered the work of others, in the second chapter we elaborate our own framework, drawing on and developing some of the existing work as well as setting out new ideas. The chapter more or less replicates the concerns of the first in addressing four issues. First is the definition of the welfare state. The second part focuses on gender relations, describing how we define this concept and how we observe gender relations across the eight countries. Discussion in the third part of the chapter concentrates on the relationship between these two key concepts. The fourth part turns to matters of comparison, outlining our approach to comparison as well as setting out a justification for the selection of country cases.

The following four chapters employ this framework to examine key aspects of the relationship between the welfare state and gender in the different national settings. They are organized on the basis of the three lenses of care, work and welfare (with two chapters devoted to the latter). These four chapters follow a roughly similar format. They start out by introducing the topic, paying attention to how the welfare state might be thought of in relation to whichever domain is the focus of the chapter. The middle, and largest, part of each chapter explores the relationship empirically, while the last part is devoted to a discussion of power relations and contests that are embodied in the set of activities or sphere that is the focus of the chapter.

Chapter 3 concentrates on care. Its initial focus is on public policies around care. These are shown to be complex and to vary widely across countries. Having set out the policy background, the chapter moves on to consider key features of the social organization of care. These include the volume of informal care and the conditions under which this and paid care are carried out. Some of the implications of being a carer are then investigated. Mothers of young children are the focus for this purpose. Their labour market participation as well as their financial situation are examined in turn. The contests around care and the power relations involved in it form the chapter's third and final theme.

Work is the topic of the fourth chapter. Having set out some key aspects of the relationship between the welfare state and paid work, the chapter undertakes a detailed analysis of gender inequalities and differences in the labour market. Among the issues considered are women's access to the labour force, some qualitative aspects of women's relationship to paid work, and how the welfare state is associated with gender differences in the structure of the labour market. Earnings as well as the implications of participation in paid work for male and female roles are illuminated in these analyses. In its penultimate section the chapter sets out some key contests that arise in the domain of employment.

The fifth chapter centres on the welfare state and income. The redistribution of resources is explored through an analysis of gender differentials in income and poverty. For this purpose, households headed by women are compared with those headed by men. A detailed investigation of income levels and risk of poverty among two critical groups of households – those headed by lone mothers and those of women in later life – then follows. Taken together, this analysis serves to answer questions about how women and men are integrated into the economic order, the extent to which women can maintain households without a male income, and the significance of the mechanisms used by the welfare state to deliver support to women and men as heads of households. As with other chapters, attention in the final section is devoted to a discussion of some contested issues relevant to welfare and income.

Chapter 6 explores the distribution of resources within the family. Women's and men's personal access to resources, the autonomy exercised by them over their use of time, and the balance of resources within households are all explored in turn. In directing the empirical gaze to the individual, this analysis moves beyond conventional practice. It will enable us to make statements about the division of resources in what is customarily treated as the private sphere. Money and time are the two resources considered. The final matter for empirical consideration is the family's role in redistributing resources between women and men. In this and other ways, the family is recognized as an important site of redistribution and a place in which gender inequalities and conflict may exist.

Chapter 7 draws on the information presented in each of the preceding four chapters to present a composite picture of each country, as well as to explore patterning in how gender and the welfare state are related across countries. It first characterizes the national situation in the eight countries through an analysis that integrates care, work and welfare. Attention then turns to the cross-national picture and to similarities and differences among them. Drawing out similarities allows for an exploration of how countries cluster into cross-national patterns, whereas the exploration of key differences highlights the factors that are unique within and across nations. A further section goes on to analyse the significance of these similarities and differences in explaining variation.

The concluding chapter develops the main issues raised by both the theoretical and conceptual discussions and the empirical findings. Such issues are seen to be of two main types. In the first part of the chapter, we draw out some insights from our work for the study of how gender and the welfare state are related. This is followed by a consideration of the value of the comparative methodology adopted and a contrast between our findings and those of other comparative welfare state research. Our work also has implications for policy and policy development across nations. These are drawn out in the second part of the chapter in terms of the pressure points around care, work and welfare and a discussion of the political contests relating to them.

Through this we explore future policy challenges across the eight welfare states.

A list of references and a technical appendix follow. The technical appendix explains the key features of the LIS data base and how it was used for the analyses presented in chapters 5 and 6.

1

Studying the Welfare State and Gender: The Insights of Existing Work

This chapter introduces the main literature on the welfare state and gender. This has been quite a polarized literature. Historically, scholarship on the welfare state, fashioned in the main by political scientists and social policy analysts, paid little or no attention to gender. As is the case with other areas, it was only when a feminist lens was turned on the welfare state that its gender dimensions were unveiled. The split between mainstream and feminist literatures is now so familiar that a conventional review of the literature would be rather hackneyed.[1] Rather than going through each of the main works or providing a chronological account, we adopt in this chapter a more innovative and instrumental approach. A review of literature is normally conducted with the aim of familiarizing the reader with how the topic has been approached and underlining the distinctiveness of one's own approach. Our intent here is less one of acquainting the reader with the key approaches and more one of engaging with the literature for the purpose of developing a satisfactory approach to the subject matter. Four themes structure the chapter:

- how the welfare state has been conceptualized;
- how gender and the relationship between it and the welfare state have been understood;
- how agency can and has been considered;
- how comparison has been undertaken and organized.

We will draw from a broad set of literature – the gender-focused work, what can be labelled the 'conventional welfare state literature', and that falling into neither category.

1.1   Conceptualizing the Welfare State

The welfare state has been interpreted by three main literatures: social policy, political economy and feminist. The first literature, which developed mainly in Great Britain, problematizes the way in which the rule of law is translated into policy, and policy in turn is put into practice. Guided by an interest in administrative matters and how problems can be solved by specific types of policy response, this literature compartmentalizes social policy into particular fields, such as health, education, housing and so forth. As a result, the social policy approach lacks an overarching concept of the welfare state. The underdevelopment of theory within the discipline generally has not helped. Social policy has concerned itself most with delivery and what happens to policies as they are implemented, i.e. social administration (Donnison et al. 1975; Brown 1985; Glennerster 1985). This has led to particular types of research interests. Managerialism, the delivery of social services, and the degree of professionalism among staff are strong themes. A view of social intervention as a benign process pervades this literature, especially the early work (Tawney 1931; Titmuss 1974). Resource distribution has been another interest of the social policy approach. Social services, as well as the system of welfare benefits and taxes, are examined for their impact on incomes and opportunities. This has led to a body of work that explores poverty and inequality and shows society to be riven by division (Townsend 1979; Le Grand 1982; Hills 1995). Social policy, on this interpretation, is intricately involved in a range of social cleavages and in privileging some sectors of the population. A further body of social policy analysis has focused on the regulatory functions of policy. This type of work examines how welfare acts to regulate people's lives: the receipt of welfare is shown to exert control over behaviour, and welfare professionals are portrayed as agents of social control. This view depicts those who deliver welfare services as acting in their own interests or in the interests of the state (Piven and Cloward 1972; Ginsburg 1979; Lipsky 1980).

The social policy approach excels on the small detail of policy, and has proved that the implementation of measures cannot be read off from legislative content or indeed political intent. This literature, which has long had an interest in outcomes and effects, has, in addition, given a rich account of the experiences of those at the receiving end of public support.[2] In considerable contrast, the departure point of the political economy approach, the second set of literature on the welfare state, is the organization and politics of welfare in capitalist societies.

The political economy approach focuses on the influence of politics and political actors in the context of an organized welfare state. Not only does it connect democracy and capitalism, it holds democracy to be a necessary condition for the existence and functioning of developed welfare states. An early advocate viewed the welfare state as an almost inevitable product of the maturation of democratic societies, with welfare provision, in turn, enhancing citizenship and democratic participation (Marshall 1950, 1964). Against the backdrop of a long-term interest in explaining the growth and development of the welfare state, a more recent literature has sought to theorize welfare state reform as a distinct process (Pierson 1994; Taylor-Gooby and Svallfors 1999; Bonoli et al. 2000). The influence of ideology, and of particular political actors such as political parties, trade unions and employers' groups have been prioritized as an explanation of the welfare state (Furniss and Tilton 1977; Shalev 1983; Korpi 1989). This view leaves no doubt but that the welfare state involves relations of power, and the approach has been particularly concerned with stratification along class lines. Comparison has been the lifeblood here. Focusing on international welfare state variation, scholarship highlights that there is no one way of organizing welfare. This is a literature that is not centrally concerned with the nuts and bolts of policy, however. Rather, its interest lies in how the welfare state embodies and activates a range of economic and political interests. Theorizing the form of the welfare state within and across societies is a special concern. If the social policy literature focuses on resource distribution as it affects welfare, then that on political economy finds redistribution interesting because it influences a series of power balances in society. Here is its political science lineage at work.

Feminist scholarship, too, offers a set of insights about how the welfare state is to be conceived. It has highlighted especially the norms and assumptions that are embedded in welfare policy and provision. In this and other ways it provides a counterpoint to the conventional work. While feminists were not the first to consider the normative architecture of policy, their work serves to reveal how ideology pervades social provision. Gender norms are to be seen in how social programmes assume and reinforce a family breadwinner role for men and a maternal, wifely, caring role for women (Shaver

1991). The work undertaken on the British welfare state has been especially good at dissecting individual programmes to reveal how their conditions of entitlement and ways of operating are infused with gender-related norms, beliefs and assumptions (Land 1978, 1989; Lewis 1992; Lister 1992). To the extent that a similar emphasis was present in US scholarship, it has been realized by tracing the development of programmes over time (Koven and Michel 1990; Skocpol 1992; Gordon 1994; Mink 1995). This approach shows how ideologies and discourses, especially those pertaining to motherhood, have informed social policy making over the long haul (see section 1.2.2 below). Some feminist work has, therefore, suggested that the welfare state should be conceptualized in more micro terms than has been the case with the political economy approach. The content of welfare state programmes, such as the conditions governing entitlement and the unit to which benefits and services are directed, has been shown to have a huge impact on the welfare of individuals and on relations of power within families and society. A related insight of feminist work has been the significance of welfare state services. These are held to be deserving of study in their own right. Not necessarily revealed by the structure of cash transfers, they are of immense significance for the distribution of women's time between care and work.

The agency dimensions of the welfare state emerge prominently in feminist work. Ideological as well as other forms of welfare state agency, especially at the individual level, are emphasized. More than any other, feminist work has sought to bring the welfare state to life – to reveal it as a presence in women's lives. There have been two strands here. The first, predominantly Scandinavian scholarship, draws attention to the special relationship between women and the welfare state. Helga Hernes (1987) and other feminists have suggested that women's lives are more dependent upon and determined by state policies than are those of men. They elaborate the nature of women's closeness to the state in terms of three sets of relations: as citizens, employees and clients. Nancy Fraser's (1989) work could also be seen as developing an understanding of the welfare state as a political presence in the lives of women. Focusing on the ideology of, and discourses around, welfare, Fraser reveals that the needs of means-tested benefit recipients (most of whom are women) are not met on their own terms but are framed within categories developed by the welfare state, categories that are themselves gendered. While juridical, administrative and therapeutic procedures make the interpretation of needs appear to be non-political, they result in women being treated as dependent clients or subjects and, as the majority of recipients of means-tested benefits, open to intrusive activity by welfare bureau-crats (Fraser 1989: 154).

However, this political view of the welfare state has tended to eclipse the redistributive agency of social policies. In other words, the analysis has for the most part examined the principles of provision rather than identifying how these translate into actual transfers of resources. As a consequence, too little information exists on the welfare state as a redistributor of financial and other resources be-tween women and men. Another shortcoming of much feminist work is that it has been rather weak on acknowledging and studying change. This may have to do with the relatively fixed notion of interests that underlies the scholarship. It is difficult to register change, especially improvement, when operating with a conception of the welfare state as serving either men's interests or those of capitalism.

Summarizing the insights of these different literatures, the welfare state could be said to be the social face of the state. It is to be understood as a particular state form, whereby the public authorities garner resources and assume responsibility for organizing their redis-tribution. The functioning of the welfare state is ultimately dependent on, and indeed is the result of, the organizational forms associated with advanced capitalism. The family is integral to such forms, as are, of course, democracy and the market. At the most basic level, the welfare state provides income and resources to individuals and fam-ilies. The overall objectives of welfare state intervention are more varied than this, however, and may include reducing poverty, redis-tributing resources (income or material resources as well as oppor-tunities), providing security and welfare, organizing private and public life. Another set of welfare state activities relates to the organ-ization for service provision, especially health, education and social services. Furthermore, the welfare state involves the creation of a bureaucracy, to be understood not just as a body of personnel but as a set of rules and procedures. These rules and practices, which are given life in the conditions attaching to benefits or services, are value-laden and rich in assumptions about social life (including the appro-priate roles of women and men). They are therefore an important social statement in their own right. They have a significance also in regard to the processes they set in train. The rules governing entitle-ment lead people through a process of claiming and, should they be deemed entitled, into a relationship with the state and its representa-tives that extends into society itself.

1.2 The Relationship between the Welfare State and Gender

Having considered alternative conceptualizations of the welfare state, we now turn our attention to the theoretical frameworks within which the relationship between gender and the welfare state has been cast. This has been considered mainly by feminist literature. While conventional scholarship now integrates the family more readily into its work (e.g. Esping-Andersen 1999), gender is not part of the theoretical framework, and empirical consideration of gender is largely limited to how welfare states operate to affect the family. Feminist scholarship offers a far more complex conceptualization of the relationship between the welfare state and gender. It could be said to have used two overriding frameworks: the state and patriarchal political relations on the one hand, and family, care and social relations on the other. Although these literatures developed in tandem, they will be treated as distinct for the purposes of review.

1.2.1   The welfare state and political relations of gender

An interest in theorizing patriarchy as a system of political relations was one of the original themes in feminist work. Indeed, patriarchy in feminist hands rivalled the analysis of capitalism in conventional scholarship. Different forms of power relations between women and men have provided an overriding focus. The welfare state is conceptualized as part of, and party to, a broader set of power structures in society which act, primarily but not exclusively, to perpetuate male power. Work on patriarchy has been illuminating on several different counts, especially in terms of the questions it posed. An understanding of patriarchal relations as embodied by the welfare state emphasizes the social control and regulatory functions of the welfare state and how these are exercised over women. Challenging a benevolent view, the welfare state is represented as a site of power relations, the experience of receiving welfare a process of social control and regulation especially from a patriarchal perspective. In contrast to the conventional literature's emphasis on society-wide power relations, this perspective brings power relations among individuals to light. Wilson (1977), for example, charts how the state acts to control women by discriminating against them and prescribing for them the role of mother. She argues that understanding the welfare state requires an appreciation of its actions in relation to the family and how it provides support in a fashion that reinforces an ideology of the traditional family. In her view, 'social welfare policies amount to no less than the State organisation of domestic life' (Wilson 1977: 9). Not only are gender-related control processes enacted by social policy, the welfare state is seen to play a role in more general forms of social regulation. Williams (1989, 1995) expands the analysis of the welfare state's policing function to incorporate control along racial lines. Scholars have also tried to establish links between the structure of the welfare state and the form and nature of political relations. Questions are raised about whose interests are served by the welfare state, and in particular whether men benefit from it at the expense of women. This line of analysis queries, for example, whether the principles of entitlement to benefits are such that they construct different social rights for women and men (Sainsbury 1996). Two themes are apparent: how social security privileges men and male power over women; how social services are organized in such a way as to supplement, rather than supplant, women's unpaid work. The two-track welfare state – a set of rights-based insurance arrangements for men and means-tested benefits primarily for women – has been an insight of this scholarship (Fraser 1989; Nelson 1990).

A related focus of feminist work, especially that of political theorists, is the public–private divide. Such a split reserves the public, political sphere for men and the private sphere for women, and functions as a mechanism to exclude women from the body politic. Analysis of the division of public from private serves especially to highlight its political significance as well as its changing nature historically (Okin 1979; Eisenstein 1981; Elshtain 1981). The split between public and private is said to be a split between the state and family, a fissure between production and reproduction (Showstack Sassoon 1987: 165). One consequence, it is argued, is that men have been able to create the state and the welfare state in their own image. Overall, while the public–private split has not given rise to a large body of theory, the concept has been useful in problematizing boundaries which might otherwise be taken as natural. It is informed by the view that all welfare state intervention is political and can be located in relation to the divide between public and private life.

Citizenship has provided a further frame for scholarship on the political relations of gender. By bringing the nation-state to the fore and focusing on the relationship between the state, collectivities and individuals, citizenship reveals what it means to be a member of the community bounded by national law and public provision. The concept contains a direct line of analysis to resource flows and resource distribution, and hence to the welfare state, because at least part of what it means to be a citizen is defined in terms of rights of access to social services and public resources. In particular, in collectivizing certain sets of resources and removing them from the free play of market forces, social citizenship establishes a counter-logic of exchange to that prevailing in the market. Citizenship marks inclusion in or exclusion from the national community and is therefore a major line of differentiation. Feminist analysis has found rich terrain in the problematic nature of female citizenship. Pateman (1988), for example, shows how both the potential routes of full citizenship for women – attaching rights to work or to care – are impossible to achieve within the confines of a patriarchal welfare state.[3] Citizenship not only connotes the quantitative but also speaks to qualitative aspects of identity in so far as they are constituted by membership of the state and the privileges and responsibilities attaching to that. Its main comparative potential lies in the extent to which it can problematize the link between political participation and representation and access to social benefits. While women's political participation and representation have been identified as markers of women's access to citizenship, questions remain about whether women use political power to pursue 'women-friendly' policies (Skjeie 1991; Phillips 1998; Bergqvist et al. 1999; Siim 2000).

1.2.2   The state, care, social relations and the family

Feminist work on care, social relations and the family offers an alternative theoretical approach to the welfare state. We refer here to a literature that includes work on the provision and receipt of personal services to meet care needs. This is another way of seeing how welfare state programmes shape the lives of women and men. This literature places emphasis on the quality of social intervention and how welfare states influence social relations within and outside the family. This is to some extent a counterpoint to the view of the welfare state as a set of patriarchal relations, in that the welfare state is seen as contributing to, but not necessarily determining, social relations. While power relations are included in this work, there is a tendency also to emphasize interdependence over oppression as characterizing social relations. This work is somewhat more open towards the impact of the welfare state, in that it (a) enquires into the nature of power relations rather than assuming them to be patriarchal, and (b) locates the welfare state's agency in a complex set of social relations.

   Care has been identified as a somewhat unique social phenomenon, one that slips between the tight categories of the social sciences (Graham 1983: 14). Closely related to welfare, care has been defined in broad terms to encompass the range of human experiences associated with feeling concern for, and taking charge of, the well-being of others (Graham 1983: 13). The scholarship has been quite multi-dimensional, drawing attention to the labour involved in care, care giving as a constituent part of women's identity and the emotional dimensions of care.[4] Far more than paid and unpaid services, care has been elaborated as located in relations that are characterized by personal ties of obligation, commitment, trust and loyalty. The distinctiveness of care as a model of social relations is emphasized in a literature that elaborates care as a social as well as an ethical practice. In the latter regard, care is developed as a set of values to guide human agency in a variety of social fields (Sevenhuijsen 2000). While this work does not always start with the welfare state, it usually has something important to say about how the welfare state engages with (the generic activity of) care. In fact, the welfare state's influence is huge. Not only does it serve to define the location of care, it exerts singular influence on whether care is paid or unpaid and on the general conditions under which it is carried out and experienced.

This is one of the few areas of welfare state scholarship that has emphasized the relational elements of the welfare state – social programmes are represented as responding to people within the context of their social relations and as helping to shape what constitute appropriate roles and behaviour. This literature has also served to draw together the analyses of the family, the community and the state, demonstrating how these have imprinted on them the social and economic relations that shape women's position and the kind of labour they perform (Graham 1983: 22–3). Scholarship has in particular acted to uncover many of the 'welfare-conferring' activities of the informal sector. Thinking in terms of care opens up a way of analysing links between the welfare state and the family on the one hand and the welfare state and the community or voluntary sector on the other. In turn, it offers a new perspective on the reasons for the welfare state, suggesting that the social organization of care rivals the management of employment-related risks as an explanation for welfare state development (Jenson 1997). A further advantage is that care as a generic activity helps to transcend spheres conventionally defined as distinct (such as the family and the market). Hence, care can be employed to trace patterns across spheres. Care has a third advantage, in utilizing a defining feature of women's lives to undertake a broader analysis of the social organization of welfare. Moreover, it does this in a way that is sensitive to agency, bringing care givers and care receivers to life as active agents.

While care incorporates activities other than the care of children, it is not surprising that motherhood has been a predominant theme of feminist work on the welfare state. Motherhood, or rather the social construction of motherhood, has enabled feminists to make comparisons between welfare states as far apart as those of Sweden and the USA (Skocpol 1992; Gordon 1994; Mink 1995; Gornick et al. 1997; Gornick 1999). Welfare states have been analysed in terms of how policies have constructed women as mothers and have endorsed maternalism as an ideology. In the hands of historians, this has involved the search for what Mink calls the 'maternalist idiom' in social policy (1995: 174). Gordon (1994) identifies maternalism as an ideology that incorporates many different interpretations, having been used as an argument for mothers' employment or for protecting women's role in the home. This maternal theme is also uppermost in work on the analysis of welfare state variation in terms of breadwinner models (Lewis 1992, 1997a). Welfare states are compared and contrasted in terms of how they treat mothers, and in particular whether they regard women as mothers or workers (Leira 1992). Lone motherhood has been a specific sub-theme of this literature. In contemporary analysis, the study of lone mothers is seen as revelatory of how welfare states treat women (Hobson 1994; Duncan and Edwards 1997; Lewis 1997b).

While one might expect a focus on motherhood to connote a family-centred analysis, this is not the case. Apart from some work in the early days, the family has not been theorized in its own right in feminist work on the welfare state. Mary McIntosh (1978) provides one of the few theoretical considerations of how the welfare state's gendered effects are centrally linked to its treatment of the family. In quite a functionalist analysis, she interprets the welfare state as propping up the traditional family form. Other than this, feminist work has tended to focus on particular family relations rather than the family as a whole. Feminists have always had reservations about the family, fearing that analysis serves to reify it as a collective unit. Hence the family has tended to be in the background of much feminist work – the family-related roles of women (e.g. mother, wife) have been taken as the point of departure, rather than the family *per se*. It may be that the family is making an appearance in its own right, however. Daly (2000) integrates the family into the conceptualization of the welfare state and examines how social programmes affect the well-being of the family and the distribution of resources among individual members. In addition, a burgeoning literature from feminist economics studies how economic inequalities are worked out within the family through bargaining or co-operative conflict (Sen 1990; Agarwal 1997).

Overall, feminist work, whether focused on political or social relations, has been informed by a strong theoretical sense of either the state or the welfare state. Its interest in theorizing has been realized to greatest effect in work on patriarchy, citizenship and care. The approach taken to the state and gender relations has been critical. Certain fundamentals about the relationship between the welfare state and gender are revealed. The welfare state is shown to be systematically (although not uniformly) engaged in, or associated with, relations of power between women and men. The welfare state, secondly, embodies a set of interests, whether these are viewed as emanating from the interests of men, those of the nation-state, or actors associated with capitalism. Welfare provision is therefore a process of control and regulation. The theoretical limitations of feminist work on the welfare state are in some ways to be understood in terms of the limitations of its core concept, patriarchy. Patriarchy has been something of a theoretical strait-jacket. In offering a unidimensional analysis of social relations in terms of dominance and subordination, patriarchy provides no terms for examining the relations among women as a differentiated group. It has, in addition, blinkered scholars, so that the exercise of other forms of power in the welfare state and the possibility that the welfare state has emancipatory effects for women have been overlooked. To some extent, though, feminist work has itself provided a corrective to this tendency, for it has within it a dialogue concerning the strengths and shortcomings of early work. The care literature, for example, emphasizes social relations, interdependence and connectedness, and elaborates women's relationship to the welfare state in terms of three roles (as citizens, employees, clients), thereby serving to place the qualitative aspects of welfare state provision side by side with its more quantitative dimensions.

1.3 Developing an Agency Perspective on the Welfare State and Gender Relations

The work considered to date does not provide all the co-ordinates needed for a satisfactory conceptualization of the relationship between the welfare state and gender. For one thing, the agency or dynamic aspects of this relationship, while adverted to by different perspectives, have not been developed sufficiently. Secondly, the temporal dimension has been more or less omitted. In this section, therefore, we want to draw attention to two sets of literature that offer some relevant insights.[5] We refer to the literatures on claims making and the life course.

1.3.1   Claims making

The claims-making perspective rests on an understanding of welfare as a source of contest and political struggle. The main proponents of a claims-related perspective on welfare are Peattie and Rein (1983).[6] These authors are concerned to develop the language and vocabulary of a theory of claims, especially for the purposes of describing political economy at the level of the individual and the household. Peattie and Rein's work connects macro and micro in that, while claims and claiming have an individual aspect, claims originate in particular sets of norms and values and are processed through a series of social conventions and systems of legal and customary entitlements (1983: 20). Their conceptual treasury consists of claims, claims packages, claims systems, claims rationales and the process of claiming. While they do not explicitly define them, they imply that claims are a set of demands that are institutionalized in social roles. Claims confer, along with income, position and status. Claims can be stable or unstable (in that the amount of resources subject to stable claims varies across societies). Claims packages consist of a unique assemblage of claims that a household (or any unit) puts together in order to maximize its welfare within a given claims system. A system of claims is part of social convention, or an always evolving system of power relations. Peattie and Rein identify three realms within which claims are generated and honoured: government, family and market.[7] Societies can be characterized and compared in terms of their overall system of claims. These constitute the distinctive way of organizing the overlap and interaction between claiming in the three realms. When it comes to making claims – which is the agency component – Peattie and Rein regard them as being asserted in terms of what they call 'claims rationales'. These are normative arguments that contain both factual and ethical components.

This approach has many points of interest from our perspective. First, it is sensitive to variation. For example, various systems of claims are regarded as both internally negotiable and culturally variable (Peattie and Rein: 28). Given this, the approach theorizes variation as resulting from the predominance of particular principles of claiming and combinations of claims across spheres – in Peattie and Rein's language, different 'claims structures'. The claims-making perspective is especially proficient in understanding the welfare state as a political domain – one in which contests take place over who gets what. In this and other ways, it has a number of gender-sensitive aspects. For example, Peattie and Rein include the family as one of the three claims-making realms, and they refuse to attribute claims from employment a privileged status within their theoretical framework. The fact that they recognize that the principles underlying the different realms become blurred at the margins may well have a resonance for gender, which tends to cross spheres. Not only do claims around gender stretch across different boundaries of social life, they are to be seen at their sharpest where the state encounters the family or the family meets the labour market. This is a very agency-oriented perspective, in that it centres on change generated by agency around claims. The approach also has limitations, however. It cannot easily explain the form of the policy response to claims (why, for example, some countries institute systems of social insurance rather than social assistance), or why some claims are regarded as legitimate while others are not. One wonders also if it is sufficiently differentiated to capture significant variations among claims and among those who are pressing them. That said, its dynamic and contest-oriented potential renders the idea of claims making attractive for the present purposes.

1.3.2   The life course approach

The life course approach shares with the claims-making perspective a central focus on the dynamics of the welfare state, and adds to it an understanding of dynamic processes within individual biographies (Leisering and Walker 1998; Leisering and Leibfried 1999). This approach focuses centrally on the patterning of individual lives, and especially on how the institutions of the welfare state exert a formative effect on the temporal organization of life. Early social policies, such as prohibition of child labour and the introduction of compulsory schooling, helped to shape the differentiation of childhood and old age as genuine phases of life (Leisering and Leibfried 1999: 24). Biographies are normalized and rendered continuous by three core components of the welfare state: education (which supports entry into work, lays down career tracks, and provides training opportunities); old age pensions (which serve to secure and organize the life span); and special institutions of risk management (like health and unemployment insurance, social work, and social assistance, which act to bridge crisis periods in life). The risk management functions come into play only when the idealized expectations of a normal biography fail to materialize. They are, then, safety nets for 'deviant' life courses and are especially important in the middle phases of the life course (Leisering and Leibfried 1999: 29). All three welfare state components effect change by virtue of their definitional, integrational and formative functions. They structure and differentiate the life course; they influence the connections between the three main stages of life (childhood/youth, employment/family, old age); and they affect the patterning of social, economic and gender-related divisions (i.e. social stratification).

Not only does a life course approach capture the development of welfare states historically, it is in tune with some of the key challenges facing contemporary welfare states. It is a perspective that addresses the welfare state directly, seeking to explain both the nature of provisions and some of their social effects. The perspective points out that social insurance and social services act as structuring mechanisms, and that welfare states (broadly conceived) play a major role in directing the course of social life. The approach is rather uneven in this respect, however, since it better addresses the beginning and end of the life course than the middle. This middle stage, the period of child bearing and rearing, is arguably the most gender-differentiated phase of life. Hence, the links between gender inequalities and social policy are somewhat neglected.[8] The approach is, nonetheless, especially valuable in drawing attention to the temporal order of life as a focus of welfare state intervention. Social policies define the onset of childhood, adulthood and later life, and signally influence the conditions under which people pass through these life phases. Also interesting for our purposes is a capacity to focus on continuity as well as discontinuity in life courses. The relation between continuity and discontinuity may well be important from a gender perspective. Whereas continuity typifies the male life course, discontinuity in the sense of movement between different spheres of activity is a better descriptor of the average female life course. The cross-national potential of the perspective is also striking, in that it has theoretical terms to deal with variation. For example, it allows one to explain differences in national welfare state patterns in terms of the normative models of the life course underlying them and the extent to which such models emphasize different fields of life course activity (Leisering and Leibfried 1999: 7). The perspective has the added advantage of being dynamic. Leisering and Leibfried are at pains to point out that the approach both produces and presupposes the individual as active subject. Thus, the term 'life course' has a double meaning: first, in the sense of a regulated path that lives should follow and, second, in the individual's encounter with his or her own history, captured by the notion of biography (1999: 37).

The claims-making and life course approaches share a notion of agency that operates at the individual level as well as at the level of the welfare state. Understanding agency at the individual level is attractive not least because it imbues people with power and the possibility of resistance to a particular social order. Operating with a notion of the agency of the welfare state throws light on the power of state action to shape individual lives by fashioning people's material and ideological circumstances.[9] The claims-making perspective in particular lends the welfare state a dynamic cast, with political contests around welfare articulated through the structure and process of claims making. We also take from this literature an appreciation of the political nature of the welfare state, how it shapes interests as well as resources, and its impact, at an ideological and practical level, on gender roles. We draw further on these perspectives in the next chapter.

1.4 Comparison and the Study of the Welfare State and Gender Relations

The matter and methods of comparison form another core set of interests for our work. This section considers to what purpose comparison has been employed in studies of the welfare state and gender. There is in fact a formidable body of comparative literature. In the hands of conventional scholars comparative work has addressed itself to three general areas: welfare state growth and development, welfare state regimes, and evaluative studies of the welfare state. Work from a gender perspective has taken a somewhat different approach, and this will be considered after the discussion of the three themes of mainstream work.

1.4.1   Explaining welfare state development

A considerable part of early comparative endeavour was dedicated to an investigation of the causal significance of economic or political factors for welfare state development. This work tended to be highly quantitative, concerned to subject hypotheses about welfare state development to empirical testing.[10] It treats the welfare state as one element in the development of modern capitalism and democracy (Cutright 1965; Wilensky and Lebeaux 1965; Wilensky 1975). The growth of the welfare state is understood as either functional to modernization or as a by-product of it. The welfare state, then, is not so much examined in its own right as seen as the outcome of the development of modern industrial society (Alber et al. 1987: 459). The operationalization of the welfare state is relatively simple – social expenditure is taken as the measure of welfare state development.

From this perspective, the most interesting question is why countries vary in their levels of social expenditure. Statistical analysis is the preferred medium for testing the relationship between social expenditure and a wide range of causal variables, such as levels of economic growth, the degree of unionization and the dominance of left parties in government (see e.g. Stephens 1979; Castles 1982; Pampel and Williamson 1988; O'Connor 1988; Korpi 1989). For the purpose of testing theory, a relatively large number of countries (typically twelve or more) is used.

This literature draws its comparative strength from pinpointing processes that operate across countries, thereby avoiding the danger of falling into nation-specific explanations. It also has ambitions to test and develop theory. One of the main shortcomings relates to the use of social spending as a measure of the welfare state. Social expenditure is a crude indicator, revealing nothing about programmatic differences and failing to capture the quality of benefits or the conditions under which people receive social transfers and services (Amenta 1993: 758). Furthermore, analysis of social spending is silent on welfare state effectiveness, since it cannot address patterns of need among the population and ignores the contribution to welfare made by institutions other than the state, notably the family, community and voluntary sectors (Boje 1996: 22–5). In addition, the work has not satisfactorily explained welfare state growth, since controversies remain about which of the competing factors offers the most complete account of welfare state development (Esping-Andersen 1987, 1990; Amenta 1993; Mabbett and Bolderson 1999). For these reasons, this approach is not only outmoded, it is also of limited use for a study in which the qualitative dimensions of welfare state provision are to the fore.

1.4.2   Welfare state regimes

The second mode of comparing welfare states has relied on typologies of regimes as the principal methodological tool. It has, to all intents and purposes, superseded the first genre of comparative studies. This kind of approach starts from a position of diversity in social policy formation and in the strategies chosen by political actors (Kangas 1994). Work on welfare state regimes is most closely associated with Esping-Andersen, who, using a range of empirical measures, demonstrates how welfare states cluster into regime types (1990, 1999). Liberal, corporatist and social democratic regimes are distinguished according to a specified set of criteria such as the degree of de-commodification (freedom from the market), the stratifying effect of the welfare state, and the relationship between the state and the market. The complex of measures used bears witness to Esping-Andersen's concern with qualitative variations among welfare states, a characteristic that sets his work apart from the earlier work on welfare state development. The use of the term 'regime' is significant in that it reflects an understanding of the welfare state as part of an integrated system that articulates a particular policy logic (Esping-Andersen 1987: 6–7). Again, in contrast to the earlier genre of work on the welfare state, which assumed that factors elicit identical effects across countries, variation is inherent in the notion of a welfare regime, and there is no expectation that regime types would necessarily converge in response to globalization. It could be argued, then, that the most important contribution of Esping-Andersen's work methodologically has been to indicate that welfare state variation is not distributed in a linear fashion, but is instead clustered.

Regime analysis is typical of case-oriented research in exploring the qualitative aspects of welfare states and understanding welfare regimes as integrated wholes. The strengths of regime analysis derive, mainly, from an appreciation of qualitative variation and an understanding of the welfare state as embedded in, and part of, a wider social order. Using a typology of regimes also has the advantage of creating the opportunity to cover a wider range of countries than is typical of the small numbers usually studied in case-oriented research. It is not surprising, therefore, that much of the more recent comparative work on the welfare state has fallen within the regime analysis tradition. Of all the comparative literatures, regime analysis has attracted the most scrutiny from feminist scholars. While much of the reaction has been critical, the notion of welfare regimes has found a distinctive feminist interpretation. One tendency has been to develop a new set of regime classifications focused on male breadwinner models (Lewis 1992, 1997a). The other response has been to augment Esping-Andersen's existing measures of welfare state activity to capture women's relationship to the welfare state (Orloff 1993, 1997). These will be discussed further in section 1.4.4 below.

There are a number of unresolved issues in the regime literature, especially stemming from the use, and limitations, of typologies as a methodological device. In particular, the literature is often unclear about the distinctions between ideal and real types as methodological tools. For example, it is not clear whether Esping-Andersen's typology is based on ideal types of welfare state or existing welfare state models. Further, the utility of producing classificatory typologies is open to question, given that the empirical picture of the welfare state that emerges is both partial and static. Typologies are drawn up at a

particular point in time, and welfare state change renders them in-
accurate and outdated (Taylor-Gooby 1996; Cox 1998). Finally, a
typology draws attention to differences between types at the expense
of exploring variation among countries classified similarly, such that
small-scale, but nevertheless highly significant, differences are overlooked.

1.4.3 Evaluative studies of the welfare state

The third approach to the comparative analysis of social policy is
evaluative, using comparison as a way to understand the impact of
particular policies or the effectiveness of the welfare state in reaching
given goals. This approach is qualitatively different from the other
two. More focused on policy and its effectiveness, empirical results
are considered interesting in their own right, rather than as tools to
develop or test theory or to elaborate concepts. Most commonly, such
studies evaluate welfare states according to national levels of poverty
or the distribution of income among particular sectors of the population (e.g. Gardiner 1993; Blackburn 1994; Atkinson et al. 1995;
Atkinson 1998; Korpi and Palme 1998; Vleminckx and Smeeding
2000).[11] The terms of reference may, however, be broader than poverty or income distribution and refer to concepts such as social
inclusion, solidarity and security (Paugam 1996; Hills 1998; Goodin
et al. 1999; Gordon and Townsend 2000; Atkinson et al. 2002;
Stewart 2002). Much evaluative work follows from the interests of
supra-national institutions or agencies (such as the European Union
(EU), Organization for Economic Co-operation and Development
(OECD) and the International Labour Office (ILO)) and, partly as a
consequence, varying domains of policy and a wide range of countries
are to be found in these studies. The methodological approach
adopted by studies in this tradition is fairly standard. They rely on
statistical analysis of data in the form of variables, often for a large
number of countries. The main contribution is empirical rather than
conceptual. Evaluative work has fostered methodological and technical advances with regard to both the collection and analysis of
cross-national data, most notably LIS, which currently produces
comparable income data for some twenty-five countries.

Evaluative studies of the welfare state have enriched our understanding of empirical variation across a large number of national
settings. We know that there is considerable variation in the design
and implementation of social policies cross-nationally, and that small,
as well as large, differences in the content of policy can lead to
divergent outcomes. The involvement and interests of supra-national

institutions, the changing profile of national populations, the diffu-
sion of economic and social policies, and changes in policy will, no
doubt, create a permanent place for these studies within comparative
work. However, questions remain both about the methodology of
these studies and their contribution to our understanding of the
welfare state. Looking first at methodology, cross-national evaluative
work is marked by a number of difficulties. With notable exceptions
(Atkinson 1995), the literature has remained quite unreflective about
the methodological challenges posed by comparison. The comparability of data and concepts tends to be taken as given, and the processes
by which data are rendered comparable treated as either unproblematic or as technical matters. In conceiving of and operationalizing the
welfare state in a narrow way, this literature has strong similarities
with the earlier work on welfare state development – the first comparative literature considered. The majority of evaluative studies have
focused on income transfers rather than cross-national variation in
the provision of services or the broader redistributive processes of the
welfare state.[12] A more serious limitation of this work stems from the
fact that it requires the effects of the welfare state to be isolated from
other 'confounding' factors, such as the operation of the labour
market. There have been some notable developments in measurement: Mitchell (1991), for example, attempts to specify the impact
of the welfare state by differentiating between pre-transfer income
(i.e. income from the labour market and private savings) and post-
transfer income (income net of taxes and cash transfers). Innovative
though this work can be, there is a trade-off in relation to complexity.
Cash transfers are only a partial measure of welfare state activity or
outcome. Reducing the welfare state to its role in income redistribution is an over-simplification and goes against the thrust of other
literature considered in this chapter, which emphasizes the social role
of the state as well as its economic functions. Further, in common
with many evaluative studies, this kind of work fails to identify which
policy brings about which outcomes (Johnson and Rake 1998).

1.4.4   Feminist comparative work

A comparative focus has been a relatively recent interest of feminist
work. The early work spoke in very general terms and was convinced
that the sets of relations it identified were universal. However, there is
evidence of organic development in feminist approaches, and recent
literature has actively sought to investigate variation.

Jane Lewis (1992) sets out to develop a model of regimes that is
sensitive to national variation. Her work is a direct challenge to the

conventional regime-oriented literature, led by Esping-Andersen (1990), which she criticizes for ignoring gender-related variations in social policy. She suggests that welfare states can be grouped, independently of other criteria, on the degree to which they adhere to a male breadwinner ideology. Lewis operationalizes such an ideology in terms of the norms and assumptions about women's roles, especially motherhood, that are encoded in social policies. According to her model, developed European welfare states are grouped on a continuum formed by strong, modified and weak male breadwinner models. Sainsbury's (1996, 1999) work is also to the fore in welfare state comparison. She is interested in how gender differentiation is written into income support policies and the consequences of these policies for gender inequalities. Variation in the principles of entitlement to cash benefit programmes forms the core of her analysis. She seeks to link outcomes with the design of policies not just in terms of normative assumptions, but in the conditions attaching to cash benefits. She examines a range of income maintenance programmes in Britain, the Netherlands, Sweden and the USA, and reveals the importance for women of the fine print of social provision. Moreover, she demonstrates that while men's route to benefit receipt is straightforward, women gain access to benefits in a series of roles (mother, worker, breadwinner, carer, wife) and via a series of different programmes. Finally, there is Hirdmann's model of gender contracts. Although this was developed to capture historical variation in Sweden, Duncan (1995) has attempted to adapt it for cross-national application. He argues that national gender contracts may take the form of a housewife contract, a dual role contract or an equality contract, with a number of countries currently in transition between types (Duncan 1995: 272–3). However, the variation in welfare state programmes is not brought directly into play in his elaboration of these types. In line with Hirdmann's analysis, Duncan views the welfare state as reflective of, rather than initiating, such gender contracts.

There is another form of comparative feminist literature in which scholars are motivated by an interest in the design and effects of specific programmes across national frontiers. Ginn and others, for example, compare pension arrangements in a number of countries, so as to identify women's independent access to income in old age (Ginn and Arber 1992; Ginn et al. 2001). Gornick et al. (1997) examine how social provision, both income support and services for children, affects women's employment. Glendinning and McLaughlin (1993) compare the care needs of the elderly across a number of European welfare states and how policy has responded to them. Sørensen and

McLanahan (1987, 1989) provide another example of this approach, and look at how national variation in social security provision affects poverty and the distribution of income between women and men. Programme-specific, this literature tends to isolate different aspects of the welfare state in order to capture the impact of social policies empirically.

On the basis of the literature reviewed we can see that comparison has been utilized for more than one purpose. We intend to use a comparative methodology not just to compare, but also to explain. We want to explore diversity and, in contradistinction to evaluative studies, to trace the linkages between the welfare state and key aspects of the social order. Centrally focused on the welfare state, our approach is also distinct from studies of the origins and growth of welfare states. Only the work of Lewis (1992) comes near. But, by contrast with Lewis, who wanted to identify the differences between nations as variations on a particular underlying model, our approach is more open. We move beyond the scrutiny of policy for its normative content to examine the complexity of women's and men's lives as they are lived in a number of countries. This bottom-up approach, rooted in the empirical reality of gender differentials and inequalities, allows us to learn how policy plays out at the individual level and avoids imposing a single policy logic on any national welfare state or indeed across states. Comparison is used by us to reveal those features of national welfare arrangements that are particular to countries and those that are general across countries. We are not especially interested in identifying regimes. While the regime concept has the advantage of encapsulating variation on a range of factors, it is too constricting, because it limits the number of factors that can be considered and constrains how variation is interpreted. Complexity and configuration most interest us. We will search for the similarities and differences across our cases so as to draw out the unique and complex configuration of factors making up each case and explain, through juxtaposition of different country cases, the underlying patterning at work.

1.5 Overview

The different literatures serve to underline important features of the welfare state and gender relations. First, resource distribution and the impact of policy on well-being, income and other resources emerge as vital. However, a kind of economism characterizes much of the conventional literature, seen especially in the focus on redistribution and the economic functions of the state. This makes it less than amenable to an analysis of gender, either in a redistributive or a broader sense. Thinking from the perspective of gender requires a broad understanding of welfare state activity. This includes the redistribution of resources, the organization of the life course and the engagement of the welfare state in shaping social roles. We believe that a gender perspective must bring the power-related aspects of the welfare state to the foreground. This means that male–female power relations have to be given prominence and also that the welfare state needs to be seen as contested. Rather than being a 'settlement' of some sort, from a gender perspective the welfare state is an active site and source of adjudicating particular claims. This makes it difficult to focus solely on a set of outcomes associated with the welfare state (whether conceived of in terms of balance of power or resources). In addition, the analytic gaze is turned on to the processes set in train by the welfare state. A further insight concerns the role of the market and the politics associated with it. It is clear that social policy undergirds the functioning of the market. This occurs not just in obvious ways – such as the support of the unemployed – but also in less obvious ways – for example, the conditions attaching to benefits may serve to regulate both the work-force and the labour market. Feminist work underlines how the welfare state underpins the family and contributes to the definition and location of care and the roles associated with care. The welfare state proffers material and ideological support for certain social roles, most notably that of motherhood, and frequently bolsters or actively supports gender segregation of such roles. The welfare state reinforces divisions along gender lines, as well as those of class and income group. In short, welfare is political and reaches deep into society.

These ideas will be developed further in the next chapter.

2

Framework of Analysis

Drawing in part on the insights of the work reviewed in the last chapter, we now elaborate our own framework of analysis. Towards this end, the two concepts that lie at the heart of the book – the welfare state and gender relations – are defined, and their relationship specified. This will serve the dual purpose of detailing the concepts to be used in the analysis and, in returning to some fundamental definitional issues, opening up the possibility of a different approach to the study of gender relations and the welfare state. The chapter is divided into four parts. First, it presents a range of definitions of the welfare state and, having done so, delineates the approach adopted in the current research. Second, it elaborates our conceptualization of gender relations. Third, it brings these two concepts together and specifies how we intend to capture empirically the gender dimension of the welfare state. The final section is devoted to comparison, describing the comparative framework to be used and presenting the rationale for the choice of the eight countries.

2.1 Defining the Welfare State

As was clear from the literature discussed in the last chapter, the welfare state has been conceptualized in many different ways. Often, however, the definition of the welfare state is not made explicit, so its meaning has to be read from how the concept is applied. A clear definition is critical for the present work, since it focuses centrally on the activities of the welfare state and covers so many countries. In this section four definitions are briefly outlined before we draw from them to develop our own.

The first set of scholarship identified in the previous chapter was the social policy approach. This literature focuses not on the welfare state at all, but rather on a collection of public policies and services (education, health, social security and so forth). From this literature has come a tendency to study benefits and services in isolation from one another, with the result that, although the literature has excelled on details of policy, it has proceeded without an explicit, overarching concept of the welfare state. The welfare state tends to be equated with a specific institutional form of social policies (e.g. the Beveridgean welfare state). Such definitional looseness has led to shortcomings. It has, for example, effectively foreclosed debate on what constitutes social policy,[1] and whether divisions such as those between social policy and economic, cultural, foreign and criminal justice policy are intellectually defensible. The work of comparative researchers has thrown the limitations of this approach into sharp relief. Differences in administration and national context mean that a social programme operating in one country will rarely find an exact mirror in another. Family policy, for example, is institutionalized through a dedicated ministry with a specific set of goals in some countries, while in others the support of the family is implicit in a range of benefits and services and cuts across administrative boundaries. Moreover, other important axes of cross-national variation, such as the degree of state intervention, become apparent only when looking at the welfare state as a whole.

The second approach, deriving from political economy, understands the welfare state to be a particular form of the state. It locates the development of the welfare state within a broader project of state building and democratization. In this approach the welfare state is defined as an embodiment of relations of power, especially in terms of how its programmes and outcomes are identified with the interests of particular classes or economic actors. A largely comparative scholarship has sought to identify the political struggles that determined the form of the welfare state. These have included the influence of left- and right-wing parties and the corporatist mechanisms through which trade unions and employers are brought into the policy-making process. When it comes to the content of social policy and the connections among policy spheres, this approach has only limited capacity to capture the smaller detail of cross-national variation and to link it to outcomes for individuals and families. Further, these studies have adopted a narrow definition of power, understanding it mainly in terms of the formal political arena. As well as discounting the importance of relations of power in the family, such a definitional narrowness means that much of women's political agency is overlooked,[2] and the influence of social movements such as feminism on welfare state development underplayed.

As it developed, this literature nurtured an interest in the welfare state as an institution, and this led to a concern to analyse the effect of factors internal to the welfare state on growth and retrenchment. The professionalization and centralization of activities within a welfare bureaucracy have been elaborated as a key feature in the growth of welfare states. Welfare bureaucrats develop particular expertise and capacities and are identifiable agents within the policy-making process, and indeed in society at large. Later variants of the political economy approach have given an insight into the machinery of government and show how nations may get 'locked into' particular paths of policy development, with policy innovation more likely to occur if it requires the extension of existing capacities rather than the development of a new bureaucratic machinery (Pierson 1994). The behaviour of state bureaucrats has also been marshalled in the analysis of policy reform, although debate continues about the nature of bureaucrats' interests and their capacity to pursue them.[3] Defining the welfare state as an institution and an embodiment of power relations has some weaknesses, however. An exploration of the formal mechanisms of government and the elite cadre of policy makers gives little sense of the actual content of social policies or how they are experienced by users or recipients. In drawing its analytical framework from political science, this definition risks being overly governmental in focus. Thus, an interest in formal political mechanisms serves to exclude non-governmental provision of welfare (by the family or voluntary sector). Additionally, the focus on government action obscures the welfare implications of government inaction. Non-provision may be an important mechanism for creating or reinforcing social divisions. For example, non-provision of caring services has important implications for gender inequalities.

A third definition derives from a view of the welfare state as an ideological mechanism, leading to the institutionalization of individual and social values. The ideological practices of the welfare state have been subject to a variety of interpretations. Marxist writing has highlighted that, in addition to its role in furthering capitalist accumulation, the welfare state legitimates the interests of capital (O'Connor 1973). Social interventions are interpreted as a mechanism for quieting social protest, defining and controlling deviant behaviour, and thereby maintaining social divisions (Ginsburg 1992). Feminist work is quite strongly represented here, especially that which has seen the welfare state as the embodiment of patriarchy (Wilson 1977). From the opposite end of the political spectrum, the welfare state has been identified as altering social values (in particular, reducing the value attached to paid work and removing the stigma associated with claiming state support), with the result that, for some, welfare states are inevitably accompanied by a culture of dependency (Murray 1984, 1996). Analysis of the welfare state's normative impact has been complemented by a recognition that the welfare state reflects and embodies social values more broadly held – in particular, ideologies about welfare.

One shortcoming of these definitions of the welfare state as ideological practice is that the agency of welfare recipients falls from view. Yet as active subjects, they may be either complicit with or resistant to the welfare state. Another important shortcoming is that a singular logic of policy, be that patriarchal, anti-libertarian or capitalist, is implied. An underlying problem here is that it is assumed that ideology can be embodied or expressed in a consistent and unitary fashion through welfare policies. Insights from the neo-Marxist, feminist and post-structuralist literatures reveal that, by contrast, the state and the policies emanating from it may be contradictory in nature, and therefore unable to promote consistently a particular social ideology (Laclau and Mouffe 1985; Pringle and Watson 1992). Hence, while health and education services can be interpreted as meeting capitalists' interests, since a healthy, educated work-force improves profit margins, such services also increase the power of organized labour and may undermine the conditions of profitable capitalism (Gough 1979; Offe 1984). Similarly, contradictory gender ideologies can be seen where welfare provision enables women's independence (allowing them to live as lone parents, for example) while creating a new form of dependency on the benefits and services of the state (Showstack Sassoon 1987; Gordon 1990). Further, nationalist and racist ideologies have also been identified in welfare. These cross-cut one another and operate in concert and sometimes in conflict with patriarchal ideology (Williams 1989, 1995; Lister 1997). As a result, the treatment of women and men is shaped by the coincidence of a range of ideologies.

Finally, under a much broader definition, the welfare state has been identified as being a particular society 'in which the state intervenes within the processes of economic reproduction and distribution to reallocate life chances between individuals and/or classes' (Pierson 1991: 7). The welfare state as a means of social transformation and its embeddedness in a broader social order are each invoked by this definition. Such a definition has analytical flexibility on a number of levels. First, by drawing attention to the reallocation of life chances as an object and/or outcome of welfare state intervention, the redistributive impact of the welfare state may be seen to fuller effect. The welfare state is placed at the heart of the analysis of social life, rather than viewed as a by-product of other processes (such as political change or industrialization). Secondly, the identification of the welfare state as part of society allows one to look more broadly at the social structure, especially the provision of welfare beyond the state. The approach comprehends the welfare-conferring activities of the family, employers, the voluntary and charitable sectors in more than a subsidiary fashion. In contrast to the focus on codified policy offered by the previous definitions, the notion of the welfare state as being embedded in society allows one to see the welfare state as a social as well as an economic actor. Finally, the notion of the welfare state in society has the potential to incorporate the widest range of social actors, and so operates with an understanding of agency that extends beyond the formal political sphere. In particular, this definition can be sensitive to the agency of the recipients of welfare services, rather than viewing them as the passive objects of welfare intervention (whereas approaches concerned with institutional structures or professional management tend to eclipse the experience of those on the receiving end).

These definitions of the welfare state help us towards developing our own. Given the comparative interests of the current analysis, any definition used should be able to capture variation and be meaningful in all the national settings included in the study. It is therefore essential that the research take a comprehensive and general view of the welfare state. Hence, we are sympathetic to the welfare state defined as being part of society, in which a sociological understanding of the activity of the welfare state is combined with an explicit recognition of welfare provided by other institutions. However, we wish to extend this understanding further by incorporating the welfare state's involvement in ideological processes also. This invokes both normative process and power relations. We understand the welfare state to play an important role in creating or reinforcing specific sets of social values, including the values and expectations attached to social roles such as worker, spouse and carer. In this and other ways it shapes power relations and serves to constitute gender interests. The diverse activity of the welfare state in redistributive, political and social processes is central to this understanding. We can therefore envisage cross-national variation in welfare states' involvement in the regulation, production, distribution and politicization of welfare. Further, the involvement of non-state actors and institutions (most notably the family and the labour market) in welfare provision is emphasized. This understanding of the welfare state in society highlights the significance of national context to variation. These issues will be further elaborated later in the chapter.

2.2 Defining Gender and Gender Relations

For such a widely used concept, it is surprising how infrequently gender has been defined.[4] In effect, its usage has been rather careless. Three exercises of clarification are essential in the specification of gender. The first relates to how gender is understood, the second centres on how gender is to be observed, while the third involves a clarification of the explanatory potential of gender.

In the most limited definition, gender may be understood as a classificatory concept to categorize the differences between individual women and men. Such a definition tends to work to a dichotomous logic. It is, therefore, difficult to extend it beyond a description of sexual difference rooted in biology. Starting from this definition, one is actually required to make a conceptual leap in order to understand gender as a property of collectivities and institutions (Connell 1987: 139). Neither a dichotomous categorization nor a biological under-standing of gender helps much in seeing gender as part of society. For this purpose one must treat gender as a social practice. As social practice, gender is continually created and reconstituted by the activ-ities of women and men, as well as of social institutions such as the family, the welfare state and the labour market. A notion of gender as social practice moves us away from thinking about gender as fixed and incorporates the agency of individuals, collectivities and insti-tutions in supporting or resisting existing norms and power relations. This injects a dynamic element into the concept and creates the expectation that contesting notions of gender, arising from the inter-ests of different social actors, provide a motor for change (Connell 1987: 134–9). Our concern to capture the dynamic and relational aspects of gender means that we prefer the term 'gender relations' to 'gender' and, while we may use 'gender' as shorthand, we have in mind gender not as dichotomous categorization but as sets of norms and relations embedded within social structure.

The second clarification relates to how gender relations are to be observed. If one adopts a broad understanding of gender relations as social practice, it is clear that analysis focusing on women alone will provide only limited insight. Although one can observe a movement in scholarship away from a women-only approach to one that conceives of gender as a comparison between women and men, this movement remains partial, and many texts slip back into a 'women only' mode.

For us, any legitimate use of gender relations must include a male–female comparison. The point of this is not the obvious one – that such practices affect men and women as individuals – but rather that gendered social practices have consequences for the relationships, public and private, between women and men as categories of social actor. Gendered norms and practices traverse the public–private divide and hence must be observed in the family as well (what we later call 'private welfare') (Hartsock 1998). Overall, this approach allows us to take account of the heterogeneity that exists among women and among men according to different statuses (e.g. parent versus non-parent), different characteristics (such as stage of the life course and ethnicity) and differential access to resources. To capture relevant aspects of status and characteristics, the analysis will focus on 'differences', whereas access to resources is conceived of in terms of an inequality paradigm.

The third clarification centres on how gender is employed in the explanation of social phenomena. To employ gender relations in an explanatory capacity, one must be clear what particular agency is being invoked. While the literature does not always make this explicit, such agency lies in gender-based power relations. One can see gender power relations as being played out across the spectrum. We are especially interested in looking at them in the welfare state and, via this, the labour market and the family. However, while we recognize gender as a feature of the social order, we do not believe that it completely describes social phenomena. Room has to be left for structures of power other than those originating in gender relations (most notably, capitalism) in the framing of the gender dimension of welfare states.

We define gender relations as a composite of three elements. These are resources, social roles and power relations. 'Resources' refer to goods and capacities at one's disposal; they both express and influence life-style, social status and well-being in fundamental ways. Their distribution is frequently contested. From a gender perspective, time and opportunities have to be set alongside the more common understanding of resources as money or financial assets. A gender analysis also suggests that the combination of resources matters, and that individuals require quite specific combinations of resources, depending on their circumstances. For example, to take up employment, a mother requires somebody to substitute for her time as well as a wage that makes it worth her while to be in paid work. Social roles are the second element of gender relations. They refer to the extent to which norms and behaviours are social and patterned for women and men. Parental and family roles are the most obvious examples of how social norms prescribe particular behaviours for women and men. For individuals, roles provide a set of guidelines about how to behave, as well as conferring and affirming aspects of identity. Social roles are relevant also at a larger level, in that for society they serve to bring regularity and, ultimately, social order. Welfare states help to determine the form and meaning of social roles by, for example, treating men as the providers for their families. Welfare states also affect the choice of roles available to people, not least because they help to set out the rewards and penalties attaching to particular roles. Their effect on social roles is therefore an important aspect of the agency of welfare states. There are close links between roles and power relations, the third component of gender. Indeed, power relations derive from and are closely associated with roles, as well as other social phenomena. With a focus on power relations we intend to open up our analyses to the possibility that the welfare state affects the power resources of individual women and men and their distribution between them as (part of) social groups. The relative power of different groups (and interests) may be mirrored and expressed in the activity of the welfare state. The transfer of resources, via taxation and social security, is obviously important here. There is a more subtle power relation operating as well, however, in which the welfare state mediates between interests and, where contests arise, acts as arbiter and judge. For example, there is a selection process involved in deciding on the circumstances that are deemed to merit support from the state. Additionally, casting policies (and thereby competing claims of different groups or sets of activities) in particular modes serves to constrain the ways in which issues and contested claims are dealt with subsequently.

2.3 The Welfare State and Gender Relations – Towards a Framework of Analysis

Now we turn to the interrelationship between the welfare state and gender. This interrelationship requires clarification on two fronts. First, the processes and impact of the welfare state need to be conceptualized with regard to how they affect gender relations. Second, the gendered content of the welfare state needs to be examined.

2.3.1 The gender dimension of the welfare state

As argued above, capturing the gender dimension of the welfare state requires that the definitions of both be broad. With regard to the welfare state, we here follow the feminist and other literature in treating the programmatic substance of social policies as normative. Welfare states are ideological; the normative content of social programmes is powerful in creating and reinforcing appropriate behaviours for women and men. Such effects are to be seen in the valorization and affirmation of social roles and the organization of life into a series of phases or stages that centre especially for women around the relationship between roles and behaviour relating to family and work. The welfare state therefore reflects existing gender relations as well as contributing to their continual reconstitution. Highlighting the normative elements of the welfare state acts also to link the content and form of social policy with political struggles and discourses. Programmatic content reveals which needs are legitimated and thus attract public support. The conditions governing entitlement also reveal the kinds of hierarchy into which needs or social rights are placed *vis-à-vis* each other. For example, where entitlement is conditional on means testing, the well-being of recipients is placed in the hands of bureaucrats, and the individuals involved are therefore subject to control and regulation. The fine print of programmes and the conditions governing access to them are significant also for the degree to which they affect choices available to individual women and men. The opportunity to combine different social roles, such as mother and worker, is of particular importance to gender relations. The generosity of support and the extent to which welfare states orient their benefits and services on a family or individual basis are also vital. Taken as a whole, the programmatic substance of the welfare state uncovers where the boundaries of social intervention are drawn. To investigate welfare state programmes as a whole, then, is to enquire into a broader set of questions about which activities are paid and unpaid, whether relations fall within or outside the control of the state, and whether spheres are treated as public or private or some kind of combination of both.

Our framework is sympathetic to agency on the part of the welfare state. We view the welfare state as a presence and set of relations in people's lives. The agency effected by the welfare state invokes the complex of processes set in train by social policies. The financial role of the welfare state is most familiar, a legacy of class-based analysis that regards welfare as a compromise between economic actors achieved mainly through financial redistribution. Feminist work has highlighted that financial redistribution affects not just poverty and income inequality, but also the degree to which people are enabled to achieve financial independence. Less obvious is the welfare state's agency in relation to time. The life course approach draws attention to the role of the welfare state in shaping the temporal order.

Developing this further, we would point to how the welfare state, through its service provision, actually redistributes time and in this way affects people's (especially women's) choices about the use of time (Scheiwe 1993). To some extent the debate about welfare state restructuring in terms of cash versus care is a debate about whether the welfare state's redistributive efforts are better focused on money or time. There is another type of agency effected by the welfare state as well: the shaping and redistribution of opportunities. This is understood to have both a concrete and an abstract dimension. The welfare state's role in relation to concrete opportunities is to be found, for example, where it offers leaves from employment, labour market-related training and placement and jobs (in the public sector). The less concrete aspects of the welfare state's effect on opportunities could be summarized in terms of constructing the life course and defining work and care. These aspects become important only when one understands the welfare state as influencing the opportunity to work, to care, or to engage in a combination of both. To summarize, our framework considers the welfare state as a (re)distributor of money, time and opportunities as they play out across the life course.

We recognize along with the feminist literature and that on claims making that power relations are an integral aspect of the welfare state's operation. Our framework is conscious of the contested nature of welfare, epitomized most visibly perhaps by the process through which claims are pressed, treated and delivered. This kind of understanding is important to a gender perspective, since the division of resources between women and men is of fundamental importance to the welfare state's own functioning. A focus on power makes the boundaries of provision particularly interesting, and directs attention to what the welfare state does not do in addition to what it does do. At least part of the reason why the welfare state is powerful is its role as broker of contested claims. Further, specific policies may privilege certain social practices. So, for example, the welfare state, in utilizing a breadwinner model, acts to reinforce this form of relations between women and men. Finally, recognizing the welfare state as a site to which competing claims are brought by different interests and at which they are decided recognizes that people, including welfare recipients, are active in contesting or complying with prevailing norms.

2.3.2 Care, work and welfare as the linkages between the welfare state and gender relations

Through which lenses can we observe the links or relations between the welfare state and gender? There are three lenses through which the relations between the welfare state and gender are best observed. These are care, work and welfare. As we use them, they are at once states or conditions, sets of relations, and activities. As states or conditions, they provide a descriptor of circumstances. As sets of relations, they are defined by interactions and social relations with others. As activities, they are generic to social life. The fulfilment of personal needs is the foundation of our first subject, care. This concept is different to that of work and welfare, in that it connotes activities and acts of receiving as well as providing. For example, care needs cannot be met without the provision of some kind of good or service, and welfare states are increasingly expected to be involved in this. The interpretation of care needs, the direct and indirect provision of care and, through that, the shaping of the social organization of care all fall within the ambit of today's welfare state. Our second term, work, is used to refer to productive activities. Work is most significant for how it affects one's relationship to economic resources. Therefore, labour market activity will be one of the most important routes for exploring work empirically. However, our conceptualization of work involves a problematization of the division between labour that is paid and that which is unpaid. What interests us particularly is the role of the welfare state in creating or institutionalizing such a division. The third lens, welfare or well-being, is used to refer to relative access to the resources of time, money and opportunities. It will be obvious that this understanding of welfare is derived primarily from the activities that welfare states undertake to enhance welfare or well-being, and incorporates how this affects both household units and the individuals within them.

2.4 The Approach to Comparison

The rationale for adopting a comparative approach in the current study is that we want to make explanatory statements. Comparison will allow us, in the first instance, to treat welfare states as complex and integral wholes and, in the second, to explore the conditions under which welfare states affect gender relations. Only by investigating whether similar conditions lead to similar outcomes across countries can we explain the linkages between the welfare state and gender. There is another reason why our approach has to be comparative. The phenomena about which we want to make explanatory statements – the welfare state and gender relations – can be understood better by an examination of the variation existing both within national settings and across them. Thus, we explore national policy configurations, with inter- and intra-national variation examined as a matter of course. Such multiple levels of analysis reflect a concern to explore, on the one hand, the distinct way in which gender norms and assumptions are written into the structure and practice of different welfare states and, on the other, the effects of these. The nation is the preferred unit of observation because the phenomena on which we focus are macro-social in nature. In particular, the nation-state is the most appropriate reference unit for social policy (and, perhaps not unrelatedly, the unit for which most information is available).

The key features of our approach can best be understood by positioning it relative to existing comparative methodologies.[5] Our work is closer to the case-oriented than the variable-oriented methodology. That is, it aims to draw out how factors come together and interrelate across a small number of cases, rather than searching after a general 'truth' through the testing of theoretical propositions across a large number of cases. For us the national setting is far more than context or background. It is, rather, part of the explanatory framework. Isolating factors from the setting in which they operate may lead to misunderstanding. Our view of causality is complex, rather than mono-causal. Put simply, what interests us is the layering of factors one upon another and the placement of social relations in their varied contexts. Furthermore, we are as interested in qualitative as in quantitative outcomes. Our work, however, is less true to the case-oriented approach, inasmuch as we examine eight national welfare states (a larger number of cases than the two or three typically considered in case-oriented research). We realize that as the number of instances increases, the number of causal conditions that can be considered rapidly decreases (Kangas 1994). This requires a clear strategy for dealing with variation. The theoretical framework elaborated above serves an important function in this regard, by using concepts (care, work and welfare) that operate at a sufficiently general level to capture both commonality and variation across cases.

There are, of course, limits to our methodological approach. In common with all comparative work on the welfare state that relies on empirical elaboration, our analysis is constrained by data availability. In particular, the lack of longitudinal data for all countries considered limits our analysis of the redistributive effects of the welfare state. Further, analysis of domains such as care is constrained by the scarcity of data that accurately identify care givers and receivers. In addition, our research does not provide an account of whether and how the welfare state is experienced at the receiving end as a mechanism of social control. As with all comparative research, our analysis represents a particular balance between generality and complexity. For example, our empirical chapters are weighted more heavily in favour of analyses that span the eight countries rather than presenting material on a case-by-case basis.

2.4.1   The selection of countries

Our comparative objective is to examine the linkages between national welfare states and gender relations and to ascertain whether and how the welfare state matters for gender relations. One of the guidelines for our research design and selection of cases, therefore, is to have a diversity of welfare states represented. Existing knowledge of the universe of welfare state variation plays a key role in the selection process.

The selection of countries is made on the basis of the relationship between the welfare state and gender and the nature of variation therein. Cases are selected in order to control for differences between welfare state forms and gender relations. This variation is interpreted in terms of the treatment of care, work and welfare within the national setting, and especially by the welfare state. Sweden, at one extreme, operates on a model of universalist social policies, is very supportive of employed motherhood, and, on a wide range of measures, demonstrates the lowest degree of gender differentiation of any advanced welfare state. Care, work and welfare are to all intents and purposes rendered public goods by a very interventionist welfare state model. Italy is perhaps an opposite case in that its welfare state is segmented and restricted in coverage, and gender relations are underdeveloped as an explicit focus of public policy. The family is arguably the most important provider of resources and services, not only as regards care and welfare but also in relation to work. The USA is an extreme case in another sense: its 'small' welfare state offers limited social protection and leaves welfare and care very much to the sphere of private relations and the market. Apart from these three countries, five others have been selected so as to bring depth to the comparison and control for variation. Existing literature on the welfare state indicates that these countries fall roughly into two groupings. One grouping is that of the continental European welfare states. Their model of welfare aims for universal coverage of the work-force by social insurance, rewards a lifetime's employment, and ties benefit entitlement closely to labour market status and participation. To explore diversity within this group, France, Germany and the Netherlands were chosen. Of these, Germany is the most supportive of a traditional gender division of labour. Both care and the welfare of women are closely tied to family status, and it is work in the form of the wages paid to men that determines the well-being of the family. The Netherlands shares some features of the German model, but both the welfare state and the labour market are more flexible. This, among other things, makes for greater part-time employment of women. Care is highly privatized in the Netherlands, in that the welfare state does not provide a high level of relevant services. France is usually described as a continental social policy model, but when it comes to the family and the nature of female roles, it varies significantly from both the German and Dutch patterns. Its inclusion will allow us to examine a public infrastructure that offers a rare, non-Nordic, example of an approach that is strongly supportive of employed motherhood. Care has a more public character than in the other two countries, but work and welfare are closely tied together for both women and men. Ireland and the UK (and indeed the USA) share elements of a liberal approach to the welfare state, with income transfer systems that are oriented above all to the prevention of poverty. None of these countries is explicitly supportive of the financial independence of women, whether one judges that in terms of support for employed motherhood or the provision of a living income for women. In all three, care is primarily a matter of family relations, and tends to be targeted only by limited action on the part of the state. These countries differ from each other in the degree of support that they extend to families with children and the role of the state in providing services.

In line with the vast majority of comparative studies, the nation-state is taken as the primary unit of analysis. A possible challenge could be launched to this by arguing that welfare states are not bounded entities, but rather should be interpreted in light of the growth of influence of supra-national institutions, such as the EU, or in terms of processes like internationalization. However, such an argument does not sit easily with the mass of empirical data that highlights national variations in welfare state form and the role of the nation-state (especially the welfare state) in determining how globalization and other developments are experienced at the national level (Sykes et al. 2001; Yeates 2001). Nor can it be easily accommodated with the fact that supra-national policy making allows considerable variation in the detail of social policies at the national level. This is, after all, a matter of subsidiarity. Operating with a relatively large number of countries means that our use of the nation-state as the unit of analysis does not preclude the examination of cross-cultural patterns as they are manifested in social policy. There are sufficient cases to be able to draw out the overarching commonalities among, for example, those that share a particular political ideology. This allows us to examine the potential clustering of nations into groups that share a common policy tradition (Therborn 1993).

2.5   Overview

Revisiting definitions of the welfare state proves useful in drawing attention to the normative agency of the welfare state and the processes in which the welfare state engages. The former relates to the constituent elements of the welfare state, invoking a view of it as both a body of law and rules and a set of cash transfers and services. While this provides a useful elaboration of content, it becomes meaningful only when it is considered alongside the agency or activity of the welfare state. The focus in this study, then, is not just on what the welfare state is, but on what it does. The literature considered in this chapter and the last highlights the fact that the welfare state is involved in a range of processes. In an attempt to organize the different forms of agency, we distinguish two key sets of welfare state activities. The first, the most concrete and certainly the most familiar, pertains to resource distribution. It is no secret that the welfare state reorders access to resources, with consequences for material well-being and social inequality. This is in many countries the *raison d'être* of the welfare state. Money transfers do not capture fully welfare state resource distribution, however. Time is another resource that is, in part anyway, in the gift of the welfare state to redistribute, most prominently through care-related services and benefits. While redistribution may be seen as representing a power settlement of some kind, it does not exhaust the significance of the welfare state's association with power-related matters. This leads on to a second form of welfare state agency – how it frames and engages in activities that affect the power balance between women and men. Political contest is inherent in the welfare state. This is to be seen in its control over resources and its power to frame contests. There are two aspects of relevance here. First, the welfare state is not a neutral or passive participant, but is active in both shaping and negotiating power relations. By virtue of its authority and the fact that it mediates between claims, it imbues certain ideas, roles and practices with power. Viewing it as a site and sometimes source of contest allows one to see that any settlement around welfare is temporary. Discourses concerning reform are therefore very important, for they can reveal the power-based nature of opposing ideas and competing claims to welfare state support. Secondly, there is a gender aspect to welfare state activity, in that it exerts a significant influence on the balance of power between women and men.

Reflecting on gender as a concept is also rewarding since it allows us to clarify gender as a set of social practices that find expression in the dynamic relations between women and men as well as in differentiation in the structural position of women and men as social groups or categories of social actors. The view of gender relations elaborated in this work sees them as constituted by access to resources, social roles and power relations. This framework of gender relations was further elaborated by specifying the lenses through which the links between gender relations and the welfare state are to be observed. Care, work and welfare are fundamental to society across the eight countries, and have meaning in each.

Finally, our interest in variation in welfare states and gender relations can be pursued only through a comparative research methodology. Drawing on a case-oriented approach to comparison, this research analyses a relatively large number of cases. The countries – France, Germany, Ireland, Italy, the Netherlands, Sweden, the UK and the USA – were selected with an eye to the significance for explanatory purposes of similarity and diversity across national welfare states.

3

Gender and the Provision of Care

This chapter focuses on the social and economic relations of care. It draws out the relevant features of care as it is organized and carried out within and across countries and in terms of its consequences for gender relations. We begin in the first section with the policy backdrop, outlining the key features of care as it is addressed by public policy across the eight countries. Since care is in some ways a relatively new exigency for welfare states, some time is devoted at the outset to identifying underlying policy models, paying special attention to linkages across policy domains and to how the different welfare states resemble or differ from each other in the way that they fashion care as a social good. The second part of the chapter searches after the empirical or actual organization and provision of care in everyday life. The volume of care and the conditions under which care is carried out are the subject of discussion here. In its third part, the chapter identifies some implications or effects of the different public policies (or lack of them in some cases). In this regard, it looks especially at the employment and income-related effects associated with the social organization of care. Given the lack of information on the identity of carers for adults, such effects are examined primarily in terms of the implications for mothers. The extent to which care is linked with or is a source of contest, debate and power relations forms the substance of the fourth part of the chapter.

3.1 The Governance of Care

3.1.1 Defining care

Care is defined with reference to the activities and relations involved in caring for the ill, the elderly and the dependent young. It is remarkable in a number of respects. It is at one and the same time a form of interpersonal relations and a social exigency or necessary activity in society. Hence care is particularistic – in the sense that it pertains to intimate human relations and activities – and yet at the same time general – in the sense that it is part of and integral to society. A second remarkable feature of care is that, rooted in relations of personal involvement and also to some extent personal service, there is a moral element in care that distances it from the usual boundaries of work (Feder Kittay 2001: 41). Having taken some time to mature as an academic concept, care is today an established field of study, especially in sociology and social policy. Not only is care recognized as a promising line of academic enquiry, but it is coming to be the axis of much feminist analysis of welfare states. Running a risk of over-simplification, one could say that care has had two main currencies in the literature: as a concept utilized to interrogate and account for the life experiences of women, and as a tool for the analysis of social policy (Daly and Lewis 2000). In the former guise, the concept draws attention to the material and ideological processes that make up care and at the same time confirm women in the social role of carer. Care has been identified as work with a woman's face. In the analysis of social policy, care has been the subject of scholarship that focuses on how social policy has sought to manage the demand for and supply of care. As a defining feature of both private life and public provision, then, care serves to reveal how the linkages between family, state and society are gendered.

Taking the literature on care overall, there are a number of points worth emphasizing. The first is that social policy is hugely important in determining the form and consequences of care in society. This is not to say that public policy has always and everywhere actively engaged with care – as we shall see in the pages that follow, this is a variation. But when public policy has treated care as a social exigency, the possibility of an alternative vision of women's lives and family life is introduced. A second point is that the political economy of care extends beyond public provision. While the state may provide supports and services and regulate the conditions under which care is undertaken in the public realm, most care is provided informally in families and communities and has costs attaching to it (even if these are not always visible). A broad political economy is therefore involved. These two insights inform this chapter throughout.

3.1.2 Policy parameters of care

Care is quite unique as a concern for social policy, which is more accustomed to meeting financial need and generally holds itself aloof from the relational implications of its own practice. Care is also very complex.[1] At least part of the complexity derives from the fact that care, although it tends to be more readily conceived of in interpersonal terms, is present also at the macro or collective level. To the extent that welfare states respond to the needs associated with care, they are altering the division of labour, cost and responsibility among the state, market, voluntary/non-profit sector and family. In addition, making provision for care involves welfare states in recasting what were heretofore in almost all national settings private forms of solidarity and exchange. Relations of gender and generation are especially affected. A second dimension of complexity arises from the fact that making provision for care may entail the satisfaction of (one or more of) three needs: a need for services, for time and for financial support. The underlying point here is that although welfare states may choose to respond in a uni-dimensional fashion, care as an exigency for public policy has at least three dimensions. A further complicating aspect of care is that it is a policy good with a number of constituencies: the person experiencing the set of needs that comprise care and the actors who seek or are assigned to satisfy that set of needs. Finally, and related to the last point, care can be either or both formal and informal. Even in the most advanced welfare states, care is never provided completely in formal (professional) settings.

Pared to its essence, the welfare state either provides care directly or provides resources to enable people in private life to (continue to) provide it. This is to over-simplify the situation, however. The policy landscape surrounding care in European welfare states is actually quite crowded. One can identify four general types of provision, each with its own compensatory aim or logic:

- *Monetary and social security benefits*, such as cash payments, credits for benefit purposes, tax allowances. These compensate people financially for either the provision of care or the costs incurred in requiring care.
- *Employment-related measures*, such as paid and unpaid leaves, career breaks, severance pay, flexi-time, reduction of working

time. Time and income compensation for earnings lost are the main 'goods' conferred by these provisions.

- *Benefits or services provided in kind,* such as home helps and other community-based support services, child care places, residential places for adults and children, and so forth. These provide care directly, thereby substituting for private provision.
- *Incentives for provision other than by the state,* such as subsidies towards costs, vouchers for domestic employment, and vouchers for child care.

These influence the supply of care and have a direct effect in shifting the locus of care.

3.1.3   Provision of care-related supports and services

What matters empirically is how different measures are brought together by welfare states into an overall architecture. What are the main contours of variation in how the eight welfare states in this study make provision for care?

Taking children first, the two measures most telling of how public policies treat care are parental, as distinct from maternity, leave and public child care facilities. What matters most about the former is whether it is paid or unpaid and also the generosity in terms of both the level of payment and the duration. In regard to child care, coverage in terms of the proportion of the age cohort reached can be considered to be the most significant factor. Table 3.1 shows how countries compare in regard to their provision on each of these measures.[2] The amount of variation is striking. Looking at the second column, we can see that, when maternity leave is combined with parental leave, countries vary widely in terms of the duration of leave. Germany and France offer a very long period of leave (162 weeks), whereas the USA has no mandatory, nationwide programme of job-protected leave (either maternity or parental). Ireland and Italy tend towards the less interventionist end of the scale, with 18 and 25 weeks respectively of employment leave. However, the absolute length of the leave available is a less reliable measure of 'quality' than the duration of leave that is paid. This, reproduced in the third column of table 3.1, shows the cross-national comparison in a somewhat different light. Sweden now precedes Germany in offering the longest period of parental leave – the equivalent of 43 weeks of paid leave in comparison with Germany where it is 32 weeks. Italy is the next most interventionist provider – the average Italian parent can avail themselves of the equivalent of 25 weeks of paid leave to care for

Table 3.1   Provision for children, early to mid-1990s

	Consecutive weeks of maternal and parental leave	Equivalent of (maternity and parental) leave, weeks paid in full	% of cohort attending/ places available in publicly funded services for children 0–3	% of cohort attending/ places available in publicly funded services for children 3–6
France	162	Medium (13.5)	Medium (23)	High (99)
Germany	162	High (31.7)	Medium (22)	Medium (85)
Ireland	18	Low (9.8)	Low (2)	Low (55)
Italy	25	Medium (25.1)	Low (6)	High (91)
Netherlands	42	Medium (16.0)	Low (8)	Medium (71)
Sweden	64	High (42.6)	High (33)	Medium (72)
UK	40	Low (8.6)	Low (2)	Low (60)
USA	12	0	–	–

Source: Adapted from Bettio and Prechal 1998: 21, 32, 47

young children. There is a substantial drop then to 16 weeks for the Netherlands and 13 for France. The UK and Ireland are the least interventionist in regard to the distribution and nature of family roles, offering 9 and 10 weeks respectively of fully paid leave (effectively only paid maternity leave). The patterns of provision and the cross-national comparison remain fairly consistent when the spotlight is turned on the provision of child care services (last two columns of table 3.1). France, Germany and Sweden are the highest providers, and Ireland and the UK the lowest. Italy and the Netherlands are similar in favouring private provision for younger children but public provision once children reach the age of three.

Welfare states treat care for the elderly quite differently from that for children (table 3.2). Whereas leave for parents is one of the most widespread types of policy response to the need for care of children, residential provision and also cash payments to those who either provide or need care are the customary policy responses to the need for care of the elderly. Indeed, in line with a European-wide trend towards home-based care, the welfare states under consideration here are increasingly willing to make a payment specifically for the activity of 'private' care for the disabled and the elderly. The UK was the first country in Europe to pay for private (in the sense of informal) care for ill and elderly adults, with the introduction in 1976 of a social security payment for a person providing care. Ireland quickly followed the UK's lead, but the international pattern is far from homogeneous in

Table 3.2   Provision for the elderly (65+), early to mid-1990s

	Whether a payment for care exists	% of the elderly in institutional care	% of elderly receiving home care services
France	No	Low (2)	Medium (7)
Germany	Yes	Medium (3)	Low (3)
Ireland	Yes	Medium (5)	Low (3)
Italy	No	Low (2)	Low (1)
Netherlands	No	High (10)	Medium (8)
Sweden	Yes	Medium (5)	High (13)
UK	Yes	Medium (5)	High (13)
USA	No	–	–

Source: Adapted from Bettio and Prechal 1998: 41, 52

that other countries have chosen different routes. Germany also now pays for this activity (since 1995), but makes the payment to the care receiver. Three of the other European states – France, Italy and the Netherlands – together with the USA still lack such a general cash benefit.[3] When it comes to services rather than cash, Sweden, along with the Netherlands and the UK, are the highest providers (table 3.2). Countries vary in terms of the emphasis that they place on home services as against care in institutions. Thus the UK is a relatively high provider of home care services but only a medium provider of institutional care. The relative position in the Netherlands is the reverse. Italy is low in both, and Ireland and Germany have medium levels of institutional care but are relatively low providers of public services to the elderly in the community. France tends to favour services in the community over those of an institutional nature.

Putting all of this information together allows us to establish how these countries resemble or differ from each other. First, one must separate out Sweden. It merits the epithet of a 'caring state' in that the guarantee of social security embraces not only monetary security but also the promise of professional care for those with high need (Leira 1993). Care, conceived mainly as the right to receive it, is a constituent element of Swedish social citizenship. Germany and the Netherlands form a second grouping. These states, especially Germany and to a lesser extent the Netherlands, appear to hold the view that care should as far as possible be provided by the family. Hence, there are limits placed on the extent to which the public authorities are prepared to make financial and other arrangements for a good that they view as most appropriately located in the family and civil society. The final set of countries – Ireland, Italy, the UK – resemble each other to the extent that they are characterized by inaction on some fronts but some public provision on others. While Italy tends to be more active as regards provision for children, Ireland and the UK are quite active on care for the elderly, having over the course of time increased services (in Ireland largely because of economic developments, in the UK because of these together with changes in the notion of family solidarity) and more actively promoted the provision of a care-related cash payment. France is somewhat of an exception. While it resembles Sweden in some aspects of its approach to child care, the norm of family care is quite strong, and certainly in larger families care is managed in such a way that it is most appropriately provided by mothers. The USA is another exception, by virtue of the very low prevalence of public services.

Against this policy backdrop, what is the empirical reality of care across the different countries?

3.2   The Provision of Care

3.2.1   The volume of informal care

In all countries the vast majority of care is informal (in the sense of being provided on an unprofessional basis in the care recipient's own home) and unpaid. In regard to care for the elderly, one report suggests that across the fifteen member states of the EU and Norway informal care is five times more prevalent than formal care (European Commission 1999: 20). This varies cross-nationally, though.

Focusing on informal or unpaid care, table 3.3 presents the most recent information on the numbers of people (in the six EU member

Table 3.3 Percentage of the adult population whose daily activities include caring for children or for sick, disabled or frail adults without pay by sex, 1996

	Caring for children		Caring for adults		Both children and adults	
	women	men	women	men	women	men
France	23	12	5	3	27	14
Germany	28	16	7	4	33	19
Ireland	40	17	7	3	44	19
Italy	37	15	9	4	41	18
Netherlands	41	31	8	5	45	34
UK	37	21	10	6	43	26

Source: Eurostat 2001b: 117

states covered by this study apart from Sweden) who are involved in providing unpaid care to children and sick, disabled or frail adults on an everyday basis. Informal care is quite a widespread activity. For example, in the EU just under one in four of citizens aged sixteen and over is involved in looking after children (their own or those of others) on a daily basis without pay (Eurostat 2001a: 82). The proportion caring for adults on a similar basis is about 6 per cent. These, it is important to point out, are not the same people. In fact, between a quarter and a third of the EU's citizens are involved in providing unpaid care. Taking the six countries as a whole, informal care impinges most in the lives of Dutch, Italian, Irish and British citizens.

Care for children is much more widespread than that for adults. Of the countries included in the study, the numbers of people providing unpaid care for children are highest in the Netherlands (at around 35 per cent) and lowest in France (at around 16 per cent). Ireland is another country with a high percentage of people involved in informal care for children, and it is followed by Italy and the UK. Germany has a somewhat lower proportion, closer to France than those other countries. Turning to unpaid care for sick or disabled adults or older people, not only are considerably fewer people involved in providing this form of unpaid care, but there is less variation cross-nationally. The UK followed by Italy and the Netherlands are the countries with the highest proportion of the population involved in caring for sick, disabled or frail adults. France is again at the lowest end of the scale.

In terms of the identity of the unpaid care providers, women are twice as likely as men to be involved in providing both child care (31 per cent compared with 15 per cent) and care for ill or elderly adults (8 per cent as against 4 per cent) (Eurostat 2001b: 28). In Italy and Ireland, the gender disparity is especially marked, being nearly three to one. The Netherlands is an interesting exception in regard to the high percentage of men (31 per cent) who are involved in providing unpaid child care as part of their daily activities; it thus has the smallest gender disparity of any country. Following sex, age is the next most important factor in the identity of the care provider. For example, across the EU carers of children are predominantly drawn from two age groups: those in the 30–39 and 40–49 age brackets. In regard to the care of sick or disabled adults and older people, it is people aged fifty years and over (especially those in the 50–59 age bracket) who take the major responsibility (Eurostat 2001b: 28). It is important to note that the identity of the carer and also the gender distribution of care work depend to some extent on the location of care. In Great Britain, for example, when care is being provided for someone in the same household, men are as likely as women to be the provider, but when the care recipient lives in another household, women are much more likely to be the carers (Arber and Ginn 1999).[4] Overall, however, caring is a highly gendered activity in European countries, except for the Netherlands and to a lesser extent the UK.

In terms of the amount of time expended, the average number of hours spent on unpaid child care in the EU as a whole is 34 hours per week (Eurostat 2001a: 82–3). Care is more demanding of women's time – they devote an average of 41 hours per week to it, compared with a male average of 21 hours. In regard to care for adults, the amount of time expended is less – 21 hours per week on average across the EU. While this type of caring also takes up more of women's time than men's, the gender disparity in time expended (22 hours for women, compared with 18 for men) is less than it is for child care. This information is not available on individual countries.

3.2.2   Conditions of paid caring

When enquiring into the conditions of care work, one must look not only at care workers in the labour market but also at the conditions under which such work is carried out informally. Information in both cases is very scarce, and there is almost no cross-national material available. As a result, we can piece together only some of the story, especially since most of the available information is for people who are employed as carers.

In regard to employed care workers, among the best sources are a recent OECD (2001c) study of early childhood care and education in twelve countries and a research programme by the European Foundation for the Improvement of Living and Working Conditions on the promotion of employment in household services in EU countries (Cancedda 2001).[5] This work, together with that of Christopherson (1997), the OECD (1998) and Moss (2001), reports considerable variation as regards the conditions of care work and the career opportunities available to those who carry out this work for pay. One of the seeming constants across nations, however, is a feminization of the caring sector. As the sector has grown, women have formed an ever larger majority of paid care workers. Up to recently the caring sector had seen hardly any organizational change. However, not only has it begun to expand considerably, there have been changes in the regulatory frameworks governing the provision of services, as well as moves towards decentralization and privatization of the financing

(OECD 1998: 183). The result is a growth in a largely unregulated labour force, much of it in the private sector.

Taking child care on its own, there is almost always a hierarchy among care workers, at its least pronounced in the Scandinavian countries. But across countries, out-of-school care provision for children is relatively neglected as an occupational sector, with the result that wages are low and there is little or no regulation, training or career structure. Moreover, there are areas within this sector – family-based care, for example – that are in many countries open to whoever wishes to enter them. One factor which makes a significant difference to working conditions for child care workers within and across countries is the degree to which early childhood services are integrated within one (educational) system. Where this is the case, as for example in Sweden, conditions tend to be better. However, in other countries, especially France, Ireland and the USA, early child care is divided between the educational and welfare sectors, with the latter (which tends to cater for the younger children and to be known as the 'child care' sector) having poorer working conditions and also a generally lower status. Despite the fact that the UK is moving towards a more integrated system, child care workers there and in the USA are paid at a rate close to the minimum wage (Christopherson 1997). In the USA, for example, a survey of child care workers found that they earned less than half the average earnings for the female labour force as a whole, and a third of male average earnings (Whitebook et al. 1990).

The occupational structure in regard to care for the elderly is more universally two-tier and, therefore, bifurcated. One level involves some medical assistance with or without personal care, and the other, lower level centres on household work sometimes combined with personal care (Christopherson 1997). The overwhelming majority of the latter workers across countries are employed on a part-time or casual basis, and turnover rates are high. Moreover, the elderly care sector is, according to the OECD (1998: 179), situated at the low end of the earnings scale in the broader social and care sector. There are few career prospects, and many of those involved in paid care for the elderly carry out their work in very isolated circumstances.

There is no comparable information available on the conditions under which people provide informal care. In terms of the nature of the work involved and the experience of carers, research suggests a conflict between the image of caring work, which is typically portrayed as requiring few skills, and the reality, in which quite a complex set of resources are required (Christopherson 1997: 6).

3.3   Income and Other Implications of Caring

There is no straightforward or easy way to measure the implications of being involved in care or the outcomes associated with care-related policies. This is because we have too little information on who is providing care and the conditions under which they are doing so. Such information shortages frustrate the identification of a clear category of 'carer'. Informal care for ill and elderly adults is especially hidden. Only rarely likely to be full-time, it is often fitted in around existing economic and other activities, including retirement. To know the effects of care or the implications of policy on it is therefore difficult, if not impossible, especially if care results only in minor adjustments to normal activities. The 'big bang' of motherhood is the easiest aspect of care to identify. The labour market behaviour of mothers of young children allows us to build up a picture of how caring is associated with absence from or reduced participation in the labour force. Given this, we are going to take the situation of mothers of children under five years (and in the case of larger families children under fifteen) to interrogate some of the costs associated with providing care for children. In terms of the range of implications of caring, existing work suggests that caring has two possible effects (Jenson and Jacobzone 2000). In the first instance there is a substitution effect, whereby time devoted to informal care reduces labour market participation, either by a complete withdrawal or by a reduction in hours. The second is an income effect, caused by income forgone due to investment in caring work which is either unremunerated or offers only a low level of financial compensation. In seeking the financial implications of caring, therefore, we are especially interested in two sets of effects: chances for participation in employment and the effects on income.

3.3.1   The labour market-related implications of being a carer

There is considerable evidence that caring affects labour market participation (Jenson and Jacobzone 2000). As Carmichael and Charles (1998: 762) put it, care involves an opportunity cost in the form of forgone labour supply of female carers who are of working age.

When women who were economically inactive or working part-time were asked in 1997 about the reasons for their current economic status, the proportion citing personal or family responsibilities was as shown in table 3.4.[6] Clearly, the extent to which caring is associated with constraints in relation to labour supply is something that varies hugely cross-nationally. Only 1 per cent of economically inactive

Table 3.4 Percentage of inactive women and women in part-time employment citing personal or family responsibilities as the reason for their current employment status, 1997

	Inactive*	Part-time**
France	1	29
Germany	19	69
Ireland	4	46
Italy	37.5	24
Netherlands	40	50
Sweden	5	–
UK	22	48
USA	68.8***	–

Sources: * Eurostat 1998: table 111
  ** Eurostat 1999a: table 2
  *** Bureau of Labor Statistics 1998. The statistic refers to women aged
      between 25 and 54 years only, and is for 1996

French women, compared with 69 per cent of their US counterparts, cite personal or family responsibilities as the reason for why they are not in the labour force. The USA, Netherlands, Italy, the UK and Germany appear to be the countries where care responsibilities exert the strongest and most direct effect in preventing women from entering the labour market. Such a reported effect of caring in Ireland, and to a lesser extent France, is surprisingly low. It may, however, be significant that upwards of three-quarters of inactive women in these two countries gave no reason for their economic status. In general, the results from women working part-time confirm both the significance of caring and the way it patterns women's labour supply cross-nationally. We can see that caring constitutes the greatest identified constraint on the female labour supply in the USA, the Netherlands and the UK, and the least in Italy and France. Ireland occupies a position somewhere in between these extremes. Putting the data together, in the Netherlands caring would appear to be as likely to keep women out of the labour market as to direct them into part-time employment. The relationship is similar but weaker in Italy. In the other countries, caring is more likely to result in part-time employment for women, especially in Germany, Ireland and the UK. Overall, it appears that caring has the strongest negative effect on women's labour supply in Germany, the Netherlands and the UK, and the weakest in Italy and France.

Of course, these results have to be set in the context of the overall proportions of women who are in and out of the labour market. Hence, we need to explore the labour force participation of different groups of carers. This information is most widely available for mothers. Table 3.5 shows the comparison for the age group 25–49 years between the employment rate of mothers with young children and women without children.

To take all women in the age group first, Ireland and Italy are outliers, with employment rates in the region of 50 per cent, compared with an average of 70 per cent. Hence, before we even take account of the effects of motherhood, these two countries stand apart by virtue of relatively low female employment rates. Germany, the UK and the USA are the countries where motherhood has the greatest impact on women's employment rate, however, reducing it by up to about a third in comparison to women without children. Motherhood also exerts a rather strong effect in Ireland and France, with mothers' employment rates down on those of childless women by over a fifth. However, in Italy and the Netherlands the effects of motherhood on employment are (surprisingly in the case of the latter) rather minor. In Italy, where there is a very low female employment rate overall, motherhood (of young children anyway) does not significantly differentiate between women in and out of employment. The case of the Netherlands may not be directly comparable to the other countries, in that mothers' employment is almost exclusively part-time, so overall employment rates are somewhat deceptive.

This is not an exhaustive account of the relationship between motherhood and participation in employment, however. One of the great insights of feminist scholarship on the labour market is that the effects of children on women's labour market participation are not to

Table 3.5 Employment rates of women aged 25–49 years, 1998

	All women	Childless women	Women with children 0–5	col. 3 – col. 4
France	68.6	73.2	57.0	16.2 (22%)
Germany	69.1	74.3	50.1	24.2 (33%)
Ireland	55.6	59.7	46.0	13.7 (23%)
Italy	51.0	52.5	45.7	6.8 (13%)
Netherlands	69.8	73.2	60.7	12.5 (17%)
UK	72.1	78.8	55.4	23.4 (30%)
USA*	67.6**	85.2***	61.5***	23.7 (28%)

Sources: Eurostat 2001a: 106
  * OECD 2001a: 211, 134
  ** The statistic refers to women aged between 16 and 64 years and to the year 1999
  *** The statistics refer to women aged between 20 and 60 years and to the year 1999

be understood in absolute terms, but rather are refracted through a number of lenses. Chief among these is the number of children. Table 3.6 shows how this set of effects operates across countries by comparing the gap in the activity rate between mothers of different-sized families to that of women with no children for all countries except Sweden and the USA (for which no data were available).

Across countries the number of children makes a considerable difference to mothers' activity rates. Increased numbers of children tend in general to erode mothers' economic activity to the point where women with three or more children have their labour market participation reduced by around 40 percentage points. In terms of cross-national comparison, these results tend to confirm those above, in that children have the strongest effect on women's participation rate in Ireland and Germany, and the least in France, the Netherlands and Italy. However, while motherhood always matters (except for sometimes in France and Italy), any such general effects are mediated by the number of children. There are some countries where the number of children makes a significant impact. France is a case in point; it is only when women have three or more children that their economic activity rate is significantly affected. This is true also in Italy. The relationship is generally similar in the UK and Germany, but the effect of having children on women's labour force participation is stronger for all family sizes in these two countries as compared with Italy and France. The pattern in the Netherlands and Ireland is somewhat different, in that even one child has a strong downward effect (although of the two countries the labour supply-depressing effects of subsequent children are stronger in Ireland). If we take fertility rates and existing family size

Table 3.6 Absolute difference between the activity rates of mothers with different numbers of children as compared with women without children aged between 20 and 45 years, 1997

	Mother 1 child	Mother 2 children	Mother 3+ children
France	0	−9	−36
Germany	−12	−25	−42
Ireland	−19	−30	−42
Italy	−6	−12	−27
Netherlands	−18	−23	−34
UK	−13	−18	−41

Source: Eurostat 1998: calculated from graph 27, p. 263

into account, the effects of larger family size on reducing female labour supply are likely to be most severe in Ireland and the UK given current demographic patterns.

Overall, if we view the costs of care in terms of constraints on female labour supply and mothers' employment, the Netherlands, Germany and the UK are the countries where the costs attaching to care are the greatest. It is important to point out, though, that other research on the UK has found that the effect on women's labour supply depends on the volume of caring that they have to do (Carmichael and Charles 1998). The study of Carmichael and Charles found that a threshold of 20 hours (of caring a week) made a significant difference in terms of labour supply, and hence earnings capacity. This finding of the labour market effect being mediated by the intensity of care giving is also reported for the USA by Boaz and Muller (1992). If we turn our attention to mothers specifically, the Netherlands, the UK and the USA are the three countries along with Ireland where having young children most affects employment rates. France and Italy are different. In France it is the number of children that makes for significant differences in activity rates of mothers and non-mothers. In Italy women's economic activity patterns are so compromised anyway that being a mother (especially of one child, which is the norm in Italy) does not make for a lot of difference. Very little information is available on Sweden and the USA, but these appear to be more similar to France than to the Netherlands, Germany and UK.

3.3.2   Income-related effects of being a carer

When it comes to investigating income, data constraints together with the paucity of research on the topic again limit the analysis. One study that is available from the UK (Carers National Association 2000) suggests that caring is associated there with considerable financial hardship and has a strong negative impact on income. For example, 77 per cent of the carer respondents reported being worse off since becoming carers, and almost one in three were reliant on the safety net benefit – Income Support. In the following sections we are compelled, because of information shortages, to confine our analysis of the financial implications of caring to mothers.

The income-related effects of motherhood can be measured in a number of ways. For our purposes, gaps in wages or earnings and poverty rates are the most telling indicators. With regard to wages, Harkness and Waldfogel (1999) used the LIS data base to identify the effects of gender and family situation on wages. Information is available for only four of the eight countries, however. The gender

Table 3.7 Mean hourly wages* of different groups of women as percentage of mean hourly wages of men (age group 24–44), mid-1990s

	All women	Women without children	Women with children	col. 3 − col. 4
Germany	86.6	88.2	85.5	−2.7
Sweden	83.9	85.0	83.4	−1.6
UK	74.6	82.2	69.6	−12.6
USA	78.3	82.9	75.6	−7.3

Source: Harkness and Waldfogel 1999
* Wages are defined as gross annual earnings divided by the number of hours worked

comparison, as well as that for women with and without children, in these four countries is shown in table 3.7.

Of these particular countries, the gender gaps are largest in the UK and the USA and smallest in Germany, where women's wages are equivalent to 87 per cent of those of men. From the third and fourth columns of the table, one can see that it is differences for mothers, rather than for women without children, which mainly account for any cross-national variation. The effects of motherhood are strongest in the UK, where mothers' hourly wages are equivalent to 70 per cent of those of men. The situation is somewhat better in the USA, but it is in Germany where having children has least effect on women's wages. Both German and Swedish women with children are paid about the same as women without children. Regression analyses correct this latter impression somewhat though, showing that the number of children exerts a powerful influence on women's wages everywhere except Sweden. However, such effects are again largest in the UK, where the pay penalty for one child is 8 per cent (compared with 4 per cent in the USA and 2 per cent in Germany), and that for three or more children is 31 per cent (compared with 11 per cent for the USA[7]). Further investigation shows that the reason why the UK has the largest wage penalties for children is because mothers there are more likely to work in low-paid, part-time jobs and also because, even among full-timers, women with children are lower paid relative to other women than are mothers in other countries.

Since not all mothers are in the labour market, it is important to have a more general idea of their economic well-being. In this regard information on the distribution of poverty is helpful. Setting the poverty threshold at 40 per cent of median income, table 3.8 shows a number of gender-related dimensions of the relationship between

Table 3.8 Poverty and parenthood for women and men aged between 25 and 54 years, early 1990s

	Mothers' poverty rate as % of that of fathers	Mothers' poverty rate as % of that of childless women	Fathers' poverty rate as % of that of childless men	Lone mothers' poverty rate as % of that of mothers in couples	Lone mothers' poverty rate as % of that of single childless women
France (1989)	119	84	68	306	172
Germany (1994)	231	187	72	129	352
Netherlands (1991)	145	148	100	554	321
Sweden (1992)	86	57	47	69	21
UK (1995)	126	232	135	255	285
USA (1994)	171	190	113	533	256

Source: Smeeding et al. 1999

poverty and parenthood for people aged between twenty-five and fifty-four years in six of our eight nations.

The general background is of lower male than female poverty rates (for both parents and non-parents alike) and of parents being more likely than childless adults to be poor. Sweden and France are the only two nations in this comparison where parents' prevalence of poverty is less than that of people without children. Sweden is a most exceptional case in another respect also, in that not only are mothers less likely to be poor than fathers, but both male and female parents have a poverty rate that is only half that of non-parents of the same sex. The situation is very different elsewhere, however. Right across the other five countries, mothers' poverty rate exceeds that of fathers. The comparison is least favourable in Germany, where the maternal poverty rate is almost two and a half times that of fathers. This is a result of a high poverty rate for German lone mothers. In the USA and the Netherlands also, mothers' poverty rate is markedly higher than that of fathers. Mothers are not always disadvantaged relative to other women, however. When looked at in terms of disadvantage relative to others of the same sex (third column), France joins Sweden as a country where mothers have a lower prevalence of poverty than childless women. For the other countries the situation once again differs. The most extreme effects of motherhood are found in the UK, where mothers' poverty rate is more than double that of childless women (and 26 per cent in excess of that of fathers). The effects in Germany, the USA and the Netherlands, while slightly weaker, still point to motherhood as a very significant poverty 'inducer' in comparison with other women. This is true for fathers only in the UK and the USA (fourth column), and even here the poverty-inducing effects of fatherhood are much weaker in comparison with those of motherhood. The general tendency is for fatherhood to reduce men's risk of poverty, very significantly so in Sweden, France and Germany.

The evidence suggests that poverty among people aged between twenty-five and fifty-four years is tied to parenthood in general and to motherhood in particular (Smeeding et al. 1999: 20). The situation for mothers is at its most extreme in most countries when they are rearing children alone (as we shall see in more detail in chapter 5). As the last two columns of table 3.8 show, the situation of lone mothers compares most unfavourably across all countries (except Sweden) to that of mothers in couples and single childless women.[8] In regard to female lone parents, Germany joins the USA as the worst-case scenario, with poverty rates among lone parents standing at 31 per cent and 37.9 per cent respectively (compared with a national average for the age group of 3.8 per cent and 9.4 per cent respectively). One of the most striking findings in table 3.8 is that German lone mothers have a poverty rate that is thirteen times in excess of that of mothers in couples. By comparison, the disadvantage of lone mothers in other countries pales into insignificance (although in the USA and the Netherlands lone mothers' poverty rate is five times that of mothers in couples). The comparisons are generally less extreme between lone mothers and childless women (except for the UK). In general, it is important to point out that as a case of care the situation of lone mothers is somewhat extreme because it combines a number of risks. Consequently, any effects found are due not to care alone, but in addition to having to provide care without access to a male income (and in many cases also without access to market income). The larger point, of course, is, that it is impossible to know where one risk ends and another begins.

Taken together, the UK and the USA (and Ireland also, although data are less widely available) are the countries where the costs of care bear very heavily on women, placing mothers at quite a serious financial disadvantage relative to both childless women and fathers. Sweden is the opposite case to these countries – motherhood makes no differences to average wage rates, and it actually reduces a woman's risk of poverty. The Swedish case is highly unusual in the present comparison, however, and patterns in the other countries, with some exception in the case of France, suggest that the comparative issue is not whether motherhood has a negative effect on women's poverty rates, but how great is the effect.

3.4   Power Relations and Contests Associated with Gender and Care

The politics of care revolves in the first instance around the resource flows associated with it. For example, some of the costs of motherhood are to be seen in the lower hourly wages of mothers as compared with women without children. In addition, mothers in all countries except Sweden have a higher risk of poverty than fathers, and lone mothers are especially vulnerable to poverty. While exact relationships are difficult to pin down, the cross-national variation found in this set of relationships makes it clear that the position adopted by the welfare state has a significant impact. The exceptional nature of the Swedish welfare state in not just protecting mothers, but in reducing their relative chances of poverty, stands out clearly, for example. In comparing this and other welfare states, it is clear that social policies can and do affect the resource flows around care in two ways. First, they may protect the interface between the risks associated with family-related activities – for example, that of motherhood. Second, they affect the conditions under which care is carried out, including the resources associated with it, by influencing whether the work is paid or not. At issue here are the boundaries of social intervention: to the extent to which the activities involved in care are considered public, they are somehow paid, although there is variation in the level at which they are compensated.

Resource flows are themselves outcomes of other, arguably more deep-rooted processes. The second way in which welfare states become involved in the politics of care is in terms of how they influence the meaning and composition of different roles. In general across countries, care provision affirms women in the role of carers. There is variation, though, in two key respects. In the first instance, the degree or intensity of the carer role – whether full-time or a combination of full- or part-time – varies. Countries that especially tend towards a mixed carer/worker role include the Netherlands and the UK. Because of the way in which care is supported or not by public policies, the choices and opportunities available to women and men are delimited. The second source of variation is the extent to which the carer role is valorized. This leads deep into the politics of the welfare state. The exposure to poverty and to low income of different groups reflects not just their position *vis-à-vis* the market, but is a manifestation also of the extent to which family-related activities are valorized and protected.

Thirdly, welfare states' political engagement with care centres on how they frame the normative environment. Given that care at an interpersonal level is so often set within a culture of social obligation, the care giver may have little choice about providing care. It may also be the case that her or his needs are not taken into account by policy or are overshadowed by those of the care receiver (who is generally regarded as being in a more vulnerable position). One can see how policy favours one set of interests over another. While it is inappropriate to see children as having 'interests' as such, the interest-based nature of care and care policy is clear when we look at care for adults. Because they tend to view care in a uni-dimensional way, public policies everywhere make a payment to either the care giver or the care receiver. This has huge implications for the power relations involved in care, and usually acts to reinforce the power of the care giver or the care receiver (Daly 2002). A further political issue is the question of who should care. This is especially important in the contemporary climate, where changing norms about the meaning of family obligation and altered patterns of family life mean that people are no longer willing or able to care for their family members. This is centrally a matter of gender, because, as is clear from much of the foregoing, across countries care is women's work. Whereas men are viewed as choosing to care, there is an obligation on women in those societies that we are studying, as well as in many others, to be the care givers, even when this interferes with their own (income security and other) needs. Welfare states, as we have seen, are active in supporting that obligation. Hence, a further aspect of the politics of public policy regarding care is that it has huge import for individual women and men and, writ large, serves to either alleviate or intensify gender inequalities.

It would be wrong to represent the policies of welfare states with regard to care as unambiguous in intent or effect. They are not. As we have seen, across countries cash benefits for care may have the intention of supporting women in a traditional role or may act to alter the distribution of responsibility for care. Furthermore, when a programme of cash benefits and taxation allowances is compared with employment leaves, one can see some ambiguities. Where such leaves are paid, it is unclear whether they are fulfilling a wage replacement function for women, who are expected to be absent only temporarily from the labour market, or whether they are a way of making some compensatory payments to women for work that has traditionally been unpaid. In addition, the extent to which such policies are consistent with taxation and benefit policies should not be taken for granted. The sensitivity around providing for care has led to ambiguities and in some cases contradictions between income and leave policies.

3.5   Overview

The theoretical framework of this book places a premium on care. Care provides an excellent way of understanding contemporary social policy, and especially the dilemmas that societies are resolving or creating with their increasing interventions to shape the meaning of care and how it is provided. Economic matters, which are so often the lens through which public policy is framed, appear quite uncomplicated when juxtaposed with the moral and social aspects of care policy. Care is, therefore, a signature piece of society, invoking and at the same time shaping the division of labour and responsibility between women and men and the state, the family and the market.

One of the main arguments developed in this chapter is that making provision for care involves welfare states in a delicate balancing act, and that whatever arrangements are adopted have huge consequences for women, men and gender relations. We have seen that arrangements for care affect women's capacity to be employed, as well as their financial situation. Care is thus heavily implicated in gender inequality and patterns of individual and family well-being, just as variations in welfare state policy are systematically associated with variations in the situation of women and men. Whether it is the roles and relations of male and female parenthood or the conditions of paid care workers, we have seen that care does not generally bring access to a significant quantity of resources. Sweden is the exception in this regard. It is important to point out that carers in Sweden are relatively well positioned not because of the direct support and valorization of care as an activity, but rather because the employment/care interface is well supported.

With regard to care, we have seen that variation is quite wide-spread. There is a connection between the form and nature of state provision and the choices and opportunities open to women. In this respect, public provision matters. Hence, in countries such as Germany, Ireland, the Netherlands and the UK, where provision is relatively meagre (although rather different in nature), caring bears much more heavily on women than it does in, say, Sweden or France, where the public care infrastructure is much more developed. In the former countries one can see how care leaves a strong imprint on women's labour supply and their chances of being poor. However, the relationship between care, public policy and gender inequalities is more nuanced than a comparison of the extreme countries suggests. The cases of Italy and the USA are interesting because they defy a conventional explanatory framework. In Italy women's participation in employment is quite constrained, even though public provision for children, and certainly for those over the age of three, is relatively widespread. The reverse is the case in the USA, in that public provision of care for either elderly or ill adults or children is limited, but women's labour force participation seems unaffected. This seeming exceptionalism will be returned to in the later chapters.

4

Gender and Work

The economic role of women, especially married women and mothers, has been in the process of transforming as far back as World War II. The gradual movement of women into paid work and the consequential changes in both family life and the social organization of production and reproduction are fundamental to the changing nature of gender relations within and across societies. The expansion of female employment is also a vital key to how the labour market itself is unfolding. Most of the difference in labour force and employment rates among the developed economies is attributable to differences in the employment behaviour of working-aged women. Women's integration into paid work has been associated with a restructuring of employment, including the growth of service employment, more diversified working-time arrangements, and new patterns of industrial relations (Rubery et al. 1999: 13). One can also read labour market-related variation as being associated with variation among welfare states. While one cannot easily identify the welfare state's imprint on labour market behaviour, this chapter seeks to accord the welfare state as central a role as possible in the analysis of gender differences in employment. The chapter's overall goal is to establish the extent to which focusing on employment patterns of women and men reveals the existence of different employment/family/welfare systems across countries.

The discussion in this chapter is organized around three main lines of analysis. The first considers some general features of the relation between the organization of work and the structure and agency of the welfare state. The second seeks both the form and the nature of women's employment patterns and how the welfare state is associated with gender inequalities in and of the labour market. Levels of female participation in full- and part-time work are first considered. The section then moves on to investigate what might be called the qualitative aspects of women's relationship to the labour market (in terms, for example, of segregation and wage inequality). We are especially interested in how the structure of the labour market is gendered, and whether the welfare state is implicated, either directly or indirectly, in this. In the third, the focus is on a number of aspects of the relationship between the welfare state and paid work, with a view to identifying the key political dimensions of this relationship. We pay particular attention to the equality discourse, as well as the current focus on the reconciliation of work and family life.

4.1   The Organization of Work and the Links to the Welfare State

Welfare states have always been concerned about their relationship with the world of paid work and the labour market. While financial well-being and poverty have formed a key axis of growth and development, employment has been one of the main concerns of national (and increasingly international) social policy. At a societal level this is expressed in terms of a focus on labour supply and the well-being of the labour force; at a micro level it centres on individuals' work ethic and the conditions under which people undertake paid work. Social insurance is the classic way of understanding the relationship between the welfare state and employment. Organized around a series of risks that are defined as such because they occasion a loss of income from paid work – illness, accident, unemployment, maternity and old age – social insurance seeks both to encourage people to be employed and to guarantee them a certain standard of living when, for any of the above reasons, they are not. With social insurance provision as the frame, de-commodification has been one of the main concepts employed in welfare state studies to understand the relationship between the welfare state and the labour market. As used by Esping-Andersen (1990), this taps the extent to which welfare states enable people to live outside the market. It is a gauge of both the generosity of welfare state benefits and the conditions under which such benefits are granted. To the extent that it captures a broader set of concerns about the relationship between the welfare state and the labour market, a focus on de-commodification highlights how the welfare state is both an expression and a result of the politics generated by different interest groups around labour and welfare.

Feminists have been unhappy with the male bias of de-commodification, and indeed with the almost exclusive employment-oriented focus of much welfare state research. From a gender perspective, de-commodification takes too confined a view of the labour-related activity and effects of the welfare state. For one thing, de-commodification derives from an orientation to and understanding of the welfare state that is based on a typical male life-style; for another, it focuses exclusively on cash benefits; thirdly, de-commodification ignores other functions served by welfare state benefits; and fourthly, as a concept it has little or no purchase on social services. A feminist approach demonstrates that it is instructive to think in a broader way about how the welfare state and the labour market come together in society and in the lives of women and men.

One of the most fundamental areas of influence of the welfare state is on the organization of labour, work and employment in society. This occurs in numerous ways. For example, in helping to organize the provision of and for care and the well-being of individuals and families, the welfare state contributes to the structuring of the labour market and people's relations to it. The set of relations involved stands out clearly when one takes the situation of women, and variations between them and men, as the departure point. The organization of the 'private sphere' and that of paid work are seen to be inextricably intertwined, both being part of a broader system of social organization. There are a number of different levels of relations involved. First, as we saw in the last chapter, women's caring roles and activities, and hence their capacity to do paid or unpaid work, depend in a fundamental way on what is defined as appropriate social policy, both in terms of where the boundaries of public policy are drawn and in the content of social provision. Secondly, the welfare state shapes both the demand for and supply of female labour by defining care. Public caring services depend mainly on female labour and, where they exist, are major employers of women. Thirdly, the components of income support provision significantly affect labour market participation and, in the case of mothers and married women especially, influence their capacity to earn an independent income.

With regard to conceptualizing or theorizing the relationship between the welfare state and work/employment, feminist work has followed two general lines of development. The first has been to develop a framework to elaborate the set of work/family relations within a comparative perspective. The male breadwinner model has been the predominant approach here. It draws on how the differential organization of male and female employment is shaped by and re-flected in welfare state arrangements. Lewis (1992) developed this approach to compare a number of European welfare states on the basis of whether they recognize and cater for women solely as wives and mothers and/or also as workers. This led her to a threefold categorization of several European welfare states: those with strong (Britain and Ireland), moderate (France) and weak (Sweden) male breadwinner models. Lewis's work remains the most influential typology in the gender-focused welfare state literature.[1] A primary criticism to be made of it is that it has not sufficiently taken on board variations in the breadwinner role assigned to men. For this and other reasons, the model does not differentiate adequately between countries.

A second line of development in feminist work has been to focus on life chances or opportunities, understood in a larger sense than employment, and therefore to move beyond de-commodification as a significant source of welfare state variation. Many women scholars are now trying to theorize welfare state outcomes in terms of the degree to which they promote the autonomy and economic independence of women, especially those with caring responsibilities. Different end-points and conceptual hinges are deployed for this purpose: O'Connor (1992) speaks of personal autonomy or insulation from dependence; Hobson (1990) views the options in terms of exit (from a bad marriage or unsatisfactory relationship for instance); Orloff (1993) takes a step back and speaks in terms of the freedom from compulsion to enter into potentially oppressive relations; while Lister (1994) and McLaughlin and Glendinning (1994) use the concept of defamilization. While each has its distinct advantages, it is interesting in the context of the present endeavour to observe that none involves a direct theorization of the welfare state's relation to the labour market from a gender perspective. Employment is usually contextualized, placed in a broad setting that includes especially the family. If anything, a care perspective has dominated, in that the construction of and treatment of relations within the 'private' sphere are regarded as the signature piece of a gender design to the welfare state. More than contextualization, then, employment can be rather easily residualized in gender-oriented work on the welfare state.

We believe that employment and the labour market have to be analysed more directly for what they tell us about the relationship between gender divisions and welfare. For this purpose, the structure of the labour market is vitally important. In our view, employment has a threefold significance in regard to the gender division of welfare. First, there are patterns and divisions in employment that are significant in their own right for the welfare and relative power resources of women and men. Secondly, we suggest that employment has significance for the study of the relation between gender and the welfare state in the extent to which involvement in paid work represents a movement away from dependence on the family. One can conceive of this relationship either in income terms or as the degree to which women's family situations influence their employment capacity and experience (and vice versa). Finally, we suggest that it is possible to approach an understanding of the welfare state and its relations to gender inequality from the lens of the labour market. This brings to light different aspects of the state's activity. Among those for which we have sufficient information to consider here are the role played by the state in the employment of women, the state's regulatory activities (in relation to wage setting, for example), and its redistributive role (in relation to the taxation of earnings).

Taken together, all of this suggests that we conceive of women's participation in employment not as an absolute phenomenon but in a more qualitative form, especially in terms of the conditions under which women can and do engage in paid work and the differences from men in this regard. This spells a particular approach, one that is able to conceive of women's relationship to the labour market in terms of access, intensity of participation, and conditions of engagement. It is important to consider not just supply-side factors, but how gender is embedded in the operation of the labour market itself.

4.2   Women's Relationship to Employment

4.2.1   Employment, unemployment and economic inactivity

There is huge variation in women's employment rate among the eight countries (second column, table 4.1).[2] Measured on the basis of the employment rate of the total population aged between fifteen and sixty-four years, the variation ranged in the year 2000 from a 'high' of 71 per cent in Sweden to a 'low' of 40 per cent in Italy. In terms of country groupings, the USA, and to a lesser extent the UK and the Netherlands, cluster together with Sweden to form a block at the top end of the scale. Italy is out on its own in forming the opposite pole. With slightly over half of women in employment, Ireland and France are closer to the lower than the upper pole. Germany is more or less on its own in forming a loose middle way between the Scandinavian/ USA route of a highly feminized labour force and the Italian pattern of more home than paid work for women.

As the second column of table 4.1 (figures in parentheses) also shows, male participation patterns show far less variation. Typically,

Table 4.1 Employment, unemployment and economic inactivity rates of women, 2000 (male rates in brackets)

	Employment rate	Unemployment rate	Economic inactivity rate
France*	55.3 (69.3)	11.5 (7.8)	37.4
Germany*	57.9 (72.8)	8.3 (7.6)	36.9
Ireland	54.0 (76.1)	4.2 (4.3)	45.6
Italy	39.6 (67.5)	14.4 (8.0)	53.7
Netherlands*	63.7 (82.4)	3.7 (2.0)	34.1
Sweden	71.0 (74.8)	5.8 (6.0)	24.9
UK	64.6 (77.8)	4.9 (6.0)	32.0
USA**	67.9 (80.6)	4.2 (3.9)	–

Source: European Commission 2001b
  * In these countries the data on employment and inactivity rates are based on estimations by Eurostat
** Source for the USA is OECD 2001a: 211

in most countries around 75 per cent of men are in paid work. To the extent that there is an identifiable cross-national pattern, it is the so-called liberal nations, the USA and the UK, that have high levels of male employment, and the continental European countries – France and Italy – low rates. Note, though, that the Netherlands is an exception to the latter pattern, its very high male employment rates moving it closer to the USA than to its European neighbours. When it comes to the female/male employment ratio, Sweden has the smallest differential and is unchallenged in this regard. Its high female and relatively low male employment rates give it a female/male participation ratio of 0.95. The UK also has a high female/male ratio, as do the USA and France. Once again, Italy is in a class apart, at the bottom of the league.

Turning to unemployment, we can see from the third column in table 4.1 that there is also considerable variation, in terms of both its prevalence and its gendered character. Italy and France, and to a lesser extent Germany, have the greatest problem with unemployment. Unemployment is also quite a gendered phenomenon, tending to be a greater risk for women than for men. Only in Sweden and the UK does the rate of male unemployment exceed the female rate. Countries where the imbalance between women and men is especially noteworthy are France, Italy and the Netherlands, where for every 100 unemployed men there are about 180 unemployed women.

The figures on female economic inactivity (to be seen in the last column of table 4.1) throw into relief the role played by paid work in women's lives within and across nations. Upwards of a third of women across these countries are not economically active, with the variation ranging from a quarter to over a half. Italian women are the least likely to be at work or seeking employment, and Swedish women are the most likely.

The information presented thus far is persuasive regarding the fact that female employment is a source of considerable, but patterned, diversity among the eight countries. A gap of 31 percentage points separates these countries when it comes to women's employment rates. Sweden, the USA, and to a lesser extent the UK are the high female employment countries, with participation rates in the high 60s. A second tier of countries, consisting of the continental European nations, has female employment rates in the region of 50–60 per cent. The trend in female labour force participation in these countries seems to be on a steadily upward course. Since male labour force participation rates have fallen in these countries, the sex ratios are also climbing. This upward trend for women is found especially in Ireland, which has seen massive growth in women's employment in the last five years (associated with a major economic boom). For long close to Italy, which is at the bottom of the league of countries included in the present comparison, Ireland could be said to be in transition from a laggard to around the European average.

The analysis has thus far concentrated on participation and employment rates, assuming more or less an equivalence among them. However, the use for comparative purposes of absolute female participation rates as a measure of women's relation to the labour market is problematic. For, as we shall now demonstrate, such rates do not connote women's participation in employment in any simple fashion.

4.2.2   The intensity of women's participation in employment

The point has often been made that one cannot determine women's employment behaviour from gross participation rates. The intensity of women's involvement in the labour market must be examined in its own right. Reduced working time and the increasing availability of paid and unpaid leaves for child care and other purposes are just two of the factors masking the real nature of women's attachment to the labour market.[3] In the following analysis we take account of the extent and nature of part-time work and revisit participation rates and the cross-national picture in the light of them.

Starting with part-time employment, we can see from table 4.2 that the Netherlands is the part-time 'leader', with more than two-thirds of Dutch women's employment being part-time. The Dutch is a very particular trajectory, however, and is not comparable to that of any of

Table 4.2 Some characteristics of women's participation in employment, 1999

	% of women's employment that is part-time (1999)*	% total employment that is part-time (1999)*	Women's share of part-time employment (1999)**	Average hours worked by part-time women workers per week (1999)***	Women's full-time equivalent employment rate (1999)* (employment rate in brackets)
France	31.4	17.1	79.3	23.0	47.1 (54.0)
Germany	37.3	19.0	84.1	18.4	45.8 (57.1)
Ireland	30.0	16.4	77.4	18.5	43.6 (51.9)
Italy	15.6	7.9	71.5	21.7	35.7 (38.3)
Netherlands	69.0	39.8	77.4	18.2	40.0 (61.7)
Sweden	39.3	23.7	73.7	25.0	58.5 (69.7)
UK	44.2	24.8	79.6	17.7	49.2 (64.1)
USA**	19.0	13.3	68.4	–	–

Sources: * European Commission 2001b
 ** OECD 2000: table E, p. 218
 *** Eurostat 2000a: table 44, p. 148

the other countries. Its two closest neighbours in the present comparison are the UK and Sweden, but with part-time work accounting for at most 44 per cent of all female employment, these two countries are in a quite different league from the Netherlands. Italy and the USA form the lower extremity with Ireland, France and Germany in a (similarly) intermediate position (with about a third of female employment part-time). We know from other sources (Eurostat 2000b and table 3.4 above) to what extent housework or family commitments account for why women in different countries are working part-time. Such family-related exigencies account for the bulk of female part-time work in Germany – 69 per cent of all German part-time female workers say that it is because of housework and family commitments that they work part-time. This is also the case for half of all Dutch women part-time workers, 48 per cent of those in the UK, and 46 per cent in Ireland. In France and Italy other reasons are more important.[4]

It is necessary to put these female patterns in the context of the national employment pattern (third column of table 4.2). Again the Netherlands stands out – with almost 40 per cent of total employment in the part-time sector, no other country comes near it. Nor can any of the other countries match it for the proportion of men (18 per cent) whose employment is on a part-time basis (data not shown). The other two 'highish' part-time work countries are the UK and Sweden (with part-time accounting for up to a quarter of all employment). For the other countries the norm is for part-time employment to comprise around 15 per cent of all employment. As the attentive reader will have grasped, there is a strong association between part-time jobs and female employment. Hence, a huge sex imbalance among part-time workers is one of the most robust features of such employment across nations. The fourth column in table 4.2 confirms the general concentration of part-time work among women. This is a concentration that is at its most extreme in Germany, the UK and France, and is least marked in the USA and Italy. The range of variation across countries in this regard is rather small, however.

Behind these variations lies a further set of differences in the hours worked (fifth column). Part-time work is itself, to some extent anyway, country-specific.[5] Some nations tend to be long part-time work countries, while others have a pattern of short part-time work. The largest differences in the present comparison are between Sweden on the one hand and the Netherlands and the UK on the other. In Sweden women who are employed on a part-time basis work an average of 25 hours per week, whereas in Germany, Ireland, the Netherlands and the UK the weekly average is much lower, at around 18 hours. To draw out the meaning of this in real life, women working part-time in Sweden are employed the equivalent of a full working day more than their German, Irish, Dutch or British counterparts. Italy and France also tend to be long part-time work countries.

Part-time work is not the only factor complicating women's labour supply, however. There is also the matter of continuity. Unlike that of men, women's labour force participation tends to be peppered with short and sometimes long interruptions. We are seriously hampered by information shortages from identifying the extent to which women interrupt their labour force participation across nations. Without micro-survey or panel data, the closest one can come to gauging continuity is by looking at age-related participation patterns.[6] Existing work suggests that there are four general patterns of female employment participation across the life course. These are described by:

- the plateau curve (more or less continuous participation over the life course);
- the left-hand peak (signifying a lengthy or permanent exit from the labour force following the youngest periods of life);
- the m-shaped curve (which describes a pattern of returning to the labour force after a period of absence); and
- the right-hand peak (the activity rate peaking in the thirties and forties).

Europe is now showing a general trend towards the plateau curve as younger generations of women move through their working lives with fewer and shorter interruptions (Rubery et al. 1999: 83). However, there is still evidence of most of the other patterns among the eight countries in this comparison. Ireland and the Netherlands lean towards a left-hand peak pattern, with women tending to exit the labour market in their mid- to late twenties or shortly thereafter (although there is radical change in this regard among the younger cohorts of women in Ireland). The UK and France have a slight m-shaped pattern, indicating a small 'dip' in the years associated with early family formation. Germany and Italy have a more continuous pattern, although the continuity curve is much higher for Germany. In recent years Swedish women, who used to have a very high level of continuity in the labour market, have begun to remain in work in larger numbers as they grow older. This is associated with a drop in the activity rates of younger women (which may be due to either reduced employment participation associated with motherhood or increased participation in education).

These different complications have an impact on the extent to which women are actually present in the labour market. The last column of table 4.2 standardizes this by showing full-time equivalent employment rates. These rewrite the overall employment rates for women and also force us to revisit the cross-national comparison for all nations except Italy. The effect of taking account of the actual hours worked is especially large in the Netherlands and the UK: the Dutch female employment rate drops from around 60 per cent to 40 per cent, whereas that for the UK falls from 64 per cent to 49 per cent. The full-time equivalent information shows that aggregate employment rates are most deceptive for those two countries along with Germany. The resultant cross-national comparison is also altered by the switch to full-time equivalent rates, especially as regards the range of variation across all countries (which falls from 31 to some 23 percentage points). The country rankings and groupings also alter somewhat. Sweden remains in the lead, but it tops other countries by a greater margin than before – 10 percentage points. France, followed by the UK, has the next highest level of female employment participation. Italy continues to perform poorly, but is no longer isolated, for so also do the Netherlands and Ireland. These data underline how deceptive crude labour force statistics can be about women's employment.

The information in this section, which has concentrated on the structural aspects of women's participation in employment, suggests that almost everywhere women's employment participation is not only different from men's, but is compromised. The nature of the compromise and how it varies cross-nationally is very interesting. At first glance, anyway, it looks as if there is a trade-off between the hours worked and the rate of employment among women. That is, women trade on time. Women (presumably mothers and other carers) either remove themselves from the labour market, or they maintain their involvement in employment but keep their participation below a certain level. From this angle, part-time employment appears to be a safety valve (for women as well as some national labour markets). While the volume of part-time work is not a complete predictor of women's employment level, countries where it is low also tend to have low female employment overall.

Having considered access to paid work (that is, the supply side), we have to ask what happens when women are in the labour market. How are gender differences embedded in the operation of the labour market?

4.2.3   Segregation and stratification

Gender makes not only for differences in men's and women's propensity to be in employment, but also for segregation within the labour market. Despite the progressive integration of women into the labour force, a strong differentiation in the jobs held by women and men continues to be observed (OECD 1998: 15). Women to a greater or lesser degree, depending on their circumstances and the national labour market, tend to work in quite different sectors and jobs to men. This segregation has two dimensions: a horizontal one, whereby men and women are concentrated in different industries and types of occupation, and a vertical one, whereby men are more likely to work in jobs of a higher grade and status than women. We will consider each of these briefly, focusing where possible on public employment, since it is here that we can attribute agency to the (welfare) state.

In regard to horizontal segregation, phenomena such as the crowding of women into particular occupations and sectors are widely observed. A recent OECD study of seven countries[7] found that more than 60 per cent of female employees are accounted for by ten occupational groups (out of a total of between fifty and eighty groups in each country) (OECD 1998: 42). Moreover, there is no clear sign that this pattern of high female concentration has significantly lessened in the last ten years or so, except in the UK and the USA. As pointed out by the same study, the idea of a 'service relationship' is central to female-dominated occupations (together with the tendency for competencies involved in the work not to be formalized) (OECD 1998: 9). It is little surprise, therefore, that women workers are to be found predominantly in the services sector (many of these in the public sector, as table 4.4 below shows). This is true of all countries, and the degree of variation across them is limited. Italy is once again an exception, with just over three-quarters of employed women located in the services sector, compared with a cross-country average of about 82 per cent. Of the other countries, the concentration of women in the services sector is highest in the Netherlands, Sweden and the UK.

Table 4.3 compares countries on the basis of a series of standardized measures of horizontal inequality. With a value of 0 indicating no segregation, and 100 indicating full segregation, the second column in table 4.3 suggests that segregation is lowest in Italy and highest in the UK, France and Germany. Most of the countries in between are on the high side. The other data in table 4.3 confirm this pattern. Across countries around 62 per cent of women workers are in female-dominated jobs. However, women's part-time work tends to be more segregated than women's full-time jobs everywhere except Italy. The degree to which this is the case varies among countries, though. In the UK part-time work is much more segregated, whereas in Italy there is no real difference in the extent of segregation among female part-timers and full-timers. The Netherlands is another country where

Table 4.3 Horizontal labour market segregation on gender grounds, 1994

		Share of employed women found in jobs that are female dominated (more than 60% of the occupational work-force is female)		
	Index of segregation*	All women	All women full-timers	All women part-timers
France	55	67.1	64.4	74.2
Germany	54	61.3	56.5	69.8
Ireland	51	64.3	63.5	67.0
Italy	42	31.1	31.1	31.0
Netherlands	52	58.2	48.4	69.3
UK	56	66.6	56.6	79.2

Source: Rubery et al. 1999: tables 5.1 and 5.13
* The data here are based on ISCO-88 three-digit classifications

Table 4.4 Share of female employment in the public sector and the proportion of female public service workers in senior management positions, 2000

	% of women's employment that is in the public sector	% of women in senior management in the public sector
France	58.5**	44.8**
Germany	50.3	33.1***
Ireland*	51.0	13.3
Italy	50.1**	12.0
Netherlands	35.6***	15.0***
Sweden*	45.9	20.0
USA	56.3	24.4

Source: OECD 2001b
* In these countries the figures refer to women's share of employment in central or federal government
** Data refer to 1998
*** Data refer to 1999

female part-time work is highly segregated (especially in comparison to female full-time work). According to Rubery et al. (1999: 176), highly sex-segregated economies tend to be associated with high proportions of women employed in services, especially public sector services.

Moving on to vertical segregation, the key issue here is the extent to which there is inequality between women and men within occupations, especially as regards the grade or status of their positions. In table 4.4 we present the latest available cross-national information on the proportion of women employed in the public sector, as well as women's hold on senior management positions in that sector.

One can appreciate from this table how significant the public sector is for the employment of women. Apart from the Netherlands and to a lesser extent Sweden (for which the missing wider public service data is especially misleading), the public sector employs more than half of all women workers across nations. This sector is especially significant in France and the USA. The Netherlands is a clear exception here. The lack of equivalence between the general share of female workers and their share of senior management positions, to be seen by comparing the data in the second and third columns of table 4.4, shows that vertical segregation is quite widespread in the public sector. This is something that varies across countries, however. France is way out in front with 45 per cent of women in senior management positions in the public sector. Germany comes next, followed by the USA and Sweden. Senior positions in the public sector are especially hard to get for Irish, Italian and Dutch women.

4.2.4   Inequality and the role of the state

A further dimension of inequality is in wage rates and the financial return from employment. Neither this nor the role of the welfare state in regard to employment and inequalities associated with paid work have been considered up to now. These cannot be ignored, for economic outcomes are a complex amalgam of gender differences and the way in which the state acts to ameliorate (or not) such differences. One can take the privileging of different types of labour, in terms of both payment rates and how earnings and the income needs of people in different situations are treated by the taxation and social security system, as the signature piece of how the state treats gender inequality in employment. In the past, when the male breadwinner model was much more widely supported, male wages were more likely to be seen as wages to support entire families. Indeed, a founding principle of a male breadwinner model is high wages for men. To the extent that this was achieved, it reduced the pressures on the partner to take up employment for financial reasons. In the analysis to follow, we look first at wages, considering gender inequalities in pay and the distribution of low pay among women and men. We then turn to inequalities in net earnings, so as to gauge the activity of the welfare state in supporting income levels of wage earners in different family situations.

The size of female *vis-à-vis* male wages is very important in determining not just the employment rate of married or partnered women but also the financial well-being of people in different types of family situation. The gender gap in earnings is probably one of the best overall measures of the financial benefits and disadvantages associated with employment for the partner. Women's gross earnings as a proportion of those of men are shown in table 4.5.

Taking the general wage inequalities first, the variation is once again noteworthy, almost 20 percentage points separating these seven countries.[8] As with most other indicators considered in this chapter, Sweden emerges as the most positive case. In terms of earnings, Swedish women and men are very close, at 87 per cent. Most of the other countries are clustered together at around 75 per cent (which is also around the EU average). The Netherlands makes up the rear in this particular country comparison, with the UK also showing large gaps in male/female wage rates. Turning to the third column, we can see that the public sector acquits itself quite well, with women's average hourly earnings about 12 percent short of those of

Table 4.5 Women's gross hourly earnings as a percentage of those of men, 1995–1996

	Women's hourly earnings as % of men's (1995)*	Women's hourly earnings as % of men's in the public sector (1996)**
France	76.2%[#]	89.0%
Germany	76.9%[##]	80.0%
Ireland	–	88.0%
Italy	76.5%	100.0%
Netherlands	70.6%	81.5%
Sweden	87.0%	93.7%
UK	73.7%	86.3%[###]
USA***	80.8%	–

Sources: *Eurostat 1999c
  ** Government Offices Sweden 2000: 19
*** Bureau of Labor Statistics 2001: table 16, p. 31
  [#] Data pertain to 1994
  [##] Data pertain to West Germany
[###] Data pertain to Great Britain

men across countries (Government Offices Sweden 2000). The public sector is at its most egalitarian in Italy and Sweden, and is least so in the Netherlands and Germany.

Across the EU the wage gap is at its widest in the three occupational groups in which skill requirements are highest – managers, professionals and technicians – and narrowest for clerks, sales and service workers (European Commission 1998: 9).[9] The latter is especially the case in France, Sweden and the UK. In these three countries women's lower representation in high-paying jobs is a major factor in gender wage gaps. There is a remarkable similarity across countries in the degree to which wage inequalities are entrenched. For example, the wage gap increases with age (and especially so in France, the Netherlands and the UK), education and length of service (European Commission 1998: 9). This means that the return to women from education and work experience is less than it is for men. France, the Netherlands and Italy have the greatest gender disparity in the return from education. It also means that the idea of career progression, which is how employment is generally conceived, does not have the same descriptive force with regard to women's working life as it does for men's.

The existence and prevalence of low-waged employment is an important part of this constellation. In the EU in 1996,[10] 15 per cent of all employees were low-waged (Eurostat 2000b).[11] Low-paid work in the EU is by and large a female phenomenon: women made up some 77 per cent of low-waged workers, almost double their proportion of all EU employees (42 per cent). The general details for our particular countries, together with some gender-related characteristics, are shown in table 4.6 for those countries for which they are available.

The UK has the highest share of low-waged employment, followed by Ireland. With 21 per cent and 18 per cent of all employees being low-waged, both of these countries are, along with Germany (17 per cent) above the EU average. Of the remaining countries Italy has the smallest low-paid sector and is most closely followed in this regard by France. The reason for the prevalence of low-paid work varies by country. According to Eurostat (2000b: 4), it is mainly attributable in the Netherlands and the UK to low working hours, whereas in Ireland and Italy poor remuneration is the main reason for low pay. In France and Germany low hours and poor remuneration are equally important as sources of low-paid employment. Across Europe low wages are associated primarily with the service and agricultural sectors, with low-skilled jobs, with part-time as against full-time work, and with jobs of a fixed (rather than indefinite) duration.

Table 4.6   Proportion of low-waged employment, sex breakdown of low-waged work and its concentration among women, 1996

	% of low-waged employment	Sex breakdown of low-waged workers (% women/men)	Concentration index of women
France	13	76/24	1.7
Germany	17	80/20	2.0
Ireland	18	72/28	1.7
Italy	10	60/40	1.6
Netherlands	16	81/19	2.2
UK	21	81/19	1.7
USA*	–	63/37	–

Source: Eurostat 2000b
* Bureau of Labor Statistics 2001

As the third and fourth columns of table 4.6 show, low-waged work is also strongly associated with women's employment. Women tend on average to comprise around three-quarters of low-paid workers across all the countries considered. However, the sex distribution of low-paid work is something that varies cross-nationally. This sector is least gendered in Italy (40/60 in favour of men) and most gendered in Germany, the Netherlands and the UK (20/80 in favour of men). Of all the countries, it is the Netherlands where the gender imbalance in the distribution of low-waged work is most pronounced. Dutch women, therefore, appear to experience the greatest wage penalties. It should be remembered that these women are mainly mothers.

What about the role of the state? The extent to which states take a stand against low pay is important, not just in the context of labour market regulation and standard setting, but also in terms of combating gender inequality. Setting a minimum wage is one of the most widely used mechanisms in Europe for this purpose. A national minimum wage exists in five of the eight countries in this study: France, Ireland, the Netherlands, the UK and the USA.[12] In France and the Netherlands such regulation is more than thirty years old, whereas in Ireland and the UK the minimum wage was instituted only in the last few years. The level at which the wage is set varies somewhat between the different countries. It is most generous in the Netherlands (at over €1,100 a month), followed by France (at over €1,000 a month).[13] In the UK and Ireland the minimum wage is set at around €900, while it is lowest in the USA (at around €800) (Eurostat 1999b).

Taxation and social security arrangements are reflected more directly in take-home pay. Through these provisions, the welfare state assumes a more active role in determining net earnings and relative financial well-being. While data on this are not available on a gender basis, it is possible to establish the priority attributed by taxation and social security provisions to the relative well-being of individuals *vis-à-vis* families and those with different types of employment arrangements. Table 4.7 shows the relative net earnings of single, full-time workers in manufacturing industry on average wages as compared with one and two full-time earner families with two children in 1998.

As can be seen, net earnings are highest in the UK and West Germany, and lowest in the Netherlands and Italy. France tends towards the upper wage end, whereas Ireland is placed somewhere in the middle in terms of average net wages. In all of the countries, one-earner families with children have a significantly higher level of net earnings as compared with single persons (see the second and third columns in table 4.7). There is quite a lot of variation, however. West Germany and Ireland are the two countries where one-earner families with children are most privileged, with earnings levels that are between 34 and 41 per cent in excess of those of single people (left-most data in the fifth column). Italy and the Netherlands are at the opposite extreme, being the least generous to one-earner families with children. Welfare states are actively associated with these outcomes, achieving them through different means. In West Germany not only is the tax system very favourable to one-earner couples with children, tax allowances are supplemented with generous family allowances. Ireland's pro one-earner family stance is achieved partly through a favourable tax policy, but it is also a result of higher gross wages for these earners as compared with single earners. In France one-earner families with children pay little or no tax. In the UK and the Netherlands the main privileging of one-earner families with children is effected through family allowances rather than taxation.

A comparison of the third and fourth columns, as well as the right-most set of data in the fifth column, shows the relative advantage of two-earner couples with children *vis-à-vis* one-earner families. There is most to be gained from a second earner in France and least in West Germany and Italy (where a full-time second earner increases the total income only by a third or less). In Ireland, the Netherlands and the UK the net advantage to the family from a full-time second earner is to increase the take-home pay by about 40 per cent. Linking these results to taxation and social security policy, the large gain in France is associated with favourable taxation and social protection treatment

Table 4.7 Average net monthly earnings (in Euro) of full-time employees in manufacturing, 1998 (purchasing power parities)*

| | Single person | Two-child family, one earner | Two-child family, two average earners | Position of one-earner family relative to | |
				Single person	Two-earner family
France	1,360	1,671	3,048	+23%	−46%
(West) Germany	1,488	2,091	3,040	+41%	−31%
Ireland	1,334	1,794	2,950	+34%	−39%
Italy	1,303	1,533	2,244	+18%	−32%
Netherlands	1,280	1,510	2,455	+18%	−38%
UK	1,591	1,959	3,203	+23%	−39%

Source: Eurostat 2000c
* Calculated on the basis of workers on average salary

of families with children. In Germany the two-earner family with children is taxed quite heavily (almost as much as a single person), and this is also the case in Italy. In the other countries the tax regimes tend to favour families also.

We now turn to how employment is associated with power and political contest.

4.3   Power Relations and Contests Associated with Gender and Work

The results of the analyses that have been carried out in this chapter suggest a number of insights about power relations between women and men in regard to employment. The political relationship between gender and employment is framed today in terms of two main discourses or contests. One centres on the relationship between women and men as individuals – the gender equality debate – while the other is framed in more general terms – a concern about the reconciliation of work and family life.

Equality between women and men has dominated debate and political contest about gender in the public sphere. It has been especially prominent in regard to employment. Equality is a discourse of rights, one of its advantages being that it recognizes that gender is, in part anyway, composed of and constituted by differentials in power between women and men, and that these are not just expressed in the public sphere but are created there as well. To the extent that this analysis has been applied to employment, women are seen to be disempowered relative to men by virtue of differences in their relationship to the labour market. The analyses undertaken in this chapter confirm this, although there are notable variations across countries. One of the most striking differences between women's and men's relationship to employment is the generally lower quality of women's employment. The disempowering effect of inferior female employment may be said to lie in the level of job, the financial return from work, and future career prospects and financial well-being. The latter is especially important, for poor-quality employment has a lasting effect on the rights, entitlements and welfare of people as they age. Looking at women's employment in particular suggests that any patterns found are best understood within a life course perspective. This is especially valuable in drawing attention to how the social roles assigned to women and men stretch over the duration of their lives, and how social policies act to establish relationships between different phases of the life course.

Although academic and policy debates have operated with different versions of equality, the most robust differentiation is that between equality of access and equality of outcome. The former, equality of access, centres on the absence of legal and institutional barriers to entry or participation. Equality of outcome refers to the distribution of economic and other resources, opportunities and benefits, and is therefore more about tangible results. To the extent that the analyses in this and other chapters speak to matters of equality, they make an argument in favour of problematizing equality. The analyses undertaken can be taken as evidence that there is no clear, unproblematic application of either of these or other interpretations of equality to the comparison between women and men in the labour market. Access to employment is *per se* less of an issue today, when it seems that labour markets are almost autonomously expanding to draw in female labour. However, the high level of variation in female employment rates across the eight countries studied makes it clear that we cannot dispense with a concern about women's access to paid work. What is also clear, moreover, is that quality has to be set alongside access, and that an asymmetry of position and relative welfare exists between women and men as paid workers. The variation found is a complex mixture of access and quality. Thus, for example, while women appear to have quite good access to paid work in some countries, such as Sweden and the USA, they are cut off from certain types of jobs and work experience. The role of worker has a different meaning for women than for men. The welfare- and opportunity-conferring functions of the labour market, and of public employment policy, operate less in favour of women than of men.

An alternative way of framing the relationship between gender and employment is in terms of the reconciliation of work and family life. The EU has been especially influential in promulgating this set of ideas. This, while a more popular discourse today as compared with that on equality, is less attuned to gender politics. First, it tends to de-individualize women and men as political actors and female and male interests by situating both within the family. Secondly, there is an assumption that the collective or family interest is relatively unproblematic. This is in some ways reminiscent of older debates about 'family welfare' or 'family well-being' which assumed away any possible conflicts of interest within the family. Furthermore, there are real doubts to be raised about the extent to which family-related issues are prioritized in the reconciliation paradigm. Even though it is framed as a matter of balance and relative equality between the two domains of work and family, the needs of the family are downplayed relative to those of the market. Flexibility is a good demanded more of the family than the market. Overall, gender-based interests are actually played down in this debate.

Nevertheless, thinking in terms of reconciliation has two important merits. One is that it recognizes the significance of social relations. A narrow equality perspective, as epitomized by an equal rights agenda, tends to strip women and men of their relationships and societal context. This kind of approach is, furthermore, unrealistic as regards the complexity of women's aspirations and the socio-political context in which most women live out their lives (Offen 1992; Fraser 1997). The interconnectedness between women's family situation and their work situation and the fact that their power position relative to men is shaped by this set of connections is an important finding of the present study. The second strength of the focus on the reconciliation of work and family life is that it better captures the dynamic of contemporary social policy than the equality perspective. That is, contemporary welfare states are much more exercised by the need to strike a better balance between the family and the market than they are by male/female inequality.

4.4 Overview

This chapter has undertaken a detailed examination of the gender dimension of employment. We have thought in terms of women having a 'relationship' to employment, because this implies a complexity and degree of variation that are not captured by the analysis of employment participation *per se*. To the extent that women's relationship to employment is quite different from that of men, one must study it in a different fashion from conventional labour market analysis. Neither the level of participation, its continuity, the structure of jobs, nor comparative rates of remuneration can be taken for granted.

The results show a lot of variation and considerable cross-national patterning. As compared with men, women have a much reduced presence in the labour market everywhere except Sweden. One can find much evidence of gender differentiation, role segregation and inequality. Whether one searches for this in the demand for or supply of female labour or in how women fare when they are in the labour market, none of the eight countries is without deeply entrenched divisions along gender lines. This is important. But so too is the fact of considerable variation. For example, across countries, women's full-time equivalent employment rate varies by over 20 percentage points, and there is even greater variation in the proportion of women employed on a part-time basis. Much of the variation lends itself to cross-national patterning. Sweden and the USA are quite close to each other in terms of overall female employment levels. However, its relatively high volume of part-time female employment gives Sweden a 'European' flavour, rendering it more similar to the UK and the Netherlands than to the USA. France tends towards the upper end of the female employment spectrum, with fewer women in part-time work than elsewhere. Germany occupies a middle position, and Ireland is lower again (although Irish women's participation in employment has increased substantially in recent years). Italy is quite unique in the present comparison; its female employment rates put it considerably below the other countries (although the difference is not so great when full-time equivalent rates are taken into account).

Taken together, the data suggest that there are different compromises and trade-offs involved for women if they wish to be involved in the labour market. These vary in nature and intensity from place to place, but the fact of compromise or a trade-off is common across countries. Part-time work is the most widespread compromise for women, especially in the Netherlands, the UK and Sweden. Women's employment is associated with another trade-off too – low pay. The data presented indicate that women dominate the low-paid jobs, and that in some countries – Ireland, France and Germany – this is not attributable simply to the fact that they work part-time. Segregation is another widespread feature of the female employment experience. It may also be part of the trade-off involved in paid work for women. High levels of vertical and horizontal segregation are quite common in the eight countries studied.

The chapter also considered the role of the state, inasmuch as data availability would allow. The significance of the state as an employer of women emerges quite strongly. Public employment is very important for female employment everywhere, serving to push up women's labour force participation, except in the Netherlands. One of the more positive aspects of the state's agency in relation to female employment is that wage gaps and vertical segregation appear to be lower in the public sector than elsewhere. The state also plays an important regulatory role in relation to the labour market. However, because of missing data, we could not specify this effect across countries apart from the state's role in setting a minimum wage. The state's redistributive role in regard to take-home pay was easier to identify. With regard to the treatment of income of people in different family situations, there is considerable variation to be observed. This shows the welfare state at work.

5
Welfare, Household Resources and Gender Relations

This chapter centres on a key activity of welfare states and a fundamental component of gender relations: the redistribution of income among families. It examines the resources that the state makes available to households of different types, and asks whether female-headed households can secure a living income without recourse to either the state or the income of a male partner. In this analysis, access to income is taken as a marker not only of the current well-being of households but of women's and men's opportunities to access income in a variety of roles and at different stages in the life course, and hence to live free from poverty. Exploring the incomes and poverty risks of women and men across a range of household types, we seek to discover the hierarchy of resources into which male- and female-headed households are placed.

This chapter opens with an exploration of the connection between welfare state redistribution and gender relations, focusing briefly on how best to measure gender differentials in resources. The second part of the chapter undertakes a detailed, empirical investigation of resources and the part played by the state in that distribution. The resources of lone mother- and older female-headed households are a focus of particular concern here. Such households reveal how care giving affects economic resources both in the short term (as revealed by the circumstances of lone mothers) and over the life span (the incomes of older women reflecting the extent to which economic disadvantages attached to caring have accumulated across the life course). Contests in the arena of resource redistribution provide the focus of the third part of the chapter, while the fourth and final part offers an overview. Chapter 6 functions as a companion to the present analysis, turning the spotlight on individual incomes.

5.1   Gender Relations and Welfare State Redistribution

Its focus on the redistribution of income leads this chapter to the very heart of welfare state activities.[1] Although the process of redistribution can be understood in simple quantitative terms (who receives what type of resources and the nature of the hierarchy created), redistribution is a process that has important qualitative aspects. By offering protection against specified income risks, the welfare state operates to valorize certain activities and to integrate some into the economic order, while excluding others. For example, protection against the income risks associated with employment both socializes and normalizes the experience of wage earners. As a counter-example, failure to provide income security for carers results in marginalization from the economic order. Lack of coverage means that the income risks of care giving are individualized, and caring is simultaneously depoliticized, since non-intervention locates caring away from the public gaze. In the analysis that follows, we are therefore particularly mindful of how the (typically female) risks associated with care giving and economic dependency on a family breadwinner are treated in comparison with those (more typically male) risks arising from engagement in the labour market. The hierarchy of claims created by welfare state redistribution is fashioned not only by who does and who does not receive support, but also by the way in which that support is proffered. Resources may be granted as an entitlement, conditioned upon certain behaviour or linked to family or individual resources and other characteristics such as marital status, for example. Hence, the redistribution of resources may act to control and condition the behaviour of recipients. The welfare state's redistribution of resources also reflects the relationship of the welfare state to other institutions and allows for an examination of how far the welfare state bolsters or overturns the order of gender relations prevailing in the labour market and the family.

Access to resources is at the core of gender relations. Resources affect and reflect dynamics of power among individuals and within households, as well as in society at large. Alongside the short-term consequences that redistribution has for standard of living and well-being, the provision of income under particular conditions affects individuals' longer-term opportunities. By supporting particular, often gendered, social roles with a varying degree of generosity, the welfare state acts to affect the conditions under which women and men live and the choices available to them at different life stages. Additionally, the issue of whether individuals access resources in their own right or make claims as dependants or by virtue of family status (such as motherhood) is central to gender relations (Sainsbury 1996). Women's location on the periphery of the economic order or in a mediated relationship with the state can be created and reinforced by the mechanisms used to transfer income. Finally, it is important to scrutinize the privilege attached to particular family forms and, conversely, identify those family types (lone parents, cohabitants, same sex couples) that are excluded from provision.[2]

There is no straightforward way of capturing gender-based inequalities in access to resources or the welfare state's impact upon their distribution. As we explore in detail in the next chapter, analysis at the individual, as opposed to the household, level reveals quite a different picture of the balance of resources among women and men within the same family. Concentrating on households, the present chapter distinguishes the economic circumstances of female- and male-headed households of different types. The overall resources of these households, the importance of the state in the package of income that the household receives, and households' relative poverty risk are all explored. Our approach can be challenged, however. First, working within the bounds of available data means that our measure of resources is limited to income. We have argued in previous chapters that income redistribution gives only a partial account of the redistributive processes in which the welfare state is engaged. Our depiction of the distribution of income here overlooks the redistribution effected through the provision of state services (considered in chapters 3 and 4), as well as ignoring the welfare state's impact on immaterial resources, such as time (see chapter 6). Nevertheless, redistribution using tax and cash transfers is a major part of the activity of all welfare states, and income constitutes a readily available measure that travels well across nations. Secondly, our measure of the redistributive role of the welfare state is isolated to the impact of taxes and benefits on family income.[3] Hence, although our empirical measures are by necessity simplified, we understand the redistributive process in which the state is involved to be complex.

5.2 The Gender Dimension of Income and Poverty

5.2.1 The incomes of female- and male-headed households

To begin, we look at the status of female- and male-headed households.[4] This helps to reveal whether women can maintain households autonomously, or whether there are 'penalties' to living without a male income. Such analysis also shows the level of claims that female-headed households make on state resources and the degree to which welfare states protect women against the loss (through divorce, separation or widowhood) or absence of a male wage, pension or other income.

As with all measures of gender inequality, the economic position of female- and male-headed households can be properly understood only when placed within a broader national context. As such, three points need to be emphasized. First, the proportion of female- and male-headed households, as well as their characteristics, varies across the eight countries. Second, female-headed households are composed of quite distinct subgroups, and, while the absence of male income may be something they share, the differences between, say, the households of lone mothers and those of older women are considerable. Third, households headed by women have a quite distinct profile from those with male heads. While the majority of male-headed households consist of couples with or without children, female-headed households are more likely to contain an older person living alone, a sole younger childless person, or a lone parent. Hence, we are not comparing like with like, and, while relatively simple attempts have been made to adjust for household size through the equivalization of income (see Technical Appendix), these will not compensate for all the differences (age, economic status and so forth) between female- and male-headed households.

A first measure of access to economic resources is given in table 5.1, which shows the average income of female- and male-headed households as a percentage of average income for the total population. In all countries, female-headed households have an average income that is between 7 and 21 per cent below the national average. At one extreme fall the UK and the USA, where average incomes for female-headed households are 79 per cent of the national average, while for the remaining countries the equivalent figure hovers at around 90 per cent. Table 5.1 also shows the average income of female-headed households relative to that of those headed by men – this we term the gender gap in income. This gap is at its widest in the

Table 5.1 Average incomes of female- and male-headed households

	Mean income of female-headed households as % of overall mean	Mean income of male-headed households as % of overall mean	Gender gap: income of female-headed households as % of male-headed
France 1994	91	103	88
Germany 1994	93	103	90
Italy 1995	93	102	91
Netherlands 1994	92	102	89
Sweden 1995	90	105	86
UK 1995	79	107	74
USA 1997	79	108	73

Source: Luxembourg Income Study, authors' analysis
Incomes equivalized to OECD scale

UK and the USA, with female-headed households receiving incomes that are respectively 74 per cent and 73 per cent of those of male-headed households. This gap is driven by exceptionally low incomes for female-headed households as well as unusually high incomes for those headed by a man. Sweden has the next largest gender gap (86 per cent), while Germany and Italy experience the narrowest of gender gaps (90 per cent and 91 per cent respectively). It is no coincidence, perhaps, that the three countries with the largest gender gap are also those with the largest proportion of female-headed households and, associated with this, the highest proportion of lone mother households (this we explore in more detail in section 5.2.3).

The gender gap presented in table 5.1 is calculated using net income: it is therefore a measure of income after the state has levied tax and made cash transfers to households. The next task is to examine whether the welfare state narrows the gap between the incomes of female- and male-headed households. For this purpose, we distinguish income from the labour market, private pensions and investments (labelled 'market income' as a shorthand) from taxes and transfers (labelled 'impact of the state').[5] The distribution of market income (plotted in figure 5.1) is revealing in itself. Female-headed households fare the worst in the UK, where they have, on average, less than half the market income of households headed by a man. The situation in the remaining countries is slightly better; yet even so, female-headed households command an average market income of around 60 per cent of that of male-headed households. There is considerable variation in the extent to which the eight welfare states

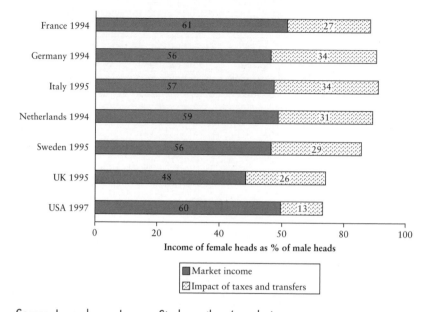

Source: Luxembourg Income Study, authors' analysis
Figure 5.1   The incomes of female-headed households relative to those that are headed by men, pre- and post-tax and transfers

intervene to narrow this gender gap. For example, in Germany female-headed households command 56 per cent of the market incomes of equivalent male-headed households, but their incomes are raised by 34 percentage points by taxes and transfers, with the result that households headed by a woman have, on average, a net income of 90 per cent of those headed by a man. State intervention is of a similar magnitude in Italy, while in the Netherlands and Sweden the gap is narrowed by approximately 30 percentage points, and by just over 25 percentage points in France and the UK. An obvious outlier is the USA, where state redistribution narrows the gender gap by only 13 percentage points, with the result that female-headed households command an average of 73 cents for each dollar of income of male-headed households.

Disaggregating sources of income reveals that female-headed households command only a limited amount of income from the market: across all countries, few women can sustain a household without intervention or assistance. There is, however, considerable variation in how far the state intervenes to support female-headed households: in Germany and Italy, high levels of state redistribution bring the average female-headed household almost in line with those with male heads, and the more moderate redistribution effected by the French, Dutch and Swedish welfare states also results in a significant narrowing of gender differentials. By contrast, in the UK the poor starting position of female-headed households means that, even after quite considerable state transfers, they command less than three-quarters of the income of households headed by men. This leaves such households in a very similar position to those in the USA, in which there is significantly less redistribution in favour of households headed by women than in any other country under study.

5.2.2   Gender and the risk and persistence of poverty

Protection against poverty is considered to be a primary function of the welfare state, as well as a basic measure of the well-being of households. The extent to which female- as well as male-headed households can live free from poverty gives a clear indicator of their integration into the economic order, and provides important information about the quality of women's and men's lives as well as their short- and longer-term opportunities. Against a backdrop of considerable cross-national variation in the amount of redistribution toward female-headed households, it is particularly pertinent to enquire into both the degree to which the eight welfare states are protecting female-headed households from poverty and the impact of the welfare state on gender differentials in poverty.

Table 5.2 draws on published European data of poverty rates (based on a poverty line of 60 per cent of median income) for those male- and female-headed households that consist of a single person (a

Table 5.2   Poverty rates for female- and male-headed single person households, 1997

	Female-headed	Male-headed	Total	Gender poverty ratio (female to male)
France	21	18	17	1.2
Germany	27	19	14	1.4
Ireland	51	34	20	1.5
Italy	23	16	19	1.4
Netherlands	22	22	13	1.0
Sweden	20	26	12	0.8
UK	41	24	22	1.7
EU 15	27	19	18	1.4

Source: European Commission 2001a: table 3c

categorization that excludes lone mothers). Rates of poverty for women's and men's households are shown alongside a gender poverty ratio (in the last column of the table). The gender poverty ratio indicates whether women living alone are at greater risk of being in poverty than equivalent men: a figure of 1 would indicate an equal risk of being in poverty, and figures in excess of 1 show that female-headed households face a higher risk of poverty. The norm for all countries is that poverty is feminized. In fact, across the EU women living alone are almost one and a half times more likely to be in poverty than men in the same circumstances. Ireland and the UK stand out for their above average poverty rates: half of these female-headed households are classified as poor in Ireland, and two-fifths in the UK. In terms of the gender poverty ratio, however, the two countries diverge somewhat, with Ireland's ratio close to the EU average of 1.4, while in the UK women living alone are 1.7 times more likely to be in poverty than men in a similar situation. Germany and Italy form a middle group of countries, with poverty rates near or below the European average and a similar gender poverty ratio. In France, poverty rates are low overall, and this is accompanied by a relatively narrow gender poverty ratio. The Netherlands and Sweden form exceptional cases, combining low overall poverty rates with a roughly equal risk of female and male poverty in the case of the Netherlands, and in the case of Sweden a poverty risk for male-headed sole person households that exceeds that of equivalent female-headed households.[6]

This picture of poverty among women and men living alone throws new light on the relative resources of female- and male-headed households. Germany and Italy, which appeared highly redistributive on previous measures, have a gender poverty ratio that is very close to average. There are, nevertheless, echoes of the patterns found to date among the different measures: the relatively strong position of female-headed households in France emerges clearly from all measures, as do the relatively poor circumstances of similar households in the UK. Moreover, Sweden conforms to its by now familiar pattern with the lowest (in fact, negative) gender poverty ratio.

The next task is to establish the role of state taxes and transfers in alleviating poverty and affecting gender imbalances in poverty. Drawing again from published data, table 5.3 compares the poverty rates for all women and men as they would be if families received only income from the market with poverty rates after the state has levied taxes and paid cash transfers. For each, a gender poverty ratio is calculated (as above).[7] There is remarkably little cross-national variation if we look at the poverty rates that would prevail if only market

Table 5.3 Poverty rates for women and men before and after state transfers, 1997

	Poverty before state transfers			Poverty after state transfers			Reduction of women's poverty resulting from	
	All women	All men	Gender poverty ratio	All women	All men	Gender poverty ratio	Pensions	Other state transfers
France	43	39	1.1	17	17	1.0	58	42
Germany	42	35	1.2	15	13	1.2	70	30
Ireland	42	39	1.1	21	19	1.1	33	67
Italy	45	40	1.1	20	19	1.1	92	8
Netherlands	40	34	1.2	14	12	1.2	54	46
Sweden	48	41	1.2	11	12	0.9	49	51
UK	46	39	1.2	25	20	1.3	48	52
EU 15	44	38	1.2	18	17	1.1	65	35

Source: Authors' calculation based on European Commission 2001a: tables 3a and 6
Poverty line 60 per cent of median income. Income equivalized to modified OECD scale. Income measured at the household level and assumed to be shared equally between adults in multi-person households

income were available. The country ranking that emerges from this measure of poverty is quite distinct; if families received only market income, Sweden would have the highest poverty rates of all countries and a gender poverty ratio in line with its European neighbours.

Swedish taxes and transfers, however, reduce women's poverty by more than three-quarters. Although the state exerts a significant impact on poverty in all the remaining countries, differences in the degree of state intervention result in poverty falling into a familiar pattern of cross-national variation. Once state transfers have been taken into account, the poverty rates of women vary from a low of 11 per cent in Sweden to a high of 25 per cent in the UK. Even though state transfers have a substantial impact on the rates of poverty, they do little to alter the gender poverty ratio. In fact, in the UK, state intervention slightly increases the ratio of female to male poverty. The way in which women's poverty is reduced is also intriguing, and the final columns of the table show the percentage of poverty reduction attributable to state pensions versus other state transfers. Germany and Italy, both of which have a surprisingly low gender gap in incomes, are outliers here also. In both countries, women are protected from poverty by virtue of the pension system: in Italy, 92 per cent of the reduction in women's poverty is a result of pension provision, whereas for Germany the figure is 70 per cent. In the remaining countries there is evidence of a much greater mix, with around half of the poverty reduction resulting from other state transfers, while in Ireland a full two-thirds of poverty reduction is brought about by state transfers other than pensions.

Capturing the characteristics of those whose incomes fall below an income line at one point in time gives us only limited information about the experience of poverty. Snapshot measures do not distinguish those experiencing a temporary dip in income from those who have lived in poverty for an extended period of time. The experience of persistent poverty has a crucial gender dimension. Poor women are in the main lone mothers or older women who frequently have limited opportunities to enter the labour market. As a result, women are even more heavily represented than men among the persistently poor (Ruspini 1997, 1999; Blank 2000; Burgess et al. 2001). To get some measure of persistent poverty, we examine those who fell below the poverty line in each of the three years from 1994 to 1996. Figure 5.2 uses an index measure of persistent poverty (where 100 represents the average rate of persistent poverty) and reveals that across all countries women have an above average risk of experiencing persistent poverty. There is, however, no clear association between single year measures of poverty and gender gaps in persistent poverty. The UK, for

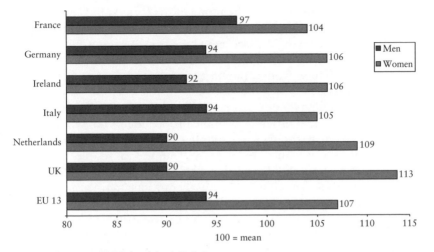

Source: Eurostat 2000d: table A.2.5.2

Figure 5.2 Proportions of women and men experiencing persistent poverty, 1994–1996

example, has high poverty rates overall and a significant gender gap in persistent poverty. By contrast, in the Netherlands, low rates of poverty coexist with a large gender gap in persistent poverty.

This complex cross-national picture of incomes and poverty begs an explanation, and we now turn to an examination of resources of different household types, looking first at lone mothers and other households with children before examining the incomes of older women and men.

5.2.3 The economic resources of lone mothers and other households with children

The central questions here are what resources are made available to support parenthood and how far lone mothers are protected from the income risks of raising children without immediate or direct recourse to a male income. An understanding of where the responsibility falls for providing the time and economic resources needed for child bearing and rearing are crucial to any picture of gender inequality (Folbre 1994; Joshi and Davies 1996; Joshi 1998). The division of responsibility has two key facets: first, how the costs of children are divided between the state and the family, and second, their distribution within the family, i.e. the proportion of costs borne by women and men.[8] This latter aspect can be determined only through an examination of women's and men's individual incomes, and we return to this issue in chapter 6. For the moment the focus is the institutional division of the costs of children: we measure the strength of the claims that can be made on the welfare state by virtue of having children and complement this by an examination of the income advantages and penalties that follow from different types of parenthood, particularly lone motherhood.

Before examining incomes, it is worth noting that there are considerable cross-national differences in the proportion of households with children and, in particular, the number of households headed by a lone mother (constrained by data, we employ a simple definition of lone mother households as being a sole adult woman residing with at least one dependent child). The number of lone mother households falls into a distinct cross-national clustering: at one pole are the UK, the USA and Sweden, with relatively high proportions of lone mother households (6.3, 5.4 and 4.8 per cent of all households respectively); a middling rank is made up of Germany, France and the Netherlands (all close to 3 per cent); and at the other pole is Italy, where fewer than 1 per cent of households are headed by a lone mother.

Looking first at all parents, it is again instructive to examine incomes from the market alongside the claims that parents make on state resources. On the basis of market income alone, households with children enjoy incomes close to or above average in Germany, the Netherlands and the USA. In all three countries, however, taxes and transfers act to reduce these incomes, so that the average net income of households with children is nearly a fifth below the national average. By contrast, although the tax and transfer system operates to reduce the income of households with children in Sweden also, this reduction is less marked with post-tax and transfer incomes of households with children just 6 per cent below average. France is unusual, in that the transfer and tax system works in favour of those with children, making their income position slightly better than that of their German counterparts. Hence, with the exception of France and Sweden, having children does not lead to a strong, or indeed any, claim on state resources such that families in all countries bear the costs of children in the form of below average incomes.

Against a backdrop of parenthood giving but limited claims on state resources, we now explore the income 'penalty' attaching to lone motherhood. This is measured as the difference between the average incomes of lone mother households and those of the whole population. The penalty for lone motherhood is at its greatest before the state intervenes (figure 5.3). This is particularly the case in the Netherlands and the UK, where lone mother households have market incomes that are approximately 80 per cent below the national average.

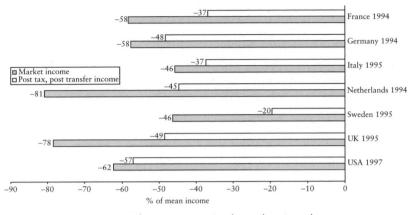

Source: Luxembourg Income Study, authors' analysis

Figure 5.3 The income 'penalty' of lone motherhood

In Sweden and Italy, by contrast, the market incomes of lone mother households are 'just' 46 per cent below the national average. The extent to which the state intervenes to reduce the income disadvantage of lone mother households is revealed when we compare market incomes with incomes after taxes and transfers. In the Netherlands and the UK, the transfer system has the biggest impact on the incomes of lone mother households; yet, even after considerable state intervention, the mean income of lone mother households comes to barely half the national average. Compare this to Sweden, where state intervention reduces the financial disadvantage of lone mothers to 20 per cent of average income. A comparison between France, Germany and the USA is also revealing. The market income disadvantage in all three countries is very similar, with lone mother households having a market income that is around 60 per cent below average. After the state intervenes, lone mother households enjoy very different income levels across countries. In France a high degree of state intervention reduces the lone motherhood penalty to 37 per cent of average income, but in Germany the impact of the state is much less (lone mothers having a net income that is 48 per cent below the national average), and in the USA state intervention barely affects the income disadvantage experienced by lone mothers. It is interesting to note how little correspondence there is between the degree of welfare state intervention and the adequacy of the incomes of lone mothers. This reflects cross-national variation in the market incomes of lone mothers, driven largely by differences in the degree to which they participate in the labour market (see chapter 4).

Since state transfers make up a substantial part of the income of lone mothers in many countries, their receipt merits further examination. Table 5.4 compares average receipt of all state transfers and means-tested transfers by lone mothers and all households with children. Given the previous figures, it comes as no surprise that the state is a very important source of income for lone mothers across all countries. The Netherlands falls at one extreme, with lone mothers very dependent on the state as a source of income (92 per cent of lone mothers' income is from the state). The UK and Sweden follow, with the state providing, respectively, 67 per cent and 56 per cent of the income of lone mothers. France and Germany cluster together, with lone mothers receiving a third of their income from the state. It is Italy and the USA that make up the other, low extreme. Although the state is clearly an important source of lone mothers' income, on international comparisons state transfers are but a minor contributor of resources: in Italy 14 per cent of lone mothers' income comes from the state, and in the USA 25 per cent. In contrasting lone mother households to all households with children, the distinct situation of lone mothers emerges, as does a different cross-national ranking. The Swedish welfare state emerges as the most significant redistributor of resources to households with children, providing them with a third of their income. The Netherlands and the UK fall back to the middle

Table 5.4   The state as a source of income for households with children

| | | State transfers as % of net household income | | |
		Lone mothers	All with children	All households
France 1994	All state	36	15	37
	Means-tested	12	3	2
Germany 1994	All state	36	11	28
	Means-tested	16	3	2
Italy 1995	All state	14	5	31
	Means-tested	0	0	0
Netherlands 1994	All state	92	20	31
	Means-tested	59	5	4
Sweden 1995	All state	56	33	46
	Means-tested	13	5	5
UK 1995	All state	67	19	23
	Means-tested	49	10	7
USA 1997	All state	25	6	13
	Means-tested	21	3	2

Source: Luxembourg Income Study, authors' analysis
Income equivalized to OECD scale. Means for total sample

ground on this measure (around one-fifth of parents' income comes from the state in these two countries), while the importance of the state as a source of income is less in France (15 per cent) and Germany (11 per cent). Maintaining their position at the lower bounds of state intervention, the Italian and American welfare states provide families with children with only a fraction of their incomes (5 per cent and 6 per cent respectively).

A more qualitative dimension of the experience of lone mothers is captured by the extent to which their incomes are subject to means testing. If lone mothers source their income in this manner, then the risks of stigmatization are high, and the possibilities of using intervention to exercise social control are expanded. In all countries, the importance of means-tested income is much greater for those households than it is for all households with children (see table 5.4). The Netherlands falls again at the extreme on this measure with 59 per cent of the income of lone mother households subject to a means test (twelve times the proportion received by all parents). Following close behind is the UK, where 49 per cent of the income of lone mothers is means-tested. For the remaining countries, means testing is less pronounced, yet means-tested incomes account for between 12 and 21 per cent of the incomes of lone mother households (bar Italy, where there is zero receipt of means-tested incomes).

The picture thus far is of extensive state transfer of resources towards lone mother households combined with poor access to market income. Rates of poverty serve to demonstrate how these two factors come together and whether this combination of resources results in an income adequate to the needs of lone mother households. As table 5.5 reveals, very high rates of poverty prevail for lone mother households: in Germany, Ireland and the UK, about half are in poverty, and about a third in France and the Netherlands.

Table 5.5 Poverty risks of lone mother households, 1996

| | Lone mothers' poverty rate | Poverty risk relative to | |
		All women	All men
France	31	1.8	2.1
Germany	48	2.8	3.2
Ireland	52	2.7	3.1
Netherlands	35	2.7	3.2
UK	50	2.4	2.9
EU 13	36	2.0	2.3

Source: Eurostat 2000e

While lower than the EU average, the poverty rates of lone mothers in the Netherlands are exceptionally high by national standards: lone mothers are more than three times as likely to be poor as all men, and 2.7 times more likely to experience poverty than all women. The poverty risks also demonstrate that lone motherhood is a source of considerable differentiation among women, with lone mother households between 1.8 and 2.8 times as likely to live in poor households as all women.

Viewing the economic status of lone mothers in the context of that of all households with children has been useful in a number of respects. For one, it provides an understanding of the outlier, Sweden. With strong support for all with children, the Swedish state offers considerable protection to lone mother households, whose income, while still falling below national average, is greater than that of lone mothers in any of the other welfare states considered here. Similarly, although much less of an outlier, France's significant support to all households with children appears to have positive spillovers for the economic situation of lone mothers. Beyond this, it would be difficult to predict the economic situation of lone mothers from the treatment of households with children. In the Netherlands, which offers a moderate support for households with children, poverty rates for lone mother households are high by national standards, and means-tested transfers are used extensively. Likewise, the extremely poor economic position of lone mothers in Germany, the UK and particularly the USA is not signalled by the treatment of all households with children. If we apply a strong version of Hobson's (1994) 'litmus test' – that lone mother households should enjoy economic resources equivalent to all households with children – all the welfare states represented here fail. None covers fully the combined risk of caring and of living without a male income, with the result that lone motherhood everywhere brings with it some degree of economic exclusion. However, if the 'litmus test' is more relative, Sweden outperforms the other countries by a large margin. For the remaining countries, lone mother households end up with very limited resources or in poverty. In the majority of countries, state intervention results in resources actually being taken away from families with children. By contrast, lone mother households are net beneficiaries of the state, although their access to state resources is more likely to be mediated by a means test, placing them in a qualitatively different relationship to the welfare state as compared with other families. The economic 'penalty' attaching to lone motherhood therefore comes about in spite of state intervention, and reflects the severely compromised access that lone mothers have to market income. Relatively high income levels among lone mother households in Sweden are explained by the double virtue of high access to market income and significant transfer of state resources.

5.2.4   Economic resources and poverty in later life

The ageing of the population and greater female longevity make the study of economic resources and poverty in later life central to an understanding of gender inequalities. Legal and cultural limits on labour market activity among the older population mean that there are very limited opportunities to change, and particularly increase, income after retirement. As a result, the risk and experience of poverty and low income may be qualitatively different for older people. What is more, sex differences in longevity mean that it is women who are affected most by the income risks associated with the loss of a partner. In addition to providing useful information in itself, a measure of gender differentials in resources in later life gives us a unique perspective on whether gender-based advantages and disadvantages have accumulated across the lifetime (Rake 1999). Lastly, from the perspective of the welfare state, the older population makes the single largest claim on resources, such that redistributive activities in this field can be said to speak to the form of national welfare state.

Table 5.6 provides an overall picture of the incomes of the older population. Continental European single person female-headed households have, on average, an income around 90 per cent of total mean income, and this varies little cross-nationally. By contrast, in the

Table 5.6   Average incomes of households containing an older person

	Mean income of household type as % of overall mean			
	Sole female-headed	Sole male-headed	Couple	Gender gap: income of sole females as % of sole males
France 1994	91	114	103	79
Germany 1994	92	106	98	87
Italy 1995	89	113	98	78
Netherlands 1994	90	109	90	83
Sweden 1995	92	98	102	94
UK 1995	72	89	85	81
USA 1997	74	105	100	71

Source: Luxembourg Income Study, authors' analysis
Income equivalized to OECD scale

UK and the USA, the income of female-headed households is around three-quarters of the national average. The gender gap in incomes of the older population (the last column of table 5.6), is at its greatest in the USA, where older female-headed households have only 71 per cent of the income of their male counterparts. Using this gender gap as a measure, a strong European clustering emerges, with sole older female-headed households receiving 80 per cent of the income of equivalent male-headed households in France, Italy, the Netherlands and the UK. Only in Germany, and particularly Sweden, is the gender gap narrower (87 per cent and 94 per cent respectively). Sweden is again an outlier, with relatively high incomes among sole older women (although on this dimension it falls much closer to other countries than when the situation of lone mothers is compared). A clear candidate for the other extreme is the USA, with sole older female households in a uniquely vulnerable economic position relative to other older households. In the UK, by contrast, the relatively poor incomes of older female households goes hand in hand with low incomes for all older households, such that the gender gap falls within the average range.

Given the state's role in providing income for older households (particularly single person female-headed households), we would anticipate that it plays a considerable part in establishing a hierarchy of resources among the older population.[9] This raises questions about the mechanisms used by the state to redistribute income among the older population, and particularly the degree to which older women rely on means-tested income rather than pension income from social insurance or, as in Sweden, from a citizenship-based pension. To measure this, we calculate the average per capita transfer received by single person female- and male-headed households and contrast overall state pension receipt, the receipt of non-means-tested state income and means-tested transfers.

Figure 5.4 contrasts the per capita transfers received by older sole female and male households. In the majority of countries, female-headed households receive less overall from the state than equivalent male-headed households.[10] There are, in addition, clear disparities in the way that the state delivers income to the older population. In all countries, households headed by older women are receiving significantly less income from non-means-tested sources. In France and the UK, the claims of women on their own to non-means-tested income are closest to their male counterparts (at around 90 per cent), with Sweden (81 per cent) and Germany (69 per cent) following behind. However, in Italy, the Netherlands and the USA, households headed by a sole older woman claim less than 60 per cent of the social insurance entitlements of equivalent male-headed households. In

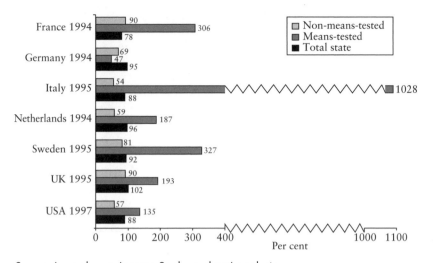

Source: Luxembourg Income Study, authors' analysis
Figure 5.4 State transfers paid to older sole female-headed households as a percentage of those paid to older sole male-headed households

addition, the income of sole female-headed households is much more likely to have been subject to a means test: female-headed households receive ten times more income from means-tested sources in Italy than male-headed households, while in France and Sweden female-headed households receive three times as much income from means-tested sources as households headed by men.

One conclusion to be drawn from these ratios is that, while the state intervenes heavily to increase the incomes of older women who are living alone, such redistribution takes a specific, gendered form. To return to a point made earlier, non-means-tested pensions do not appear to compensate women and men equally for the income risks that they have experienced over the life course. The data demonstrate that the claims of many women on pension resources have been weakened by discontinuous patterns of employment and extensive periods of caring during the active years. The economic disadvantages experienced earlier in the life course, mainly as a result of caring activities, extend into later life. As a result, a much greater proportion of women's resources derives from means-tested cash transfers. Hence, to the extent that older women are compensated, it is for their current experience of low incomes rather than for prior lifetime events.

Our empirical picture of resources in later life is completed by figures on poverty. From the poverty rates for all women and men aged sixty-five years and over (table 5.7), three country groupings

Table 5.7 Poverty rates for women and men aged 65 or over, 1997

	Women 65+	Men 65+	Gender poverty ratio
France	19	14	1.4
Germany	18	8	2.3
Ireland	30	18	1.7
Italy	17	13	1.3
Netherlands	7[§]	8[§]	0.9
Sweden	10	8	1.3
UK	34	22	1.5
EU 15	22	15	1.5

Source: European Commission 2001a: table 3a
Poverty line 60 per cent of median income. Income equivalized to modified OECD scale
Income assumed to be shared equally between adults in multi-person households
[§] 1996 data

emerge. At one pole, poverty is rare among older women and men
when they live in the Netherlands and Sweden. In the Netherlands, the
poverty rate is, in fact, higher for men, while in Sweden for every man
in poverty, there are approximately 1.3 women. Next comes a cluster
of countries – France, Germany and Italy – with middling poverty
rates, although gender differences may still be marked. For example,
German women's poverty rate is 2.3 times that of men. Lastly, a large
proportion of the older population in Ireland and the UK are in
poverty: one in three older women lives in poverty in the UK, while
the poverty rate for women in Ireland is only marginally lower. The
figures demonstrate that capacity of older women to secure an adequate income and to remain fully included in the economic order
varies enormously across countries. A poverty-free retirement remains
elusive for a significant minority of older women in Ireland and the UK,
while poverty affects only a few older women in the Netherlands and
Sweden. Nevertheless, in all countries bar the Netherlands, when they
head households on their own, older women are more exposed to the
risks of poverty than older men, with countries such as Germany and
Ireland demonstrating a marked gender gap in poverty rates.

Before concluding the analyses, let us contrast the clustering of
countries that emerged in this section with that arising from the
economic situation of households with children. While Sweden was
an outlier in its generosity of provision for people with children, it
now falls much closer to the mainstream, in that it secures near-
average incomes for the older population. However, it maintains its
record of ensuring narrow gender gaps and a lower risk of poverty

among female-headed households. The Netherlands, by contrast, which was ranked among the least generous in its treatment of lone mothers, appears to be providing most generously for women living alone in later life. The picture for Germany is rather mixed, but in Italy and France the economic situation of older women appears relatively strong, and this goes a long way to explaining the narrower gender gaps between male- and female-headed households identified earlier. The USA and the UK maintain a consistent, and poor, record. Just as lone mothers experienced the lowest incomes in these two countries, so sole older female heads of households receive the most limited resources. This suggests that in the UK and the USA female-headed households face a double economic jeopardy.

5.3 Power Relations and Contests Arising around Gender and the Distribution of Income

The redistribution of income is one of the most visible of welfare state activities. Thus the politics of income distribution are not hard to identify. This politics is also all-encompassing, since few individuals remain untouched by the collection of taxes or the transfer of resources. It is, in addition, a politics that has resonance in all the countries under consideration: identifying the different components of income demonstrated that even in those countries where the welfare state is described as small or residual, the state is a major source of income, with a significant impact on the ordering of resources among households. Although the question of who receives state resources and under what conditions is the stuff of public debate, the gender dimension may be difficult to discern. Women's and men's claims are rarely made on the basis of their sex alone, not least because women's and men's interests are defined also by their family situation and change as their roles and family status alter over the life course.

Complex also are the interlinkages between the welfare state's distribution of income and the balance of power resources within society. It is possible to disentangle three such linkages. First, the transfer of income is an expression of the power of the welfare state. Garnering and redistributing income is a political act in so far as it embodies the power of political actors to decide between contesting claims on resources. The transfer of income is most obviously an act of power where it is conditional on a means test. The requirement to meet specified conditions or fulfil certain behavioural requirements places claimants in a particular, and often subordinate, relationship to the welfare state, in which they experience the exercise of welfare state power more directly than those who receive benefits on the basis of earned entitlement. The fact that means-tested income is a larger component of the income of female-headed households suggests a certain set of power relations between women and the welfare state. Women living without a male income (especially those in the UK and the Netherlands) are shown to be more subject to bureaucratic discretion and state scrutiny, and face the prospect of steep penalties for changing their behaviour or status in certain ways. Second, the distribution of income reflects the balance of power within a given society. Powerful voices and interests shape policy and determine the beneficiaries of income distribution. The dominance of men and the greater expression given to male interests in decision-making bodies goes some way to explaining how policy is formed. The hierarchy in which claims are placed may, therefore, reflect a broader social hierarchy in which, for example, wage earners enjoy a more privileged status than carers. Third, the distribution of income affects power balances, including those between women and men. While there is no simple link between income and power, the disempowering effects of poverty, especially persistent poverty, are well known. The exposure of women with caring responsibilities to considerable income risk and the concentration of poverty among women heading their own households represent a form of political disenfranchisement. Furthermore, differences in economic resources have a bearing on women's and men's longer-term opportunities. The extent of the income 'penalties' attaching to lone motherhood and the high risks of poverty affect and reflect not only the economic circumstances of those women, but the opportunities of all women. It is clear that across all countries (with the possible exception of Sweden) women's ability to maintain a household with children is limited, and this surely operates to constrain the opportunities of women currently partnered to exit an unhappy, violent or abusive relationship.

The distribution of income has an important normative dimension also. In meeting certain claims and privileging particular groups within society, the welfare state creates a cleavage between those who are deserving of support and those who are not. There is no clearer statement of value in capitalist societies than money, and by supporting certain social roles and rewarding particular types of behaviour, the welfare state reflects, and affects, the values held by a society. On this interpretation, the fact that by international standards older women heading households in the UK and the USA receive very low incomes gives insight into the particular values placed by these two societies on the older generation and on women's caring roles. The lower incomes of lone mothers across all countries considered here suggest a continuing ambiguity about the morality of extending support to lone mothers in combination with a devaluation of their caring responsibilities.

5.4 Overview

By way of overview, we return to the questions posed earlier in the chapter concerning the qualitative dimensions of welfare state redistribution. We argued that the welfare state constituted a hierarchy of claims, and that this hierarchy reflects the relative coverage and privilege granted to women's and men's income risks. When compared in practice, the relative income position of female- and male-headed households suggests that a gendered hierarchy of claims does indeed exist in each of the countries covered here. The nature of this hierarchy varies across countries: there are some countries (notably the UK and the USA) where female-headed households have but a weak claim on economic resources, a finding that is confirmed by each measure of economic status. In other countries there is internal variation, with the claims of households headed by lone mothers and older women constituted quite differently (viz. weak claims on the part of lone mothers relative to the high incomes of older women in the Netherlands and Italy). Hence, while the overall pattern in each country represents a privileging of the claims of male-headed households over those of women, both the extent of this privilege and its source lead to cross-national variation.

Our second qualitative aspect referred to the degree to which the state integrated women and men into the economic order and, conversely, the extent to which their poverty signalled a risk of social exclusion. For France, Germany, Italy, Ireland and the UK, the poverty figures are unequivocal: female-headed households have a higher risk of both falling into and remaining in poverty. Hence, securing an income sufficient to sustain a household remains beyond the reach of many women. For those women currently part of couples, and hence presumably 'protected' from poverty by a male income, the reality is that they remain just a husband or partner away from poverty. The highest poverty risk attaches to the status of lone motherhood, although later life is also accompanied by high poverty risks in Ireland and the UK and low income in the USA. The picture is more mixed for the Netherlands and Sweden, where low levels of poverty overall coexist with gender poverty ratios that are low and sometimes even negative. Our understanding of why this might be the case in Sweden is compromised by lack of available data. The situation in the Netherlands is more easily explained, with its bifurcation in poverty rates: older women experience very low levels of poverty, while the poverty risk among lone mothers is high by national standards. This explains why the gender gap in persistent poverty remains pronounced in the Netherlands.

Focusing on the mechanisms whereby incomes are directed towards female-headed households also proves interesting. Women who head their own households are more likely to receive income that has been means-tested, so are more exposed to the social control functions of the state. This is particularly the case for lone mothers (and takes a very exaggerated form in the Netherlands and the UK), but also for older women in a number of countries. It appears that the claim of lone mothers on state resources takes a form quite distinct from that of all parents, while the claims of older women are fashioned, in part at least, by their compromised claims on social insurance or citizenship-based pensions. In all countries the costs of care are high for lone mothers, and in the UK, the USA and Ireland the effects of caring are still felt by many in later life.

Turning our focus to the role of state intervention, how does the empirical picture of the state's activities enhance our understanding of the gender dimension of redistribution? With the exception of the USA (and possibly Italy), welfare state intervention in relation to the incomes of female-headed households appears to be rather extensive, but, while gender gaps in income are frequently narrowed, they are rarely eliminated. Indeed, overall poverty rates before and after transfers suggest that state intervention broadly sustains the gendered patterning of poverty. As mentioned above, the utilization of distinct mechanisms of redistribution – particularly the greater subjection of female-headed households to means testing – emerges as a feature of a number of welfare states. The form of redistribution also varies across countries, with some interesting effects on gender. France and Sweden are unusual in the extent to which they redistribute horizontally, with relatively generous provision for families with children and, within this, lone mothers. In the remaining countries, there is evidence of a significant 'penalty' attached to all households with children, suggesting that a large proportion of the costs of children are borne privately (i.e. by families themselves). As a consequence, lone mothers are unable to secure very much income by virtue of having children, with the result that they resort to claiming means-tested, minimum income provisions. In Germany and Italy, and to a lesser extent the Netherlands, redistribution geared to the older population, and within that older women on their own, narrows the gender gap in incomes. At the same time, lone mothers are consistently disprivileged in these three countries, suggesting that the protection of widows is much more extensive than that of women for whom divorce, separation or absence of a male partner have led to the loss of a male income. The UK, the USA and Ireland experience the highest gender gaps (although our picture of Ireland is somewhat compromised by having data only on poverty rates). In the UK, a gender gap remains, despite quite extensive redistribution, and may be explained both by the limited access of lone parents to market income and the fact that the older population as a whole, and especially women on their own, have very low incomes. As far as we can tell from current data, the situation in Ireland is not dissimilar, but the gender gap is less pronounced there on some measures, not least because of the unusually high poverty risks of male-headed households. Finally, the welfare state in the USA is notable for its low levels of redistribution overall, with the consequence that the economic status of female-headed households remains relatively untouched. In this case, it is the market that is driving inequalities, with economic penalties in evidence for both older female and lone mother households.

6

Individual Resources and Household Redistribution

This chapter completes our empirical investigation by stepping inside the private sphere. Its concerns are to investigate gender differentials in individual resource entitlement and what this means for the balance of money and time between women and men and for the degree to which women and men rely on the family as a source of financial support. In short, the chapter is concerned to see how inequalities in the private sphere are associated with women's and men's relative welfare. Hinged on processes that occur within the family, the present chapter extends our understanding of gender inequalities in resources by looking at resources at the individual level and incorporating a time dimension. The analysis adds an awareness of the family's role in resource distribution to our knowledge of the family as a site of care (chapter 3). The present chapter also complements the analysis of male- and female-headed households in chapter 5, since, in looking at women and men living in the same household, it incorporates the circumstances of the majority of women who do not head their own household. Our approach is innovative: although individual claims on resources are recognized as essential in capturing gender-based inequalities (Jenkins 1990), such recognition has only rarely been translated into empirical practice (Sørensen and McLanahan 1989; Davies and Joshi 1994; Hutton 1994; Sutherland 1997).

The chapter is divided into four parts. In the first, we set the scene by discussing the significance of individual claims on resources and the resource balance within couples, as well as examining questions relating to the politics of individual welfare. Our aim in the second part is to furnish an empirical, cross-national picture of individual resources and to examine the extent to which the family itself operates as a site of resource distribution. The third part of the chapter is concerned with mapping the power relations and contests that are associated with both access to individual resources and the gender balance of resources. The chapter concludes with a fourth, overview section.

6.1 Individual and Family Resources, Welfare and Gender Relations

There are two principal motivations for departing from normal empirical practice, in which the distribution of resources is examined only at the family or household level, to seek to uncover the gendered pattern of individual claims on money and time. First, the links between individual and family resources provide crucial information about gender relations and gender inequalities. Second, the ways in which the welfare state conceives of and treats people, as individuals and within their family context, is a source of cross-national variation in both the form of the welfare state and gender relations.

Examination of individual resources indicates where women and men fall within a hierarchy of resources and, when put in the context of family resources, signals how far women and men rely upon the family as a source of financial support. While rarely problematized in mainstream literature, relationships of dependency on the family are understood here to be significant, not least because they involve distinct forms of claims making. Although all distributive systems place conditions on the access to resources, family-based claims are governed by a potentially limitless range of principles. The 'good behaviour' of recipients, socially ascribed roles, the perceived needs of individuals, the degree of family harmony or conflict, and the mood of the person who controls the resources may all play a part in shaping the outcomes of this form of redistribution. In contrast to wages and state benefits, the principles of family distribution remain invisible to all but those directly involved. As such, it is difficult to gauge whether a particular share of family resources is fair by any external criteria, and this may significantly weaken an individual's ability, or motivation, to press for increased resources. Familial redistribution remains beyond any formal system of justice; hence the possibility of the use and misuse of power is magnified. Familial redistribution is, furthermore, subject to unpredictable changes over time. This, in concert with the importance of the family for individual welfare, means that the family has considerable distributive power, and can act to overturn the economic hierarchy established by either the welfare state or the market (Curtis 1986).

As with family resources, individual claims on resources have important qualitative aspects that operate alongside their obvious quantitative dimensions. In terms of lifetime opportunities and risks, individual resources shape the potential for women and men to exit their current living arrangements as well as the economic vulnerability that follows separation from, or death of, a partner (Jarvis and Jenkins 1999). Resources therefore affect some of the most private or intimate choices that individuals face over their lifetime. The link between resources and the choice of living and partnership arrangements points out the connection between the distribution of resources and the balance of power within families, a further qualitative indicator. There is no simple link between resources and power, however (one can, for example, conceive of a household in which resource inequalities coexist with egalitarian practices of decision making). Empirical evidence nevertheless suggests that a strong link exists between individual entitlement to resources and control over their use. Thus, women's income has positive consequences for child, and in particular girls', mortality in developing economies, while in more advanced economies, expenditure on women's and children's clothing and the propensity to hold individual savings are all correlated with women's independent access to money (Haddad and Kanbur 1990; Thomas 1990; Bourguignon and Chiappori 1992).

Turning now to the role of the welfare state, the distribution of individual resources is shaped by a number of welfare state features, including the degree to which transfers and taxes are delivered to individuals or to families, the direct support proffered to relations of dependency, and the process by which claims as dependants may be made.[1] These features come together, although not always coherently, into an overarching mode of provision. Family-based provision is most strongly favoured by the German and Italian welfare states in both benefit and tax system, although in Germany a higher degree of state intervention overall means that this mode of provision has a greater impact on women's and men's resources. At the opposite pole, Sweden is quite consistent in delivering benefits to individuals without regard to their family circumstances. In the remaining countries, a mix of principles is at work, although a high reliance on means-tested delivery of state benefits, as found in the English-speaking countries of Ireland, the UK and to a lesser extent the USA, goes hand in hand with family-based modes of support.

Family and individual modes of provision not only affect resources; they also reflect and affect gender norms. Family-based provision requires that an individual be identified as head of household, principal claimant, and the person to whom resources are directed. Legal or cultural norms mean that typically this role falls to men (not least because men are more often the principal wage earners). The corollary of the naming of a head of household is that other household members are classified as dependants, denied the right to claim or receive welfare state resources in their own name (Daly 1996). Given the power implications, it is no surprise that family-based systems have come under the strongest critique from feminist analysts. However, ambiguity follows from the fact that women continue to draw considerable benefit, especially in later life, from dependants' benefits, another hallmark of familialized systems. Dependants' benefits are, furthermore, a form of compensation for the economic consequences of caring, and, while rarely generous enough to provide a living income, go some way to 'making good' the costs of care. At the other end of the continuum, individualization allows women (as well as men) to make independent claims on, and have unmediated access to, state resources regardless of their living arrangements. Equal treatment and fairness, the right to privacy within couples, and the greater likelihood that transfers will be spent on children have all been cited in support of increased individualization. The rules governing individualized systems may, nevertheless, work to disadvantage women if, for example, individualized payments are linked to earnings and time spent in the labour market. Gendered, normative processes are set in train by individualized modes of provision also. A more individualized approach to payments for children, for example, is found where payment is directed to the principal carer (typically the mother) rather than the (male) head of household. This ensures an independent income for women, with the further advantage that such a payment mechanism is likely to increase the money spent on children (Lundberg et al. 1996). Nevertheless, this may reinforce norms operating within couples that money paid directly to women is 'for the children', while money paid to men is exclusively for their own consumption (Goode et al. 1998). More subtle still, such a payment mechanism may reaffirm notions that there is a single principal carer, reflecting norms of the breadwinner / carer divide, rather than opening up the possibility of more equitable sharing of caring responsibilities.

The ways in which welfare states define and support relations of dependency directly is a further source of policy variation. Definitions of dependency range from the very narrow (in which only children are included, as in Sweden) to the very broad (where dependency continues even after a couple divorces, as is the case in the UK and the USA with regard to pension provision, for example). In terms of treatment, the magnitude of the support given to dependent relationships varies, and can be taken as a marker of the different value attached to particular family forms. For example, high levels of support for 'wifely labour' through extensive dependants' benefits (as found in Germany and, to a lesser extent, the Netherlands) bolster both heterosexual and patriarchal norms (Shaver and Bradshaw 1995). Furthermore, welfare states differ in the degree to which claims as a dependant may coexist with direct claims, such that welfare provision opens up or closes down the opportunity to combine different roles simultaneously or across the lifetime. The French pension system, for example, offers a rare example of provision that allows for a claim as a dependant to be combined with a direct, employment-based claim. More commonly (e.g. in Germany, the Netherlands, the UK and the USA) a stark choice is presented: resources can be claimed either on the basis of partnership status or on the basis of individual labour market status, but these claims may not be combined.

6.2   Individual Resources and the Gender Resource Balance

6.2.1   The distribution of individual incomes

Our desire to uncover cross-national and gendered patterns in individual resources starts with an examination of the distribution of individual incomes. This section, in the first instance, establishes the proportions of women and men with no access to financial resources of their own, people whose welfare is most at risk from family dissolution as well as from the possible abuse of gender-based power relations within ongoing relationships. In the second instance, attention is turned to the gendered economic hierarchy that emerges when individual income is the focus.

The proportions of women and men who receive no income in their own right are set out in table 6.1. For this purpose, we employ two measures of income. The first, 'personal income', consists of all earnings and social insurance benefits directed to the individual net of any taxes levied at the individual level, while the second adds to personal income those state benefits which, although assessed according to household status, are paid to specific individuals.[2] The percentage of women without personal income varies considerably cross-nationally. Almost half of all women in Italy have no personal income, a situation shared by 37 per cent of Dutch women and more than a quarter of women in France, Germany and the UK. In the USA a fifth of women

Table 6.1 Women and men recording zero personal income (as per cent)

		Women	Men	Gender ratio
France 1994	PI	27.5	11.9	2.3
	PI + SB	14.7	0.8	18.4
Germany 1994	PI	28.4	11	2.6
	PI + SB	13.3	5	2.7
Italy 1995	PI	48.2	23.4	2.1
	PI + SB	47.8	6.4	7.5
Netherlands 1994	PI	37	21.8	1.7
	PI + SB	18.9	6.1	3.1
Sweden 1995	PI	8.9	6	1.5
	PI + SB	2.1	0.2	10.5
UK 1995	PI	25.9	18.5	1.4
	PI + SB	8.2	1.2	6.8
USA 1997	PI	20.5	10.8	1.9
	PI + SB	19.3	1.6	12.1

Source: Luxembourg Income Study, authors' analysis
PI = Personal Income; SB = State Benefits

have no personal income, and even in our lowest-scoring country, Sweden, just under a tenth of women have no personal income. The risk of being without a personal income is much higher for women than men in all countries. As the gender ratio given in the last column of the table shows, in France, Germany and Italy women are at least twice as likely as men to have no personal income, while in Sweden and the UK the risk of being without a personal income is one and a half times higher for women than for men.

The second income measure adds state benefits to personal income, and signals the degree to which welfare states intervene to ensure that women have direct access to at least some income. In most countries, the state effects quite considerable intervention, and works to ensure that women gain access to at least some resources. In Sweden, state transfers reduce by around three-quarters the proportion of women without incomes, in the UK by just over two-thirds, while it is approximately halved in Germany and the Netherlands. Two countries emerge as distinct from these others, however: in Italy and the USA state transfers have little impact on the proportions of women without income. Looking at state intervention through a gender lens reveals a somewhat different picture. Across countries (with the possible exception of Germany), state transfers have a much greater impact on reducing the proportions of men without income than of women. Fewer than 2 per cent of men in France, Sweden, the UK and the USA are left without any income after state transfers have had their effect. This means that the gender ratio of those without individual income is worse when the full range of state transfers has been taken into account than when personal income alone is considered.

The proportions of women and men without individual income is a first measure of (the lack of) independent access to resources. We now add to this a consideration of where those women who do have income are located in the national economic hierarchy. To do this, men are divided into ten equal groups according to their income (in other words, we calculate income deciles for men), and women's incomes are located within that distribution. As a point of reference, if women's incomes were distributed in the same way as men's, 10 per cent of women would fall within each of the income deciles. But the picture for each country shown in figure 6.1 is quite different from this hypothetical gender equality. A feature common to all seven countries is that women are more heavily represented in the lower-income groups. The percentage of women who have income in the bottom fifth of the income distribution is close to or more than double that of men in all countries – 46 per cent of women in the UK fall within the two lowest income bands, as do 53 per cent of Dutch women, for example. It is no surprise, therefore, that large numbers of women have individual incomes that are less than the median income for men: 89 per cent of women in the Netherlands have incomes below that of the average man, 80 per cent in the UK, Sweden and Germany, 75 per cent in Italy, 73 per cent in France, and 72 per cent in the USA.[3] The almost complete absence of women at the very top of the male income distribution is also noteworthy. In all countries, fewer than 3 per cent of women have incomes that place them in the top 10 per cent of the male income distribution, and in the Netherlands and Germany this figure is closer to 1 per cent. It may come as a surprise that, of all the distributions of individual income shown here, the USA demonstrates the least gender differentials, with particularly strong representations of women in the higher-income deciles. This distribution is striking given the generally low levels of welfare state intervention in the USA and the restricted access to economic resources of female-headed households (as explored in chapter 5), and provides further evidence of polarization among women in the USA. The distribution of individual incomes also throws new light on the Swedish case. The picture that emerged from nearly all previous analyses was that Swedish women had relatively high levels of income. However, from figure 6.1 we can see that this is driven not by a strong representation of women across the

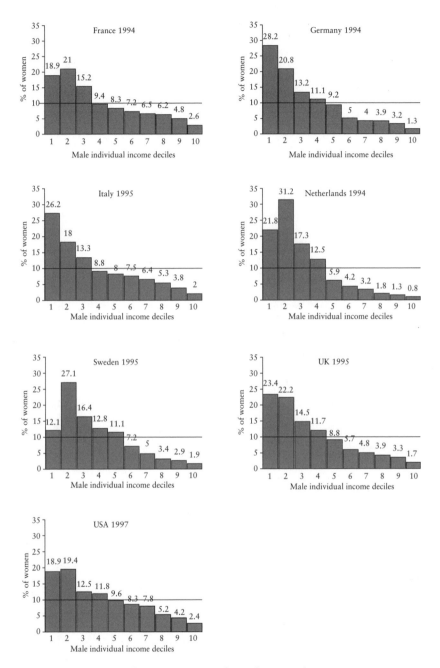

Source: Luxembourg Income Study, authors' analysis

Figure 6.1 Women's position in the male income distribution

whole of the male income distribution, but rather by a distinct clustering of women's personal incomes in the middle of that distribution. In other words, while women may be protected from the most disadvantaged resource positions, high incomes remain as much a male preserve in Sweden as they are elsewhere.

6.2.2   Gender relations and the resource balance within households

Our analysis now goes one step further into the private sphere, to inquire into how individual resources translate into a balance of resources within couples. This analysis provides two specific insights into gender relations. First, it offers a gauge of how gender relations in the domestic sphere are shaped by the inequalities arising from the labour market and the state. Second, it allows us to investigate the consequences of the welfare state for the gender resource balance (analysed by tracing the income balance between women and men within those families that are highly reliant on the state as a source of income). From an empirical point of view, it is essential to link individual incomes within couples to get a measure of the resource balances actually experienced by women and men within their families, since the connection between the distribution of individual resources and the resource balance within couples is not a simple or obvious one.[4]

To measure resource balance, women's resources are compared with the resources received by them and their partner combined. This allows for a calculation of the share of total income, wages and hours in the labour market that women contribute directly. With regard to the income measure, it is important to note that we work with an important, and optimistic, assumption that sharing takes place within families. In line with the analysis above, income is assigned to the person who receives it as far as that is possible. Some income, such as income from savings and investment, is recorded only at the family level, and in this part of the analysis only we assume that this income is divided equally within the couple. This is a 'best case' scenario, one which will be compared with the more pessimistic one of no sharing, examined in section 6.2.3 below.

Table 6.2 shows women's share of the couple's total income, wages and hours in the labour market (where 50 per cent would represent an equal balance of resources within the couple). Looking first at total income, women in Sweden have, on average, the highest share of total income (41.4 per cent), while France, the Netherlands, the UK and the USA group at a mid-point, with women's share of income around a third. Germany lags slightly behind (women's income share being 29

Table 6.2 The resource balance within couples

Women's share of	All women			Mothers		
	Total income	Total annual wages	Total hours in labour market	Total income	Total annual wages	Total hours in labour market
France 1994	34.7	32.2	35.9	38.1	32.3	33.2
Germany 1994	29.1	29.6	32.1	25.6	22.8	25.1
Italy 1995	25.2	23.7	25.5	22.4	21.7	23.5
Netherlands 1994	33.5	27.2	30.1	29.7	19.2	21.8
Sweden 1995	41.4	38.9	44.4	43.1	34.0	40.4
UK 1995	34.4	33.2	36.9	31.8	25.9	30.1
USA 1997	34.7	34.7	37.8	31.1	28.0	34.5

Source: Luxembourg Income Study, authors' analysis

per cent on average), and in Italy women contribute around a quarter of the total income of the couple. Women's share of total wages offers a rather similar picture of the resource balance within couples, since for almost all countries, the ranking and shares remain roughly the same. The Netherlands is the exception here, however, since women's share of wages is significantly lower than that of total income. This suggests that welfare state transfers are making a significant contribution to Dutch women's incomes, with the result that couples achieve a better balance of resources after the state intervenes than they would if they relied on the market alone. A final indicator of the resource balance is women's share of total hours in the labour market. Across all countries, women's contribution of time to the labour market is greater than their share of wages. This is the gender wage gap at work: women's and men's hours in the labour market are not equally rewarded, so women need to spend more hours in the labour market than men if they are to enjoy the same wages as their partners. For example, on the basis of these figures, women in the UK would have to take on an average of 62 per cent of a couple's total time in the labour market in order to bring in half of the combined annual wage.

Looking at individual incomes gives an insight into the division in the costs of care between women and men. From our work on care and the impact of children on labour market participation, we would anticipate that the presence of children introduces further imbalances within couples. Isolating mothers from other women, the last three columns of table 6.2 look at the resource shares that mothers receive directly. The expected pattern emerges for almost all countries and all measures.[5] To take an example, Dutch mothers' share of wages and hours in the labour market is on average 8 percentage points lower than that of all women. A similar, although less extreme, picture emerges for mothers in Germany, Italy, the UK and the USA, where mothers' shares of all resources are between 2 and 8 percentage points lower than those of all women. France and Sweden are exceptions. In both, mothers have a smaller share of time in the labour market, and in Sweden this is accompanied by a reduced share of annual wages. However, in neither country is this reduction matched by an equivalent loss of income. The generosity of both welfare states towards mothers is reflected in the fact that resources are more balanced for couples with children than they are for childless couples.

The analysis of the balance of resources within couples with children gives us a preliminary picture of the impact of the state on the gender resource balance. This is now supplemented with a more detailed look at those couples which have a higher reliance on the state as a source of income (table 6.3). The resource balance for these couples reflects directly on the logic underlying welfare state benefits, especially the degree of familialization and individualization and whether male heads of households are receiving state payments. In the majority of countries, a high level of dependence on state benefits leads to a higher resource imbalance within couples. The effects here vary from the mild (Sweden and the UK) to the more severe case of France, where women's share of income is 7 percentage points lower than that of all women. In Italy and particularly the Netherlands, by

Table 6.3 The resource balance within couples receiving most of their income from the state

	Women's share of income		Percentage point change in women's share of income where couple is reliant on state
	All couples	Couple receives > 50% of income from the state	
France 1994	34.7	27.7	−7.0
Germany 1994	29.1	27.4	−1.7
Italy 1995	25.2	27.1	1.9
Netherlands 1994	33.5	44.8	11.3
Sweden 1995	41.4	41.3	−0.1
UK 1995	34.4	34.2	−0.2
USA 1997	34.7	31.3	−3.4

Source: Luxembourg Income Study, authors' analysis

contrast, the resource balance is more equal for those couples reliant on payments from the state. The strong representation of pensioners among the state-dependent groups in both countries provides the explanation for this situation. Older women acquire some personal income from the pension system, and, although often not substantial in amount, this operates to increase their share of the combined income relative to what happens among their younger counterparts.

In summary, even on the optimistic assumption of equal sharing of certain elements of income, the picture that emerges is one of considerable imbalance of resources within couples. While such imbalances are less marked in Sweden, the other countries resemble one another closely in so far as women command between a quarter and a third of total resources. It is in wages that the greatest imbalances are to be seen, reflecting the coming together of fewer hours in the labour market and the gender wage gap. In most countries, mothers and women in families that are principally reliant on the state as a source of income share the experience of having even fewer resources in their own name. With the exceptions of Italy and the Netherlands, women in couples that are heavily dependent on the state pay an erstwhile hidden penalty in the form of a reduced share of the couple's income.

6.2.3   The family as a site of resource distribution

We now turn to the family as a distributor of resources, and examine the extent to which individual men and women are themselves agents of, or subject to, familial redistribution. This gives an indication not only of the likely power balance within families but, relatedly, of differences in the degree to which women and men depend on the family for their needs to be met. For this part of the analysis, we abandon our optimistic scenario of the sharing of family income components and instead operate on an assumption of no sharing, in order to reveal the percentage of couples' resources that are beyond women's direct control. Alongside these national averages, we reveal the proportions of women who contribute very limited amounts of the couple's income in their own right. This gives us an indication of the numbers of women who will be particularly affected by familial redistribution and especially vulnerable to any inequities therein.

The concentration of resources in male hands emerges very strongly in table 6.4, suggesting that women continue to depend on the family, and their male partners in particular, for resources. The percentage of income beyond women's direct control ranges from almost two-thirds in Sweden to close to four-fifths in Italy. The remaining countries cluster rather closely, with an average of 70 per cent of family income

Table 6.4   The family as a site of redistribution

	Average (mean) % of total household income not under women's direct control	% of women with less than 10% of total family resources in own name
France 1994	69.9	24.1
Germany 1994	72.1	28.5
Italy 1995	78.6	50.6
Netherlands 1994	72.4	31.4
Sweden 1995	62.2	3.7
UK 1995	71.6	24.8
USA 1997	68.9	27.5

Source: Luxembourg Income Study, authors' analysis

beyond the direct control of women. Focusing on the, theoretically at least, rather extreme case of women who command 10 per cent or less of family resources in their own name, there is evidence of considerably greater cross-national variation. Half of all Italian women have direct control of less than 10 per cent of family resources, compared with just under 4 per cent of Swedish women. For women in the remaining countries, close to or in excess of a quarter have very limited personal access to resources. This suggests that in all countries bar Sweden changing partnership arrangements have severe economic penalties for significant numbers of women, and that, while their current arrangements continue, they run the risk of the abuse of power at the hands of the person in control of family resources.

To summarize, in most countries, the average woman has direct control over less than a third of household income – in other words, her welfare is heavily dependent on the family as a site of redistribution. There is striking convergence across nations on this measure, suggesting that the gender resource balance remains an issue in all the countries we consider here. While the data cannot say how egalitarian familial redistribution is in practice, the percentage of women with very low levels of control over resources gives an indication of the degree to which women are exposed to the risks at the heart of familial redistribution.

6.2.4   Women's and men's patterns of time use

To the measures of inequalities in income, we now add some measure of gender differentials in the use of time.[6] Time has clear quantitative dimensions, and we are particularly interested in the amount of time spent in paid work, unpaid work and leisure. This should not disguise the more qualititative implications of the use of time, however. Differences exist in the degree to which women and men exercise choice about their use of time, while the lack of adequate leisure time is a form of poverty in resources as much as a lack of income. Measures of the use of time are now relatively common, although there are elements of the experience of time use which can be overlooked by survey-based measures. For example, the degree to which time is interrupted and fragmented, the pressures on time through the combination of multiple activities (housework combined with care for children, for example), and the degree to which 'leisure time' is filled with obligations to others are not easily captured, even though they may be part of important gender differentials (Phipps and Burton 1998; Bittman and Wacjman 2000).

To capture gender differences in time use, we select four measures of time balance from published data: the ratio of women's and men's time in paid work, unpaid work, leisure activities, and the absolute difference in the amount of time that women and men spend at leisure. The figures in table 6.5 reveal a considerable difference in the time that women and men spend in paid and unpaid work, demonstrating that temporal resources are also marked by gender divisions. Women spend between a third and a half of the time in paid work that men do, and even in Sweden, where female participation in employment is highest, women's average hours of paid work come to no more than 70 per cent of those typifying men. It is unpaid

Table 6.5 Gender differentials in time use

	Ratio of women's time to men's spent in*				Absolute gender gap in free time**
	Paid work	Unpaid work	Total paid and unpaid work	Leisure	
France	0.4	3.3	1.1	0.9	–
Germany[†]	0.4	3.9	1.0	0.9	–
Italy	–	–	–	–	06:14
Netherlands	0.3	2.8	0.9	1.0	00:08
Sweden	0.7	1.7	1.0	0.9	01:55
UK	0.5	2.6	1.0	1.0	01:11
USA	0.5	2.5	1.0	1.0	–1:22

Sources: *Authors' calculation from Gershuny 2000
**Bittman and Wacjman 2000: table 4
[†] Data for West Germany only; gender gap in free time calculated as men's free time less women's free time

work, however, that is most marked by gender inequalities, suggesting that gender roles in the private sphere remain much more rigid than those in the public sphere. At the lower end of the continuum, women in Sweden spend 1.7 times the number of hours in unpaid work as Swedish men, while in Germany the ratio is closer to 4 to 1. There is not only a marked gender division in unpaid work, but women's provision of unpaid labour remains relatively little changed by their employment status. This is because female employment status has only a marginal impact on men's contribution to unpaid work, and because the time spent on unpaid work does not decrease in line with increased hours in paid work (Beblo 1998). Thus, employment typically increases women's total working day. Women in full-time employment in the USA and the UK, for example, are spending almost three more hours per day in (paid and unpaid) work than those who are out of the labour force, while in Germany and Italy this figure amounts to around one and a half hours. In Sweden and the Netherlands, by contrast, women's employment status has a much smaller effect on total work hours, with women in full-time paid work experiencing a net addition to their working day of around 20 minutes (OECD 2001a: table 4.5).

Comparing all women and all men, differences in total hours in work and the time spent at leisure are much less marked than those of paid and unpaid work. Women's total working time is the same as or slightly more than men's in every country except the Netherlands. Similarly, gender differentials in time spent on leisure activities (the fifth column of table 6.5) are small, especially when compared with the differentials in income revealed above. In all countries represented here, women spend close to or more than 90 per cent of the male average on leisure activities. The absolute gap in time spent on leisure reveals a similar picture. Although Italian women experience a considerable leisure gap, enjoying six fewer leisure hours per week, the gap in other countries is slight.

There are, nevertheless, a number of interpretations of such a narrow gender gap. On one account, it may reflect the fact that leisure time is more protected from gender divisions than other forms of time use. An alternative interpretation would point to the fact that similar quantities of leisure time may serve to disguise gender differences in its quality (given that, as mentioned above, women's leisure is more likely to involve simultaneous activities and hence be subject to greater fragmentation).

As a way of summarizing, we bring together this picture of temporal balance with that of income balance presented above. Introducing time as a measure of resources gives a picture of a gender imbalance that is even more extreme than that of individual incomes. The balance of both economic and temporal resources within couples is more equitable in Sweden than in other countries. At the other extreme falls Italy, where the picture of considerable gender imbalance in temporal resources is consistent with that of low individual incomes for women. By contrast, in the Netherlands the relatively large imbalances in individual income are not matched by similar differences in the overall use of time. Dutch and Swedish women share the experience of employment having a much smaller impact on the length of their working day.

6.3 Power Relations and Contests Arising around Individual Resources and the Gender Resource Balance

The process of opening up the family to empirical scrutiny offers a number of insights into the relationship between the welfare state and gender power relations in the private sphere. Our analysis has shown one strong similarity across countries: the normalization of low or no individual resources for women and their consequent reliance on the family as a source of welfare. Even in Sweden, women's individual resources fall in the low to moderate range and, while possibly enough to protect women from the worst income risk, do not represent an opening up of the economic privilege that men enjoy. Contrary to the theoretical premiss that the family is becoming a democratized institution, made up of relationships forged between equals (Giddens 1992; Beck and Beck-Gernsheim 1995), our data indicate that significant resource inequalities mark the experience of the majority of couples across countries. Resource imbalances inevitably feed into imbalances of power within couples, and contribute to a restriction of the roles and status that women and men can enjoy. Women, particularly mothers, are more likely to occupy the role of the familial dependant, while men's greater independent access to income lends, in varying degrees across families, control over expenditure and financial decision making, as well as lowered risks upon divorce or separation. However, the immediate impact of resource imbalance on gender power relations is but one aspect of their significance: resource imbalances also restrict the roles and status that women and men can enjoy across their lifetimes. Women's and men's opportunities to form meaningful and equal relationships with one another are seriously constrained by resource imbalances and the disproportionate 'subjection' of women to the processes of familial redistribution.

The politics of this more persistent and more entrenched form of inequality merits further examination. Why is it that the more private manifestations of gender inequality remain outside mainstream political discourse and beyond the reach of much welfare state intervention? The answer to this lies partly in a normative thread that runs strongly through many welfare states, whereby intervention in the private workings of the family is deemed necessary only in exceptional circumstances. Thus family crisis or family failure provides the catalyst for resource transfers. Such crises are frequently defined very narrowly, to cover just the loss of the breadwinner income through unemployment, retirement or death. Occasionally, welfare states (for example, the Irish) make provision for family failure resulting from desertion or divorce. However, failures within stable families with a breadwinner present (such as the failure of internal redistribution to meet the needs of family members) are almost universally put beyond the reach of intervention.

Such a depoliticization reinforces the obviously private nature of familial power balance. Knowledge of misuses of power by heads of households is very limited, and a key aspect of gender power imbalance is thus privatized to the family. Even where abuses of power take a violent form, only a fraction receive a public airing. Non-violent abuse in the form of control over spending decisions and the withholding or withdrawal of income is almost never discussed publicly. Without a public airing, it is very difficult for the interests of individual women and men to become politicized, as their experience is framed as solely a private issue, with the result that links to the structural causes of this form of gender inequality are rarely made. There is another reason why interests are less clearly articulated with regard to private power imbalances: the perceived and real conflicts between the interests of the family and those of the individual. The interests of individual women and men are served by quite different policies as their family circumstances change. From the perspective of the state, family-based claims are granted more legitimacy than those of individuals. Concerns remain that meeting individual needs may further encourage family breakdown, and across most welfare states there is a continuing reservation about support of non-traditional family forms. In Germany, for example, attempts to reform tax splitting – a highly familialized system of tax assessment with strong, negative effects on female employment – were defeated on the grounds that they ran counter to a constitutional commitment to support the family.

This is not to say that the private aspects of gender relations are immune to politicization. It is perhaps no surprise that those countries

(Sweden, the UK and the USA) that have in common high rates of divorce, and large numbers of lone parents are also those in which the issue of women's independent access to income takes most prominence on the political agenda. Even so, debate is much more closely focused on curative measures targeted at women as lone parents than preventative measures that might ensure an increase in women's independent income while part of a couple. In terms of state provision, contest does arise over mechanisms of delivery and their impact on individual incomes (sometimes termed 'purse to wallet' effects). Such debate may, nevertheless, be framed in ways that disguise its gendered content. For example, policy makers may be persuaded more by evidence that women's income is more likely to be spent on children than by the need to improve the gender resource balance. It is no coincidence, then, that the direct delivery of resources to women more often occurs in the payment of child benefits than in the payment of other state transfers.

Inequalities in the division of time also reflect gender power relations. Men's absence from domestic labour may be interpreted as the result of the exercise of male power at both the macro level (in which women's social roles are delineated by their caring and domestic duties) and the micro level (whereby the division of tasks within a household is shaped by women's and men's relative power). This view is further supported by evidence which suggests that men's engagement in unpaid work involves an element of cream-skimming the most desirable tasks. On an alternative interpretation, men's absence from domestic labour may reflect their relative powerlessness within the labour market and the fact that, like women, they are unable to secure the terms of engagement in the labour market that would allow them their desired participation in domestic work. Turning to the political discourse around time as a resource, it is notable that it only rarely focuses on gender divisions in time use. Discussion of the viable alternatives to women's unpaid caring and domestic labour is interesting in this respect. Provision by the state or the market is offered as 'a solution', which, in turn, serves to frame the problem as being one of finding ways to reduce women's engagement in unpaid work, rather than increasing that of men in order to balance unpaid work more equally between the sexes. Further, the balance of time within couples and the negotiations and conflicts around this remain, as with income, rather hidden from public view. Thus solutions offered focus on the individual rather than structural causes, the responsibility being thought to lie with women to improve their time management skills until they have 'solved' their problem of time shortages.

The impact of the welfare state on gender power relations is, by way of summary, somewhat ambiguous. Both the absence and the presence of the state are here revealed as problematic for gender relations. Thus, where the state is a minor contributor to women's income or merely mirrors existing gender inequalities, its absence reflects a tolerance of gender power and resource differentials. It could be argued that the absence of the state signals a fundamental ambivalence about public intervention in the most private aspects of gender relations. However, where the state does intervene heavily, the mechanisms of directing resources at heads of households mean that gender inequalities are, at best, mirrored and, at worst, exacerbated by the intervention of the state. This, along with an awareness of how intervention in the private sphere may be seized upon as an opportunity to exercise social control, illustrates that there are no easy solutions to reducing gender inequalities and power imbalances within the private sphere.

6.4 Overview

As the analyses in this chapter have revealed, the private, intra-familial aspect of welfare is, if anything, more marked by gender differentials than the more public face of distribution of resources between female- and male-headed households. Thus, the family, far from being a haven of equality, emerges as reflective of broader gender inequalities. The distribution of individual incomes reveals some very marked gender inequalities, and, after all state transfers have been taken into account, significant percentages of women have no income of their own. This is particularly the case in Italy and the Netherlands, where very large numbers of women have no or very small amounts of resources. While state intervention has an important impact on women's access to resources in countries as diverse as Sweden and the UK, in all our nations the state operates as a more effective guarantor of resources for men. Another cross-national similarity concerns the very limited numbers of women who gain access to the highest incomes, with the majority being clustered at the bottom end of the income distribution. Measuring temporal balance alongside incomes proves an important part of the process of exploring gender relations inside the family, since imbalances are at their most pronounced with regard to unpaid domestic and caring work. In short, the gender divisions in the economic order observed in previous chapters are here reaffirmed and revealed, in fact, to take an even more exaggerated form when the focus is on individual access to resources.

From the perspective of comparative analysis, the private face of welfare requires that we revisit our picture of national configurations of gender relations and the welfare state, as well as reassess the cross-national patterns that emerged in previous chapters. Although on a couple of measures of resources Sweden maintains its status as an outlier, analysis of the gender division of private welfare tends to bring Sweden more into the mainstream. While women in Sweden are more protected against very low personal incomes than elsewhere, they share with women in the other welfare states a substantially larger share of domestic work, limited access to the most privileged economic positions, and the fact of living in couples where, on average, the majority of income remains beyond their direct control. The case of Italy also emerges as interesting on account of women's extremely limited independent access to resources and the large numbers of women who are wholly or mostly dependent upon the family for their personal welfare. While insufficient data were available for time balance in Italy, it is one of the few countries in which considerable gender differentials emerge with regard to access to leisure time. It is revealing also that there is less cross-national variation in the gendered hierarchy in the private sphere than there is in the public. The more private manifestations of the gender order are both more extreme within nations and more consistent across nations, suggesting that the private sphere has been little affected by national variations in the state or the market. One conclusion must therefore be that women's welfare continues to be shaped in the first instance by the family, and inequalities therein, such that a comprehensive view of gender relations requires that the private face of welfare be taken fully into account.

While our focus has been principally on the impact of imbalances on women, it is worth turning the argument on its head by looking at the position of men and the implications of their greater control of resources. Men's absence from domestic labour, as well as their lack of dependence on the family as a distributive mechanism, are both problematic. As the data show quite clearly, the most marked of gender divisions will not be altered without a considerable change in men's behaviour: specifically, an increase in their contribution of unpaid domestic work. Men's high rates of economic independence mean that, in addition to making 'exit' economically viable, they do not have the same interest in ensuring the just operation of the family as a distributive mechanism. This again points to the fact that the resource balance between women and men has importance above and beyond the absolute level of resources brought into the household by each.

7

Towards an Explanation of National Configurations and Cross-national Patterns

Having focused on separate parts of the welfare state in action in the various countries, this chapter brings our findings together. The overall objective is to explain the patterns found. We undertake explanation in three steps. The first part of the chapter identifies national configurations, providing an overview of, on the one hand, the form of the welfare state and, on the other, how work, care and welfare cohere into a national pattern of gender relations in the eight countries. The intent is to build up a profile of each national configuration. Our second step towards explanation, undertaken in the next part of the chapter, involves identifying the overriding similarities and differences among countries, with a particular interest in gender relations. The third step seeks to isolate the effects of particular causal factors that suggest themselves as likely explanations. The strategy here is to trace the effects of particular aspects of the welfare state in order to ascertain how well they explain the patterns found. The short overview section, which brings the chapter to a close, considers the extent to which it is possible to group or cluster countries.

7.1 National Configurations of the Welfare State and Gender Relations

The discussion here is intended to capture the complexity of national cases in terms of a set of key characteristics. This will be done for both the policy configuration and the pattern of gender relations. The objective is not only to set out the national configuration of each country, but to take a first step towards explaining why these patterns exist. In describing the countries we have been considering, we begin with those that are most similar – Germany and the Netherlands, on the one hand, and the UK and Ireland, on the other – before moving on to describe the more unique cases of France, Italy, the USA and Sweden. A guiding set of questions here concerns the extent to which there are national patterns around work, care and welfare, how these are gendered in terms of their process and effects, and how they relate to the particular form of the welfare state.

7.1.1   Germany

The idea of the social market economy is fundamental to German social policy. This philosophy is market-focused, but holds that the market needs to be made more social. A free market cannot function in a vacuum, so it has to be socially and morally embedded. Redistributive measures are central to the 'socialization' of the market, as is a high degree of regulation – of the labour market, for example. Corporatism, as embodied in the participation of employers and employees in negotiations around wages and employment-related benefits, is deeply embedded. Social policy, however, is not transformative. Rather, a primary function of this highly coherent model of social policy is to maintain the income and other differentials that arise in the market and to protect employment-related risks to income. The German system is a prototype of a social insurance-based welfare state model, with equivalence and compensation, rather than prevention and redistribution, to the fore. Pensions are very important, whereas social assistance is minimal and, where it does exist, represents a relatively disprivileged stratum of provision. The promotion of self-help and private initiative is key in this model of social policy. The family, an essential source of stability, is both idealized and bolstered by social policy. Social policy takes a traditional approach to the family in the sense that it could be said to be biased towards the support of male breadwinner/female carer families. Tax provisions, as well as cash benefits and social service provision, form a coherent package in support of families conforming to this life-style (Dingeldey 2001). The German welfare state is usefully characterized as oriented to the early and late phases of the life course. These and other features lend social policy in Germany a decidedly gendered character. Specialization along gender lines is supported and encouraged. The division of labour between women and men is one of home and market work respectively, and care is regarded as most appropriately located in a family setting. Quality (in the caring relationship) is taken as being almost conditional upon the degree to which caring is based in the family. A view of the family as the proper locus of care has informed the introduction of a payment for those caring for a child under two, which, while open to both women and men, in practice serves to institutionalize the gender division of caring work.

Against this backdrop of welfare state provision, our research has charted the rather complex gender inequalities with regard to access to financial and other resources in Germany. Gender gaps in wages are less entrenched than elsewhere, but women, and especially mothers, make but a small contribution to the income of their households. Given the cast of welfare state provision, it is little surprise to find that there are large discrepancies in the relative financial welfare of different types of female-headed households. In this social policy model, where the most supported type of family is that where the man works and the woman is based full-time in the home, female pensioners are quite well provided for, but lone mother households run a very high risk of poverty. Role segregation along gender lines is quite high. When they are employed, women and men work in different sectors of the labour market. Moreover, unpaid work remains largely in female hands, and the unpaid division of labour is generally resistant to employment on the part of mothers (Beblo 1998). A strong familial ideology spells a particular focus on policies for care. In fact, care, for both children and the elderly, is an access route to both cash transfers and relatively plentiful employment leave. However, while the German welfare state has recently introduced long-term insurance for the care needs of older people, the norm of home-based care is strong. With employment as a strong gateway to welfare state resources, women have to secure most of their resources through marriage and the family. Protection of dependency is a strong principle in German social provision, and this acts at the same time to promote dependency. Since the prevailing model of family life seems to be that of full-time care, the reconciliation of care and employment for women is not a primary object of policy. For example, services, including schools, are organized in such a way as to assume the availability of a part-time carer. Motherhood especially constrains access to the labour market. In fact, mothers of young children are almost completely excluded from paid work and have but limited opportunities to work part-time. There is a noticeable lack of flexibility in both the labour market and service provision, with negative consequences for the opportunities available to women to be self-sufficient economically. While there is the option of being supported as a full-time mother or housewife, opportunities for couples to opt for a more equal balance between paid and unpaid work for both women and men are foreclosed.

7.1.2   The Netherlands

Dutch society, while sharing much of the German pattern of social organization, locates the state in a hierarchical order whereby it is assigned the role of arbiter among a plurality of interests. Class and occupational interests are overlaid and undercut in the Dutch case with those of confessional groupings, specifically Catholic and Protestant. The state is more than a clearing-house for interests, however. It harmonizes the political demands of different groups for the prime purposes of enabling such groups' participation in the political process and maintaining their autonomy in society (Wilensky 1982). As with Germany, many of the institutional features of the Dutch welfare state are corporatist, and the history of consensus seeking in both provision and decision making is strong. The Dutch welfare state is aptly characterized as segmented (Sainsbury 1996: 30). This is true in a number of respects. For one, principles of universalism and selectivity have operated side by side. Even if the most recent period has seen cut-backs and the introduction of market provision in social insurance, the story of the historical development of the Dutch welfare state is one of the imposition of a degree of universalism on a system that had its origins in occupationally based social insurance. Solidarity has rivalled equivalence among contributors as the guiding ethos in a relatively interventionist state. Hence, solidaristic elements within the cash transfer system (such as the flat-rate basic pension) vie with strong elements of earnings compensation with a rather unclear impact on gender inequalities. A further element of segmentation is the division between social insurance and social assistance. The Dutch welfare state stands apart from its German and, indeed, other European neighbours in its relatively high use of means-tested programmes, in which women dominate as recipients. The Dutch model has been undergoing major change, however. Reforms over the last two decades have reduced access to universal protection schemes, replaced solidaristic social insurance programmes with individualistic, market-led private insurance, and social assistance more strictly targeted on the needy (Van Oorschot 1998). While reforms have been very far-reaching, it is arguable whether the position on the family has changed. Dutch social provision has long had a strong gender faultline, organized around the most prized form of family life: the breadwinner/caretaker model. Cash transfers, which are more prominent than services, take men as their object, whereas the more poorly developed social services are tailored to women in their familial capacity, being intended primarily to assist the woman in raising a happy family (Bussemaker and Van Kersbergen 1994: 23).

Our research has revealed that strong gender inequalities in access to resources are to be observed in the Netherlands. In line with the Dutch population overall, women's risk of poverty is low (markedly so for older women), but the high poverty risk of lone mothers lends the distribution of poverty a strong gender dimension. The position of lone mothers reflects how motherhood closes down full-time employment. Moreover, female part-time work in the Netherlands tends to be characterized by quite short working hours. Intra-household inequalities in the income shares contributed by women and men are very marked. Role segregation, which is strong in employment, is noticeably milder in the private sphere. That is, there is quite a degree of sharing of unpaid work, despite the fact of women's relatively low involvement in paid work. Unlike in Germany, care commands but limited access to public resources. The infrastructure of service provision for children is poorly developed, in large part because family care of children is valued as the preferred form of care. In regard to the elderly, services are biased towards residential care. To the extent that care provision has improved recently, a concern about the state of the labour market has been the motivating force. However, there is strong support in both the labour market and social security for a combination of part-time work and caring duties. The structure of the Dutch labour market is quite unique in the extent of flexibility offered around working hours in general and the fact that this seems also to be available to men (although not to the same degree as women). The relatively high degree of flexibility in the labour market, because it makes it easy to combine motherhood with limited amounts of paid work, means that Dutch women have considerable autonomy with regard to their use of time – little surprise, then, that they express a high level of satisfaction with their use of time (Bosch and Wagner 2001).

7.1.3   The UK

The UK's model of social policy is different again. Only a limited degree of regulation is exerted by the state. The prevailing philosophy supports a relatively free rein for the market. This is grounded in a long-standing concern about the distortions and perverse effects associated with state intervention. The alleviation of poverty is the most widely legitimated imperative for social policy. However, the UK has a mixed ideological heritage, which means that it is difficult to identify a single set of principles motivating state action. While there is a strong liberal lineage, universalist provisions are also evident, as for example in the National Health Service and with respect to child benefits (Glennerster 1995). These are also the elements commanding the greatest popular consensus and support. Modest redistribution is the order of the day, and protection against employment-related risks has eroded over time. In truth, the principle of social insurance was never fully established, and the story of the British welfare state over the last thirty years or so is of the gradual growth of means testing and increasing conditionality of benefits. Other than in the health domain, the British welfare state has never fully subscribed to a view of services as public goods, with the result that a mix of the public, private and voluntary sectors in welfare service provision is a hallmark of the British case. A contemporary response to the resultant gaps in service provision is quite extensive subsidies and tax reliefs, so as to encourage private, whether market or family, endeavour. The family has only rarely been an explicit focus of social policy. It is considered an inappropriate arena for state intervention, because it is a 'private' domain or because of the likely distorting or damaging effects of intervention. While most families are left to their own devices, once the threshold of what is considered normal family behaviour is breached, a whole array of services are brought to bear on families. State intervention then assumes a strong social control character in line with divisions along social class, gender and racial lines (Williams 1995). As a poverty-alleviating welfare state, women form the majority of 'clients' or beneficiaries of British cash transfers and services.

We have found that strong gender inequalities prevail in the UK in access to financial and other resources. Gender differences in poverty risks are high, driven by large numbers of poor lone mothers in combination with large numbers of poor older women. Very entrenched gender inequalities in wages and in the distribution of low-paid work are also to be observed in the UK. The story here is of both polarization between full-time and part-time employees and of deeply entrenched gender inequalities in wages and the structure of the labour market. While the wide availability of part-time work affords mothers and other women the opportunity to be in the labour market, this imposes a series of penalties in terms of pay, career prospects and working conditions, each of which has considerable consequences for the shaping of the life course (Rake 2000). There is marked role segregation in the labour market, but evidence of slightly more fluidity in gender roles in the private sphere. Caring does not bring any major claim on public resources. Only very limited services for the care of children are available, and leave and payments for this purpose are not well developed. Public provision of caring services for the elderly has somewhat greater legitimacy, perhaps because care for the elderly is more distanced from the norm of family provision than is the care of children. There is some flexibility as regards the use of time and the chance to combine motherhood and employment. The option of being a full-time carer, either of children or the elderly, is, however, not supported by public policy. This has particular implications for the well-being of lone mother families, making part-time work more or less essential if one wishes to secure a decent level of income. The care/employment interface has rarely been open to public intervention, although recent innovations, as epitomized by the introduction of a system of tax credits for those in employment, have more actively sought to alter the incentives around paid and unpaid work. When it comes to the use of time, gender inequality takes the form of long hours of paid work for men and long hours of work for women distributed between paid and unpaid tasks. Women's participation in paid work is, therefore, configured by their unpaid responsibilities.

7.1.4 Ireland

Ireland is similar to the UK in many respects, but has a greater mix of ideological influences – colonialism, liberalism and Catholicism (Daly and Yeates 1999). The colonial experience meant that Ireland's first encounters with state welfare were fashioned by Britain. Liberalism bequeathed a concern with market incentives and an extensive use of means testing. The third influence, the Catholic Church, advocated traditions of voluntarism and charity, and was strongly opposed to state intervention in the social sphere. The Church positioned itself as superior to the state, both as a provider of welfare and as a protector of the social (Daly 1999). In the Irish case it was as much Catholicism as liberalism that effected restraint on the growth of the welfare state. The political agency around the welfare state is also mixed in Ireland.

Corporatism, in the last two decades especially, has served to render economic policy more social. Rather uniquely, the corporatist social partnership has included the voluntary sector, along with employers, employees, the agricultural sector and the state (O'Donnell 1998). One consequence of this arrangement is that some aspects of the labour market are more highly regulated than one would expect of a liberal regime. Policy in relation to cash transfers is susceptible to lobbying from the many sectors of the population seeking preferential treatment. This has lent the Irish welfare state a very unique structure: there is a proliferation of distinct cash benefit programmes, often catering to very small sectors of the population. Cash transfers dominate state provision. There is a very extensive use of means testing; in fact, the benefit recipient population is fairly evenly divided between those receiving social insurance and those on means-tested programmes. Women dominate the latter. Not only are services relatively underdeveloped; Ireland has long operated with a particular idea of a welfare mix, in which the state is a partner with the voluntary (largely religious) sector. Gender and family-related matters have been a current in Irish social policy too. Families with children have been supported with relatively modest cash payments, but the influence of the Catholic Church has served to underline the autonomous nature of the family. Support for women has been closely organized around the principle of compensating for the loss of a male income. The approach here has been very particular, with any support highly conditional on both the relationship to the man and the level of available income. Intervention occurs only under exceptional circumstances, so that, overall, it is true to say that the welfare of women resides fundamentally in the family.

Gender inequalities in access to resources in Ireland are somewhat above the average for the different countries studied here. Poverty rates are very high in Ireland, with both lone mothers and older women at particular risk of experiencing poverty when they head households. The gender gap in poverty is less marked than one might expect, however, not least because of high poverty rates for men heading households on their own. Wage gaps are firmly entrenched, and there is a large low-wage sector (although this is not especially female-dominated). Access to the labour market for women was until recently rather low. Hence motherhood was a very particular status enwrapped in a traditional gender role. All the indications are, though, that this is changing quite rapidly – indeed, the movement of mothers into the labour market is one of the most striking constituents of Ireland's recent economic boom (Ruane and Sutherland 1999). But there is still high non-participation and inactivity among older mothers and married women. Labour market segregation is in the middle range, but the indications are that role segregation between women and men is high in the private sphere. Care has a bifurcated character in Ireland, but the nature of the divide is similar to that in the UK, in that it is caring for the elderly, rather than children, that grants the stronger claim on public resources. Cash benefits for this purpose are more established. The care/employment interface is a private one, in that the choices around how, when and how much to care are left largely to individuals within the context of their families. Because of the high use of means-tested benefits, need rivals

employment as a gateway to welfare state resources. One consequence is that the risk of loss of male income is recognized by the
benefit system, albeit on a contingent basis. The degree of flexibility
around the use of time is limited. While increasing, the availability of
part-time work is considerably less than in some countries, with the
result that mothers tend to be occupied on a full-time basis either in
the home or in employment. There is an imperative on men to be the
main breadwinners, and they are offered few incentives to participate
in unpaid or part-time work.

7.1.5   France

The French social model is quite particular, but, of the two general
models outlined so far, resembles the German/Dutch model more than
the UK / Irish model. The state is directive in bringing about a range of
outcomes that span the labour market and the family. This is an
interventionist state, underpinned ideologically by a particular set of
convictions about the 'good society'. Citizenship, understood as participation, is the overarching frame of social policy. The image of the
French citizen is pervasive as an object of social policy. Embedded in
child care, for example, is the idea of the child as a future citizen. Social
exclusion, rather than equality, is a guiding concern of the French welfare state, especially in recent years (Rosanvallon 1995). A 'normal', or
'good', society is seen as one in which people are able to participate in a
broad range of social spheres and develop and maintain strong bonds
with each other. Social policy, then, has an extensive role. In the service
of social inclusion, the purpose of intervention is not passive support
but rather active (re)integration into society. The French welfare state
has something of a dual character, however. It is, on the one hand,
organized around employment but, on the other, strongly supportive of
the family. Moreover, it is not accurately described (in the same sense as
the German) as a social insurance welfare state model, because it
embodies a high degree of horizontal redistribution and recognizes
the claims of those who are outside the employment system (Palier
1997). Further, it is a welfare state that has a strong service dimension,
with services around care for children especially well developed (in a
climate where public services themselves enjoy wide legitimacy).
Gender is rarely an explicit focus, but tends to be embedded in notions
about family welfare, especially families with children. While fertility
and population replacement rates are a strong motivation for French
family policy, an emergent theme is that of the quality of social and
family life. The latter may explain why France's already generous
provision of leaves for caring was recently extended to include paid

paternity leave. It is nevertheless true to say that where policies have an effect on gender relations, this tends to be a consequence of, or spin-off from, other aims.

Our empirical analysis uncovered some notable gender inequalities in access to resources in France. But resource inequalities are tempered by generous child-related provisions, which act to boost the income of women overall. One consequence is that the poverty risk of lone mother families is less than it might otherwise be. Social policy has been, and is, active on the care/employment interface. The opportunities for mothers to be in employment are high, but these depend on the size of the family, and incentives to exit the labour market increase dramatically when the number of children exceeds two (Bonnet and Labbé 2000). In sum, economic 'penalties' of motherhood are somewhat moderated by the welfare state, though for some mothers remain high. Moving on to role segregation, this is high both inside and outside the labour market. France has, for example, one of the highest levels of horizontal segregation of any of the labour markets considered, and it is evident that men make but a limited contribution to domestic work. The extent to which care is a source of claims on public resources is contingent on which sector of care is involved. Caring for children brings significant cash resources (although this is closely tied to the number of children) as well as access to public services. Public support for the care of older people is much less extensive, though. Since benefit rates are closely tied to earnings, and therefore reproduce wage inequalities, family benefits are in the front line in reducing gender income inequalities, while minima within the benefit and wage systems play an important role also. There is a lack of flexibility in regard to time in the labour market, and it is important to note that a shorter working week is not a gender-led policy, originating instead from a concern about labour supply.

7.1.6 Italy

Italy is somewhat different again, combining some elements of the strong social insurance state to be found in Germany, France and the Netherlands with a degree of non-intervention that is more characteristic of the UK and Ireland. The coincidence of liberalism and Catholicism, together with a history of regionalism and a dispersion of power, have served to constrain the activities of the Italian state. As a consequence, the welfare state is both fragmented and inconsistent. Of all the European welfare states considered here, Italy is the least interventionist and effects but limited redistribution. In addition, the country is marked by a dualism of over- and under-provision. There is a protected core made up exclusively of workers, almost all of whom are located in the public sector. Such workers are afforded high levels of job protection and are guaranteed economic security via relatively generous social insurance, particularly pensions. This results in over-protection for a minority relative to the mass of the population, for whom no minimum income or family support programmes are in place. Given this, some have identified the Italian state as meritocratic (rather than based on citizenship or need) (Trifiletti 1995: 178). This dualism has a decided north/south dimension. Ties of patronage are strong, and the Italian welfare state has a very categorical history and orientation, being closely associated with the interests of corporatist actors. The family is at the heart of welfare provision, but has been rather invisible for policy purposes. There has been no problematiza-tion of welfare provision through the family in Italy, reflected in the almost complete absence of state services in the field of care. Although not itself the object of public policy, the family plays a key role in putting together income from different sources, thereby conferring a sense of unity on a fragmented set of benefits that are inadequate in themselves and often unfairly distributed (Trifiletti 1998: 181). The almost exclusive focus on pensions reduces the relevance of the wel-fare state for women of working age. Given this, the family is central to gender identities and also to the provision of welfare. Women's market work is seen as secondary to the needs of the family. In a climate where dependence on the family is viewed as natural rather than problematic, some have spoken of women as being in a 'gift relationship to the family' (Bimbi 1993: 142).

Gender inequalities have a very specific character in Italy. Our analysis reveals that poverty rates and gender differences therein are surprisingly low, reflecting generous provision for dependants within the pension system, the practice of combining income from a variety of sources, and the low prevalence of lone mothers heading their own households. The needs of lone mothers are 'absorbed' by the family in so far as, by force or choice, they reside as members of another family unit rather than setting up autonomous households of their own (Ruspini 1999). Only a minority of women are able to access the labour market and gain entitlement to the resources and opportunities typically available to men. For those who are recorded as being in paid work, the gender wage gap is among the smallest to be found anywhere, segregation is relatively low, and women do not dominate the low-paid sector. The lives of the majority of women are very different, however. The level of resources that they can command personally is very low, especially because women's access overall to the labour market is compromised, with high rates of unemployment and inactivity. Italy therefore has strong role segregation in regard to employment (manifested by an exclusion of women), and this is mirrored in the private sphere. It is not easy to identify motherhood as the cause of inequalities, in that women's access to the labour market is already so low that motherhood has no discernible additional effect. Caring brings access to few public resources, either services or benefits. Like other dimensions of social life, the care/employment interface is private in Italy. Italian arrangements around work are also relatively inflexible, with little part-time work. This sets up a very stark choice around motherhood and limits the opportunities available to women to combine the roles of worker and mother.

7.1.7   The USA

The prevailing orthodoxy regarding the state in the USA severely delimits its sphere of action. Sharing some tendencies with the British model, a strong liberal heritage has bequeathed both a reified notion of the market and a fragmented and decidedly 'unsocial' state. The national philosophy favours economic individualism, values self-help, and has a preference for market solutions involving a minimum of state intervention or market regulation (Sainsbury 1996: 29). People are primarily responsible for their own welfare. This is not to say that the state is entirely absent from the provision of welfare. A dual, or two-tier, system exists, in many cases driving a chasm between the so-called deserving and undeserving poor. Social insurance provides mainly for retired people, whereas social assistance is strictly targeted on the very poor (who are defined in such a way as to refer mainly to lone mother families, the elderly, the blind and the disabled). Income redistribution is limited, which means that divisions created in and by the market are largely uncorrected. This is a state that lives happily with huge income inequality and high levels of poverty. Citizens are primarily economic actors, although the civil rights aspects of citizenship are also quite well entrenched (O'Connor et al. 1999: 190). Social citizenship is underdeveloped, however. In the absence of state-provided welfare services, many incentives are constructed, especially in the tax system, to bolster the private provision and consumption of welfare (e.g. significant tax breaks support middle- and high-income families in purchasing private child care). The market dominates, and the family has little or no public face. The concept of family policy is foreign to the USA, and access to public funds is contingent on 'neediness'. Nevertheless, there is some recognition of and recompense for familial roles in social insurance through the provision of relatively generous dependants' benefits. Economic individualism has fuelled some concern about women's ability to function independently in the labour market. An equal opportunities framing of gender inequalities has not only fed a legalistic approach, but has construed gender inequalities in terms of unequal capacities of women and men (Bacchi 1999). Any gender inequalities that exist are a product of, on the one hand, the limitations of this kind of approach and, on the other, the relative absence of a welfare state.

While inequalities with regard to resources are not so marked for individual women and men in the USA, our data reveals very large disparities in the level of income and poverty of female-headed households in comparison to those headed by a man. The lack of significant redistribution means that women's control over resources is closely associated with the polarizing effects of the market. Gender is one faultline, the large low-wage sector testimony also to polarization on class and race grounds. Motherhood is not a 'protected' status, but the penalties attaching to it depend to a large extent on family status, class position and ethnicity. The capacity to participate in the labour force acts especially to reduce the penalties attaching to motherhood, but the poor social infrastructure renders decisions around motherhood a matter of private concern. Role segregation is less marked in the labour market than elsewhere – in the USA, there is evidence of a female elite with significant opportunities for career progression. Role segregation in the private sphere is also less marked than it is elsewhere. Caring brings access to few if any public resources. For example, there are no mandatory leaves for this purpose in the USA, just as there are few if any care-related services organized by the public authorities. So full-time care is an option only to the extent that private resources (money rather than networks) allow. The 'small' welfare state has a particular impact on the circumstances of older women, who, relative to men, do quite poorly (even though pensioners overall are the main beneficiaries of any welfare state redistribution that takes place). Lone parents also fare poorly, reflecting their limited recourse to public resources. Access to the labour market is high overall, but limited amounts of part-time work and a long hours culture render this country quite inflexible from a time perspective. As a consequence, temporal autonomy is a scarce resource for everyone. The care/employment interface is almost completely privatized in the absence of state intervention.

7.1.8   Sweden

Put prosaically, Sweden can be said to have a 'large state' and a 'small family'. State activity dominates the labour market and dwarfs the family in ways that set Sweden apart from all the other countries considered. The Swedish welfare state tends to make public what is in other countries placed beyond the reach of the state. A broad-ranging notion of welfare citizenship prevails, whereby the income risks attaching to a variety of life histories are minimized and the state acts directly to integrate citizens into employment and, via that, into society. Employment and citizenship operate as gateways to welfare state resources for all, so that the risk of loss of a partner's income is not explicitly recognized by social protection. The high degree of individualization of benefits means that people tend, as social welfare claimants, to be stripped of their family commitments (dependants' provisions having been deliberately dropped from the social security system). Intervention has a strong gender dimension, in that the state actively engages with and promotes a particular set of gender relations. On the one hand, women are enabled to be workers, and on the other, the state assists with caring activities which in other societies are privatized to the family. Social policy has come to interpret gender equality to refer to men's family roles as well, reserving a part of the care leave specifically for men (the 'daddy month'). A high degree of labour market regulation enables this set of arrangements to function. Among the notable features are long hours of part-time work, extensive support through leaves for caring purposes, and an infrastructure and ideology of workers' rights in which gender equality is quite well embedded. The Swedish is a service-intensive state, with the twin objectives of enabling and providing employment (especially for women). It is largely tax-funded, requiring high levels of taxation, and is sustained by social democratic ideals around which there remains a high degree of consensus. Sweden's self-image is of a welfare society in which the state is the best vehicle for achieving social integration.

Looking at Sweden through the lens of gender, we found relatively low levels of gender inequality. This is the case across a range of indicators, including gender gaps in wage rates, income levels and exposure to poverty. Income dispersion is much lower than that typifying industrialized economies. This, together with effective minimum income protection and a compressed wage structure, benefits women especially (Mósesdóttir 2001). An average income is within women's reach, but their opportunity to access the highest levels of resources is limited. Any penalties attaching to motherhood take the form not of exclusion from the labour market but of differential participation in it. So, while access to the labour market is high for women, mothers work somewhat shorter hours. The Swedish labour market is characterized by high gender segregation, but this does not appear to be mirrored in private life. Judged on the basis of women's and men's time investment in unpaid work and their share of family income, there appears to be, on the one hand, some fluidity in regard to roles in the private sphere and, on the other, greater equality in terms of securing resources. Care is quite a strong source of claims on public resources, calling forth both services and cash. But the opportunity to be a full-time family carer is more or less closed off in Sweden. However, the intersection between care and employment has been made quite public, because the welfare state is interventionist with regard to both family matters and employment. Claims in relation to care tend to have their origins in the rights and needs of workers rather than in values pertaining to the appropriate nature of care. Such claims are thus rooted in an ideology of work, rather than originating in beliefs about care and the nature of private relations. So it cannot be said that care as an activity and set of relations is valorized in Sweden. Nor is it clear what the mix of provision means for the quality of care received. The existence of a large part-time sector allows women some flexibility with regard to being in the labour market, but the privileging of the dual-breadwinner family serves to delimit the options around care and the labour market. We cannot say, therefore, that women have high temporal autonomy.

7.2 Cross-national Similarities and Differences

A second step in seeking an explanation for national configurations of gender relations and the welfare state is to compare the countries by identifying similarities and differences. Cross-national similarities exist where there are differences in degree rather than in kind among the countries. Where similarities emerge, countries could be said to represent variation on a common theme (Castles 1989: 4). In other words, the countries share an underlying axis of variation, which means that they can be placed on a single continuum. This is to be contrasted with cross-national differences. These exist when the national configurations represent distinct entities and are the result of multiple factors coming together in a unique pattern. Where cross-national differences exist, variation between countries cannot be captured by statements of a 'more or less' character. Below we explore in turn the factors that draw countries together in a pattern of cross-national similarity and those that distinguish countries from one another.

7.2.1   Cross-national similarities

A number of striking similarities draw together the eight countries. These are:

- gender segregation and inequality in the labour market;
- gender imbalances in resources;
- division of responsibility for unpaid work;
- incomplete integration of caring into the support provided by the welfare state;
- women's position in the economic order.

Labour market segregation is one of the strongest similarities across all of the countries. Gender is pervasive in the structure of labour markets, shaping the conditions under which paid work is carried out, how tasks and functions are organized along occupational lines, and how jobs are differentially valued. Among the most important features of gender segregation are the divisions between full-time and part-time jobs, the hierarchy of authority and value within the labour market, and the prevalence of low-paid work. Across countries, the hierarchy of paid work is identifiably gendered, and the relative disadvantage of women in the labour market is entrenched. To understand the real significance of this, it must be placed in a lifetime perspective. There exists among men an accumulation of wage-earning and other forms of employment-based power that women rarely attain. The logic of the employment system is that it rewards continuity and seniority, commodities that are in shorter supply to women as compared with men.

A second strong cross-national similarity is the gender imbalance in resources. Women have access to fewer resources than men, both as individuals and as heads of households. Women's access to financial resources, for example, is so constrained that they are rarely other than minor income contributors to their households. This has at least two consequences. Women are, first, dependent on the family for their financial resources to a far greater degree than men. Secondly, such an imbalance plays out in the private sphere, shaping power relations between women and men. Economic self-sufficiency is not the reality for the majority of women, and poverty is an ever present risk when women head households on their own. Gender imbalances are also very marked with regard to time. Across countries there are identifiable imbalances in how women and men use their time, and in the amount of time that they expend on different tasks or activities.

A further cross-national similarity is the extent to which women assume the major responsibility for unpaid work. Our research identified a robust division of labour between women and men. Responsibility for particular tasks serves to structure and differentiate male and female domains. Overall, though, women not only do the lion's share of unpaid work, but responsibility for such work is integral to women's social roles in a way that it is not for men. These are the most entrenched of gender divisions. In no country has the movement of women into the labour market instigated a proportionate shift in men's involvement in domestic work. Hence, in comparison with men, women approach the labour market with far greater conditionality and constraint.

A further similarity drawing countries together is the incomplete integration of caring into the welfare state. Across countries, care is a strong and significant motor of policy reform and policy expansion. For example, most countries have seen a growth in service provision, in payments for care, and in employment leaves. But nowhere does care confer benefits on an equivalent basis to paid work. This means that in none of the countries are the full costs of caring being met by the state. While there is more public subsidization of care in some countries, the family continues to bear most of the costs of raising children in all countries. Incomplete integration is also to be seen at the macro level, where welfare state activities in relation to care account for only a fraction of overall welfare state effort.

A further cross-national similarity can be detected in the uneven and differential integration of women into the formal economic order. This means that women are situated in a distinct way as compared with men *vis-à-vis* the three systems of resource distribution. In relation to the labour market, for example, women's compromised access to employment in combination with the gender wage gap mean that the market is less likely to be a source of a living income for women. Although an important channel of redistribution, the welfare state does too little to realize women's financial integration. Despite the redistribution effected by taxation and benefit systems, women's own incomes rarely extend into the upper reaches of those commanded by men. Another manifestation of the inadequacy of the welfare state is that across the eight countries women experience economic penalties when they head their own households, especially as lone mothers. Women are therefore reliant on the third redistributive system, the family, which means in effect that they secure their resources by virtue of their private relationships, rather than directly through the market or the state. For each country, then, women's economic citizenship is more compromised than that of men.

7.2.2   Cross-national differences

For all that similarities can be identified cross-nationally, they should not be allowed to overshadow the differences. Significant differences are to be found across countries in:

- the possibility of combining employment and motherhood;
- inequalities among women;
- the relative privileging of different types of families;
- the role of the family in supporting women and women's risk of poverty;
- the significance of the welfare state in women's lives.

There is, first, a difference among countries in regard to whether and how employment and motherhood can be combined. Sweden allows for such a role combination in a way that is not possible anywhere else. The provision of generous leave entitlement and child care services to complement a labour market characterized by wide availability of part-time work results in a uniquely high employment rate for mothers. While such a role combination is also supported in France, a crucial difference lies in the much less uniform treatment of mothers. Alongside leaves and publicly provided child care, policy in France has actively discouraged the labour market participation of mothers of larger families. Hence, the inclusion of mothers in what is a relatively inflexible labour market has been uneven. The Netherlands constitutes yet another variant, since the main option offered there is the combination of motherhood with part-time employment. This option is fashioned by the availability of employment leaves that are moderate in comparison with those in Sweden, the limiting of public child care mainly to older children, and short hours of part-time work. While similar in some respects, the combination of employment and motherhood is even more compromised in Germany and the UK. In Germany there is more active support of full-time motherhood (particularly by the tax system), and the UK offers very limited leave and services. Of all countries, the Catholic duo of Ireland and Italy most resemble one another in this respect. The degree to which mothers can take up employment is foreclosed, on the one hand, by limited state support and, on the other, by a privatization of care to the family. However, it may be that very recent changes in employment rates – and especially the very rapid rise of female employment in Ireland – will drive a wedge between these two countries. The USA is distinct in respect of the relationship between motherhood and employment, by virtue of the fact that the economic and political imperatives for mothers, especially lone mothers, are to engage in the labour market even though the state offers only limited support for such a role combination. This results in the USA's rather unique combination of high levels of economic activity with a high risk of poverty among lone mothers.

A second difference among countries pertains to the level of inequalities among women. In some countries there is so great a polarization among women that it is almost dangerous to use the generic category 'women'. In the USA, for example, the differences between lone mothers and women in high-level jobs are arguably larger than those between women and men. Polarization among women is also to be observed in the UK, although it is less marked. In these countries, both of which experience high levels of income inequality generally, gender and socio-economic differences interact. A large divide among women also exists in Italy. A strong insider/outsider cleavage can be observed in the Italian labour market. Further exploration and better data would reveal whether this coincides with a class divide, and also how it interacts with regional divisions. For Sweden, by contrast, the range of inequalities among women is much less, and no one group of women stands out as being markedly more advantaged or disadvantaged.

A third source of cross-national variation is the relative privileging of different family types and how the welfare state places families in a hierarchy with regard to financial resources. Of great relevance here are the ways in which countries vary in their treatment of older women as household heads. While in most countries these households have a lower standard of living than equivalent male-headed households, the UK and the USA are set apart from the other countries by virtue of the inadequacy of the resources available to older female-headed households. A further example of variation in the relative treatment of different family types is to be seen in the resources made available to families with children. Taxation provisions in most countries have the effect of reducing the income levels of families with children relative to those of all households. In Sweden and France, however, generous family benefits and, in the case of France, generous tax allowances for children act to offset such an outcome.

A further notable difference is the degree to which families are expected to assume the support of women. The gaps between women's own incomes and those of other members of their families are such that women have to rely on an exchange of income within the family. The cross-national variation lies not in the fact of women's reliance on the family, but in the degree of such reliance and how this dependency is legitimated by public policy. In Germany, Italy, Ireland and the Netherlands, women are widely seen as secondary earners. Public policy support of this takes a particular form in Germany, where wage rates and welfare state and taxation benefits encourage a single-earner family model. In the other countries, an understanding that women will be supported by their families is more residual, in the sense of not being explicitly engineered by policy, and certainly not to the same degree as in Germany. Women's heavy reliance on the family is a result of poor access to market income, rather than the active promotion by the state of a male breadwinner model. The effects of French policy are more ambiguous. On the one hand, the cash transfer system is targeted at male heads of households, and the support of the dual-earner model is withdrawn when families have more than two children. On the other hand, lone mother households are the beneficiaries of significant redistribution, and dual-earner households are encouraged by the provision of care services. The USA is again different, in that, operating on the premiss of economic individualism, public policy takes few if any steps to emphasize the family as a source of support for people. Women are also treated as independent economic units in Sweden, but for very different reasons. A combination of social citizenship and economic individualism (realized in women's access to low and moderate incomes) underpins this position, such that many features of family-based support have been removed by recent reforms. The UK is in a transition between relying on family support and aiming for women's economic independence. There are vestiges of the former, but these are falling away as public policy becomes more focused on the goal of market participation for all.

A final difference to which we want to draw attention is the significance of the welfare state in women's lives. For Swedish women, the state is without doubt a strong presence in their everyday lives, whereas Italian women rarely encounter the welfare state directly. A strong public element in services and the fact that caring benefits are well established mean that the Swedish state intervenes more in the lives of women than does its Italian counterpart. The significance of the welfare state is manifested also in the nature of its relationship with women. Because such a large proportion of the resources to which women make claim in Ireland, the Netherlands and the UK is subject to a means test, the state is a controlling and stigmatizing element in women's lives. Contrast this with Sweden, where citizenship-based claims are deeply embedded.

All countries set up a series of trade-offs between women's roles and the range of opportunities available to them. However, in focusing on differences, one ends up with a sense of the particularity (although not necessarily the uniqueness) of the situation in each country. In effect, a whole life trajectory for women, such as full-time motherhood, part-time motherhood or full-time work, is privileged in each country. The problem that this creates from a comparative perspective is that the trajectory is a complex amalgam of care, work and welfare within and across countries. This therefore leads directly to the next step in the explanatory endeavour – an examination of the effect of particular factors across countries.

7.3   The Significance of the Welfare State for Cross-national Variation

The elaboration of the national configurations, as well as the exploration of similarities, differences and cross-national patterns, has paved the way for the analysis of the significance of welfare state-related factors for cross-national variation. Some such factors are suggested by the literature, some by our own empirical analysis. Among the factors we consider as crucial are:

- the degree of state intervention and the form of the welfare state;
- the bridging of the work/family interface;
- the extent to which the welfare state directly targets gender inequality and women's welfare;
- the coherence of social policy as it addresses gender roles and inequalities.

The size of the welfare state is often adverted to in the literature as key to differences in the level of welfare achieved by countries with regard to women. Is it simply the case that the larger the welfare state, the smaller the gender inequality? Even though the most redistributive of our welfare states – Sweden – also shows the least gender inequality, a correlation is more difficult to prove for the other countries. The degree of state intervention in France, Germany and the Netherlands is very similar, yet these countries manifest significant differences in gender relations.[1] Moreover, the least interventionist states – Italy and the USA – also demonstrate very distinct patterns of gender relations, while the more subtle differences between Ireland and the UK can certainly not be attributed to differences in the degree of state intervention. Given this, the programmatic and normative content of national welfare states needs to be marshalled in an explanation of gender relations.

The content or form of the welfare state, understood to refer to the construction of entitlement and / or the normative basis of claims, has figured prominently in both the feminist and conventional literatures. The coverage of the risks to income, the treatment of different categories of workers, relative levels of wage replacement, and the funding basis of social programmes are highlighted as important by the conventional literature. One of the most widely used ways of summarizing these variations is Esping-Andersen's (1990) characterization of welfare states into liberal, continental and social democratic types. It is useful to explore how far this characterization takes us in explaining the links between gender and the welfare state. Turning first to the Swedish case, social democratic principles explain much of the particularity of Sweden from a gender perspective. The promotion of welfare citizenship, founded on a philosophy of egalitarianism, leads to high levels of caring services, low risk of poverty, and the promotion of a dual-breadwinner family. There is, furthermore, an identifiable liberal cluster of countries: Ireland, the UK and the USA. To the extent that such countries show a preference for market solutions, liberalism goes some distance in explaining the high exposure to poverty risks, the imperative for female employment, and a stand-off position on the family. There is less explanatory force, however, in grouping together France, Germany, Italy and the Netherlands in a continental model. While the protection of wage earners could be taken as explaining the relatively low poverty risk in all four countries, it does not take us very far in accounting for the differential exposure of women to the risk of poverty. Moreover, these welfare states encourage rather different models of family. Germany adheres actively to the classic male breadwinner model. Italy shares with Germany the near exclusion of women from the labour market, but the role of social policy is passive in comparison with Germany. France is more supportive of a two-earner model, whereas the Netherlands favours a full-time male earner and a part-time female earner family arrangement. Overall, when viewed from a gender perspective, it is difficult to see these four countries as having the same model of welfare. Esping-Andersen's typology thus breaks down.

As compared with the conventional literature, a feminist perspective emphasizes the explanatory potential of quite distinct welfare state features. Those most often adverted to in the literature include the treatment of care *vis-à-vis* employment, the basis of entitlement, and the degree to which welfare involves processes and relations of social control. While these are undoubtedly important, we believe that, from an explanatory point of view, they have to be framed in broader terms. Hence, the remainder of this section considers whether welfare states create a bridge between the family and employment, the degree to which the welfare state targets women's welfare, and the coherence of policy with regard to gender roles.

One feature of the welfare state that has power in explaining gender differentials is the degree to which the welfare state operates as a bridge between the family and employment. Support for the care/employment interface is significant in that (a) it opens up or closes down women's opportunities at particular points in the life cycle; and (b) women's choices at these times of transition have been shown to be significant for social and economic outcomes across the life course.

In Sweden and France, care is a public concern, with the consequence that female employment is encouraged and gender inequalities reduced. Public support of care is high in Germany and the Netherlands also, but here the fact that support is organized around family-based care accounts for a greater prevalence of traditional gender roles. In a number of countries – Ireland and the UK and, at the extreme, Italy and the USA – state provision fails to create an effective bridge between care and employment. The relative absence of state benefits and services coexists with quite distinct outcomes, however. The lack of public provision has led to outcomes as diverse as market-based solutions to child care and high female employment (as in the USA) and mothers' adoption of a full-time caring role (true of Ireland and Italy). Other factors, therefore, need to be taken into account when explaining the variation among these four countries.

A second feature that our analysis highlights is the extent to which the welfare state targets women's welfare. In all the welfare states that we have considered, this is indirect and has to be read through two lenses: the level of support of family-related risks and the basis of entitlement to state benefits. With regard to the basis of entitlement to state benefits, while feminist work has tended to emphasize the distinction between individual as against familial entitlement, our work suggests that this is not a major explanatory factor for variations in gender relations across countries. One reason why the individual versus familial entitlement distinction may be too simplistic is because women rarely get benefits *qua* individuals. Rather, their claims to public resources usually rest on their family situation. Sainsbury (1996) is correct, therefore, in pointing out that the bases of entitlement need to be expanded to refer to claims that originate in marriage, care and employment. This brings to the foreground the relative generosity of welfare state coverage of family-related risks, such as divorce, separation, widowhood and lone motherhood. Our results suggest that this explains much of the variation in the financial resources available to women across countries. No welfare state covers these risks comprehensively, and policy usually creates a fissure among different types of family risk. Hence, because the German welfare state privileges marriage, widows are much better placed on the hierarchy of access to financial resources than are lone mothers. On the other hand, the even-handedness of French policy in supporting families with children without regard to marital status makes for smaller income gaps among different groups of mothers.

The coherence of social policy as it addresses gender roles is also important for explanatory purposes. The degree to which taxation, social security, care-related and employment policies come together in a coherent fashion is a source of cross-national variation. Sweden is remarkable for the high degree of normative consistency across policy domains. There is both recognition of women in a diversity of roles and a concerted policy to combat gender inequality. As a result, the Swedish approach has been broadly transformative, and gender inequalities are lower there than anywhere else. Germany too demonstrates considerable coherence both in terms of the content of policies and their associated outcomes. The imprint of policies which, across the board, are consistently modelled on a male breadwinner/female caregiver family is to be seen in the disprivileged situation of families such as those headed by lone mothers that do not conform to this model. Equally, the fact that the Italian welfare state is coherently non-interventionist is a powerful explanation of the form of gender relations prevailing there. In the other countries, more mixed models of policy can be associated with particular outcomes for different groups of women and men, but the relationship between the gendered norms prevailing in policy and the outcomes for women and men is less clear.

7.4 Overview

There is no ready or easily identifiable grouping of countries that emerges from our work. Patterns emerge on some measures, but disappear from view almost as soon as one switches indicators. In this context, it is relevant to identify the extremities of variation. Sweden emerges as a clearly distinct model, rendered different by a number of factors. On a range of measures, gender differentials are less marked there than they are elsewhere. The level of resources available to Swedish women is relatively close to the national average, a remarkable feature in international comparison. This means that sections of the female population that generally tend to be economically vulnerable – for example, lone mother households – are not so exposed in Sweden to risks such as poverty and low income. As a consequence, differentials among women are less in Sweden than they are in other countries. Care is not the overarching determinant of women's resources and opportunities that it is elsewhere. In sum, there is a diversity of opportunities available to Swedish women, which, while they do not equal those available to men, are richer in their range than elsewhere.

It is difficult to place other countries in relation to Sweden. However, France can be separated out. The more positive situation of lone parents, the rather high level of resources to which caring grants access, and the degree to which it is possible to combine motherhood and employment (although all closely contingent on number of children) are the main factors distinguishing France from the other countries. But this comparative characterization of France is more cautious than that of Sweden, since the French policy model is not as coherent (in terms of either the policy framework or the patterns of gender relations across care, work and welfare) as the Swedish.

Beyond the placement of Sweden as a distinct case, and the more tentative claim that France be categorized as distinct, it is less easy to be categorical about the placement of the other six countries. A key challenge is to identify the opposing generic model to that of Sweden. A number of countries suggest themselves as contestants for the opposing pole. One of these is the USA. The absence of state support either to families or for caring and the low levels of social protection might lead one to anticipate high levels of gender inequality in the USA. Yet, the gap in the resources available to women and men is smaller than one would expect. It seems that women in the USA manage to substitute for the relative inactivity of the state by garnering services and resources from the market. Germany too is a plausible opposing model to that of Sweden in the degree to which it frames women in terms of the family. A factor moderating the extremity of this Germany/Sweden comparison, however, is that, like Sweden, the German welfare system subsidizes some aspects of care. That is, public resources are made available in Germany to assist the family with caring. But this subsidization of care acts to privatize care within the family, whereas in Sweden it serves to relocate care away from the family. Italy also merits consideration as a possible contestant for the opposite pole to Sweden. Italy subscribes to a very traditional model of family and gender relations. Huge resource inequalities exist between women and men, and women have few chances of participating in the labour market. Care is a family responsibility, but this is because of inactivity on the part of the state, rather than a direct goal of social policy. Yet Italy is marked by exceptions and inconsistencies, the most notable among which is the less entrenched nature of gender inequalities in the labour market. Hence, while Italian women have a low level of employment participation, once they are in the labour market, their resources and opportunities compare quite favourably with those of men. The UK has just a single claim to being the opposing case to Sweden. This lies in women's very high exposure to poverty: female-headed households have the highest risk of poverty as compared with men of any country. This apart, the

UK falls between the extremes. Ireland and the Netherlands are not contestants for the opposite pole to Sweden, since on none of the indicators do they fall at the extreme. To summarize, although the comparison allows for the identification of Sweden as a very particular case, considerable ambiguities arise in assessing how the remaining welfare states affect gender relations.

8

Conclusions and Overview

This final chapter draws out the implications of our research. The insights of studying gender and the welfare state are first outlined. At issue here is how the nature of the relationship between gender and the welfare state is to be understood and conceptualized for the purposes of research. We then reflect on the benefits of a comparative approach to research in this field. The second section addresses policy. Drawing on the empirical evidence presented, it identifies key pressure points around welfare state development within and across countries. Thinking of these in terms of care, work and welfare serves to reveal both the multiple dimensions of the process of reform and the dilemmas for policy makers.

8.1 Studying the Welfare State and Gender in a Comparative Perspective

8.1.1 Insights into the study of the welfare state and gender relations

Our research gives rise to a number of fundamental insights with regard to the study of the relations between gender and the welfare state. Bringing care, work and welfare together within one framework makes for a comprehensive perspective on both gender and the welfare state. Adopting a comprehensive approach means that spheres of social life other than the economic arena narrowly defined are recognized and valorized. In particular, care and the family are not marginalized, and among the different spheres those usually referred to and constituted as 'private' are recognized as especially important for any analysis of gender relations and the effects of the welfare state. There is a point to be made also about the connectedness of different arenas of social life. It is customary for scholarship to carve up spheres, in line with the tendency for particular disciplines to take ownership of, say, the state, the market or the family. This is invidious, because social processes recognize no frontiers. The boundaries or intersections should not be taken as given, since they are interesting in themselves as sites of contest, especially those motivated by gender. In this and other ways, context is very important. Comprehensiveness thus requires a move beyond narrow conceptualizations of the welfare state to an understanding that is sensitive to the notion of the welfare society in which the state reaches deep into the social order.

Consideration of gender directs attention to the more hidden arenas of social life. It also highlights social relations, in that it serves to reveal the social embeddedness of individuals and activities. An approach should be able to countenance differences between and among women and men. Our research uncovered differentiation among (different groups of) women as an important feature of some national settings and pinpointed the role of policy in structuring women's and men's lives. Treating gender in a systematic way requires that to the more familiar resource-based study of gender inequalities we add an understanding of gender as a key element in social roles and an awareness of the way in which the state shapes and responds to gender-based power relations. Hence, rather than isolating particular differences or inequalities, analysis can seek to actively connect gender-based differences in resources, relations and interests in an overall pattern.

The welfare state needs to be seen as a set of processes that have their own agency as well as operating in concert or conflict with other forces. In effect, agency and change need to be to the fore. There are a number of approaches here also. One emphasizes the welfare state as a site of struggle, with economic, cultural and other forms of power relations ongoing in welfare. Understanding the welfare state as a site of struggle means that one should not expect policy to be logical and coherent. This leads to, second, a view of the welfare state as a political and politicized domain. In other words, the welfare state is both an arena of political relations and has itself a political agency. This view of the welfare state sheds light on the relations of power between women and men and the gender-based norms that shape such relations. It is especially important that research be formulated around a view (if not an explicit theorization) of the state and how it is located within regimes of power. Perspectives must be interrogated for the identity of the agents and the motivating agency in relation to the welfare state. Being sensitive to agency invokes change and implies, thirdly, a view of the welfare state as affecting both resources and interests in a way that may lead to change or resistance. In other words, the activities of the welfare state set in train a series of processes, and render it dangerous to approach outcomes in a narrow way.

8.1.2   Welfare state variations and comparative research

A comparative perspective has been valuable in underscoring the diversity that exists in gender relations and national welfare state configurations. The diversity in national pictures of gender relations aggregated from across the spheres of care, work and welfare would have been impossible to predict from measures of a single sphere of activity. In terms of national welfare states, this comparative research uncovered a diversity of policy practices, as well as the complex layering one upon another of political and redistributive processes. The act of comparison encourages one to look more closely at multiple aspects of women's and men's lives, with particular and unexpected national features prompting further investigation.

The comparative methodology that we have adopted is closest to the case-oriented approach, although with the unique feature of selecting a relatively large number of countries. The selection of eight countries poses challenges for data collection and the provision of succinct cross-national summaries. Yet its value lies in the inclusion of apparently contrasting cases (such as Sweden, the USA and Italy) as well as in the juxtaposition of cases that are close on a number of measures (such as Germany and the Netherlands). Of particular interest are the variables that draw our otherwise distinct nations together – such as women's individual access to income in Sweden and the USA, and the relative level of resources available to older women in Italy and Sweden. Likewise, the variations to be observed in countries that are similar in other respects are of great interest. Contrasting the German and Dutch experiences of the 'penalties' of motherhood is illuminating, as is a comparison of the gender poverty profiles in Ireland, the UK and the USA.

Having considered the benefits of the comparative approach in this work, it is useful to contrast our approach with those offered by mainstream and feminist analyses of welfare state variations. Our first point of comparison is that of regime type analysis (reviewed in chapter 1). Not only does the present analysis challenge typologization at the empirical level (we would, for example, argue that France,

Germany and the Netherlands are sufficiently distinct from one another as not to be classifiable in a single regime), it takes issue with
typologizing as a methodological practice. Typologization, which
rarely incorporates more than a few exemplars, risks freezing welfare
states in time and underplays differences among countries of a particular type, while overplaying the similarities among them. A simple
multiplication of the axes of variation used to capture welfare states
(as proposed by Orloff (1993) and Korpi (2000) among others) does
little to solve these fundamental problems. Put simply, typologization
is ill-suited to deal with the context-rich and complex information
necessary for a gender-focused analysis.

The other main branch of comparative literature discussed in
earlier chapters was feminist in orientation. This literature served
especially to guide our approach to welfare state analysis. We took
from it, for example, an interest in the normative frameworks and
power relations that are embodied in welfare states. Whereas other
feminist work has focused most on the abstract properties of welfare
states, we found it necessary to expand the framework in a number of
ways. One such innovation was to search for the links between the
design of programmes and micro-level behaviour and outcomes.
A further particularity of our approach is that we explored gender
roles and made a conscious attempt to locate women within their
caring and family-related situation as a way of understanding how
the welfare state affects gender relations. Our findings suggest that the
contrast between strong and weak male breadwinner states fails to do
justice to how policy differentiates between lone mothers, older
women and other groups. Differences among women emerge very
strongly, challenging a tendency in feminist and other work to view
women as a homogeneous group.

The complexity of national patterns of policy and of gender relations means that we are unable to assign countries to groups. To the
extent that this could be viewed as a weakness, we regard it as
deriving from the typologization methodology rather than an inherent
shortcoming of our study. Welfare states' treatment of care, work
and welfare, for example, is so complex and diverse that too many
insights are lost in the process of typologization. This confirms Korpi's
(2000) point that reliance on the state and/or the market is too uni-
dimensional to capture the complexities involved in gender relations.
For us, though, Korpi's solution of adding the market and developing
a threefold categorization of countries wherein reliance on the market
is included alongside reliance on the state and/or the family is insufficient. Across the spheres of care, work and welfare, national configurations of gender relations are frequently best represented as the

coming together of a set of variables in a unique way such that differences are a matter of kind or substance rather than degree. This is not to say that cross-national patterns cannot be observed or that countries do not resemble each other in a number of important respects. Indeed, the process of comparing countries that share some common features is very illuminating. We would argue, however, that aspects of cross-national similarity and patterning do not completely capture the comparison of national welfare states and that their particularities remain of great importance.

8.2   Pressure Points around Care, Work and Welfare and the Challenges for Future Policy

It is helpful to think of the pressure points and challenges around policy in terms of the three spheres of care, work and welfare which have guided our analysis throughout.

8.2.1   Reforms and pressures around care

Care is certainly an issue for policy, and is putting Western European welfare states under increasing pressure. The demand for care is growing at the same time as the supply of private care within the family is contracting. Trends such as women's rising participation in employment, family instability, changing norms about care as a component of family solidarity, and the ageing of the population put pressure on policy. Families (especially women) are insistent that the care of children and the elderly cannot be either a totally private or a totally public good. For these and other reasons, welfare states can no longer assume that caring will automatically be provided by the family.

It is interesting to observe that, unlike ten or fifteen years ago, gender inequalities are rarely the focus of social policy today. Rather, it is the work/family axis that is driving much policy reform. The interests that are represented most strongly in this type of policy reform are those of the market and economic actors. The search is on for the family forms that best suit the needs of contemporary capitalism. Care is therefore viewed as a constraint on labour supply; so, among other things, the issue of the quality of care, especially in terms of the needs of care recipients, falls from view. A further dilemma arising from the focus on the reconciliation of work and family life is whether new policies – such as the provision of leaves – are diverse enough to guarantee the supply of appropriate care. The related dilemma is that although care concerns both the elderly and children, policy conceives these types of care separately. Not only are care policies quite fragmented within and across countries, it is care for children that is prioritized.

Despite significant amounts of reform and the fact that much of it is focusing on reconciling family and working life, there is a wide divergence between the actual employment/family arrangements that people have and those that they would prefer (OECD 2001a). As table 8.1 shows, the model that people have too much of is the traditional male breadwinner model. In Germany, for example, this is

Table 8.1 Actual and preferred employment patterns by type of work/family arrangement, 1998

	Man full-time/ woman full-time	Man full-time/ woman part-time	Man full-time/ woman not employed	Other
France				
Actual (A)	38.8	14.4	38.3	8.4
Preferred (P)	52.4	21.9	14.1	11.7
Gap (A–P)	−13.6	−7.5	24.2	−3.3
Germany				
Actual (A)	15.7	23.1	52.3	8.9
Preferred (P)	32.0	42.9	5.7	19.4
Gap (A–P)	−16.3	−19.8	46.6	−10.5
Ireland				
Actual (A)	30.8	18.7	37.0	13.5
Preferred (P)	31.1	42.3	8.1	18.5
Gap (A–P)	−0.3	−23.6	28.9	−5.0
Italy				
Actual (A)	34.9	11.8	43.3	10.0
Preferred (P)	50.4	27.7	10.7	11.2
Gap (A–P)	−15.5	−15.9	32.6	−1.2
Netherlands				
Actual (A)	4.8	54.8	33.7	6.7
Preferred (P)	5.6	69.9	10.7	13.8
Gap (A–P)	−0.8	−15.1	23.0	−7.1
Sweden				
Actual (A)	51.1	13.3	24.9	10.7
Preferred (P)	66.8	22.2	6.6	4.4
Gap (A–P)	−15.7	−8.9	18.3	6.3
UK				
Actual (A)	24.9	31.9	32.8	10.4
Preferred (P)	21.3	41.8	13.3	23.6
Gap (A–P)	3.6	−9.9	19.5	−13.2

Source: OECD 2001a: table 4.3

the actual arrangement of 52 per cent of the population, but for only 6 per cent is it their preferred arrangement; similar levels of dissatisfaction with employment/family arrangements are to be found in Italy. The model that is too seldom available across countries is the one and a half earner arrangement where the man is in full-time employment and the woman in part-time work. In general, the two-earner family form is more sought after than the traditional model of a male breadwinner/female care giver. One has to ask how sustainable this gap between expectations and reality is, especially in countries such as Germany and Italy, and to a lesser extent France and Ireland, where the opportunity for people to realize their preferred family/ employment arrangement is very compromised. It is no coincidence that most of these are countries in which women's labour market participation is lowest.

The changing nature of the family means that welfare states are being required to rethink the ways in which they deal with people as members of families. One such reformulation of family/welfare state relations is to be found in the increasing trend for policy to grant children social rights as individuals. One sees this in Germany, Sweden and the UK, where child care is made a right of the individual child. Also, there are traces of a social rights idiom for children in the discourse around poverty in countries such as Ireland and the UK, where the entitlement of children to grow up free from poverty is represented as a birthright. Such an individualization of children's rights has not, thus far anyway, been applied to social security or taxation. The implications of this kind of development for women are worth considering, since welfare states have typically supported women in their role as guardians and carers of children. The question again has to be asked of how the future welfare of women is to be secured if children are given access to services and benefits in their own right. This kind of focus on children has, for example, no terms to see the poverty of children as a gender issue.

One should not underestimate the extent to which welfare states are promoting policies that are inconsistent in their effects on caring roles. To take but one example, the recently introduced Working Tax Credit in the UK supports a home-maker role for women married to a wage earner, whereas the incentives for lone mothers are to become paid workers. Ambiguities are to be seen also in the use of caring leaves as a policy response to the need for care and the fact that these are, in some cases, replacing direct financial support of children. Where such leaves are paid, it is unclear whether they are fulfilling a wage replacement function for women who are expected to be absent from the labour market but temporarily or whether they are a way of making some compensatory payments to women for the work that has traditionally been unpaid. People are unlikely to adjust their behaviours if they are getting inconsistent messages.

There is a set of issues around quality and especially the conditions that lead to good quality care. Worry has been expressed about the increasing trend towards benefits for care because of the implications of introducing cash into what is essentially a relationship (Ungerson 1995). A related issue is what happens when caring work is shifted to the market, and in particular whether money changes the motivations of those who do it and the character of the care they provide. Care is expensive, and this makes it more difficult for welfare states to provide care in circumstances where the demand for it is increasing.

The consensus about the proper role and behaviour of those providing care is a fragile one. It is very difficult for the welfare state to deliver policy in circumstances where norms and standards are disputed. There is no stable settlement in any country as to the appropriate division of the costs of care or the appropriate location of care between the state, the family and the market. A range of issues is to be observed in this context. Sweden, along with other Nordic states, has been forced in recent years to consider the question of who provides care, either because of escalating costs of public provision or because people are seeking the right or choice to provide personal care for young, and to a lesser extent elderly, members of their families. The continental European welfare states, which have, with the exception of France, tended to hold the view that care should be provided by the family, have been forced to rethink their position in the light of the increasingly costly trade-off between caring and other aspects of life, especially for women. The most unwilling caring states – Ireland and the UK – have also been forced to refashion their policies in recent years. In Ireland these pressures derive from social and economic developments which have swept large numbers of women into the work-force, whereas ideological developments around productivist welfare have underpinned reform in the UK.

8.2.2   Reforms and pressures around work

Women's employment is increasing in every country. The steady pace of growth conceals the transformation that is taking place. Examined at a single point in time, change seems rather slow, but the accumulation of growth over two decades indicates a fundamental shift. Both the place of work in women's lives and the organization of social life are affected. Indeed, women's life course is being redefined. When we

look across countries, there are three overriding issues that are creating pressure points for policy reform in this area.

First, the increased participation of women in employment sits
alongside persisting inequalities. Such inequalities are to be observed
in segregated employment structures within and across countries. It is
well known that there are men's jobs and women's jobs, and that this
demarcation has remained robust in the face of women's increasing
employment rates. Gender wage gaps provide further evidence of
structural inequalities in the labour market. Against a backdrop of
some narrowing of wage gaps over the past two decades, it appears
that a plateau has been reached at around the 80 per cent mark (i.e.
there is a shortfall of 20 per cent between women's and men's wages
to the detriment of women). In effect, wage inequalities seem to be
stuck.

The second issue pertains to the severity of the compromises involved for women. Rising female employment rates conceal the fact
that women have to trade off employment and family involvement.
This trade-off is not uniform across countries or across groups of
women. In some cases it is the extent of women's labour market
participation that is compromised, in others it is its continuity. As
the data in table 8.1 indicate, the unmet expectations of individuals
and families across Europe centre on the level of women's participation in employment. Only a minority of families in any country have
their preferred balance of women's paid and unpaid work. Women
are often faced with an additional compromise, involving the type
and level of job and their long-term career prospects. There are
indications that women are no longer prepared to make such compromises. For example, rising levels of childlessness and falling fertility rates indicate that the required trade-off in some countries is
severe.

The third issue pertains to the structure of the labour market. For
all that women's lives are changing, the impact of the movement of
women into employment is not generally transforming either the
structure or the organization of employment. One could characterize
the labour market as adapting to women's presence in larger numbers
rather than as radically changing. So one sees more part-time work,
some increased flexibility, and shorter interruptions of employment
for child- related purposes. But the typical male pattern of work still
prevails. It is as Rubery et al. (1999: 3) point out: the integration of
women into the labour market has been associated as much with the
maintenance and reinforcement of difference – differences across and
within nations – as with processes of convergence and equality between women and men.

How is policy responding in the face of these pressure points? With regard to segregation, policy has been relatively silent. The response that has taken place has been most likely to focus on encouraging women into typically male occupations (especially science and engineering). What is needed, however, is systemic change in regard to both the education and training systems and the structure of the labour market. Further, in terms of vertical segregation, restrictions on women's access to high-status jobs attract the most policy attention, rather than the problematic concentration of women in low-status employment. While employment-based equality was a strong theme of gender-led policies in the 1970s and 1980s, this approach to employment inequality may by now have yielded its best fruit. Policy in the future will have to address itself to more qualitative dimensions, such as skill levels, longer-term career development, and women's employment looked at from the perspective of the duration of the life course. While one can see some vestiges of such an approach in the recent move from passive to active labour market policies, such policies do not affect women in very large numbers, and are not in any case framed from the perspective of the female employment trajectory. Continuity is an essential component of career development, just as wages place a premium on seniority. Women's difficulties in attaining continuous employment under the present arrangements exert a heavy toll on their career development and lifetime earnings. Hence, taking women as the departure point, access to employment cannot be viewed in a uni-dimensional manner.

Policy is more engaged in the trade-off involved in growing female employment for women and families. The quality of economic life and the links between work and family have a presence on the contemporary policy agenda. The EU has been a dominant actor in this regard, having made concerted moves in the 1990s to enable a better balance between work and family, especially for women. Its initiatives included the working time directive (in 1998), the directive on parental leave and time off for caring for dependants (in 1999), and the part-time work directive (in 2000). A recommendation on child care was also issued. As we have seen, individual countries (especially Germany, the UK and Ireland, where reconciliation has tended to be regarded as a private matter best resolved by couples or between the woman and her employer) also find themselves having to give specific attention to the family/work balance. It is significant that these are framed as 'family-friendly' rather than as gender equality measures. They do not in practice do much to increase men's involvement in unpaid work or to significantly ameliorate the trade-offs involved for women.

As well as new policy agendas around reconciling work and family life, reform is also to be observed in mainstream labour market policy. One impetus for such reform has been the effect of cycles of growth and recession on men's access to employment. The changes in the demand for labour are such that men's chances of securing a job for life are now less assured. It is notable that the overriding policy response to the insecurity of male employment and other developments has been to focus on labour supply. In the continental European welfare states, for example, early retirement was the preferred way of responding to higher male unemployment and jobless growth. Active labour market policy has superseded such a response across Europe and the USA. Programmes seeking to insert unemployed and other benefit claimants into the labour market are now widespread. Given the continuing gender differentials in formal skills and access to employment, such policies have potential for addressing gender inequalities. However, the understanding that it is male breadwinners who need priority access to state services restricts women's access, as does the targeting of policies in some countries at very specific groups of claimants (Rake 2001).

While many welfare states operate in the expectation of women's participation in the labour market (Sweden, the USA, and to a lesser extent France and the UK), the role of women as workers remains the subject of contest in others, especially women with young children. Policy agendas are pulling in quite different directions cross-nationally. Thus, while some countries (Germany and the Netherlands) continue to seek ways of supporting stay-at-home motherhood, others (such as the UK and the USA) pursue a productivist agenda in which the employment of women especially has become a quasi-public good. As such, employment is encouraged or enforced, particularly for those women heading their own households.

To the extent that policy reform creates an obligation to be in the labour market and regards participation in paid work as being equivalent to social inclusion, it is problematic for women, especially mothers. One issue is whether the emphasis on labour market insertion devalues caring as an activity, a set of relations, and a source of inclusion. Lone mothers are very vulnerable in the face of this policy reform, because they have typically been supported by welfare states as mothers rather than as workers. The value attached to paid and unpaid work, as well as the conditions under which the state should continue to offer support to them and other welfare claimants, are also at issue. Overall, to the extent that supply-side policies have become a panacea for all employment-related problems, too little attention is being given to the kinds of changes in the structure of the labour market that are necessary for women to have real choice about how to combine employment and caring.

8.2.3   Reform and pressures around welfare

When women's welfare is examined in its own right and in comparison with that of men, a number of points emerge as critical. The distribution of income is marked by gender inequalities in both personal incomes and differentials among households. Women's risk of poverty is higher than that of men in every country (except Sweden), and particular groups of women, especially lone mothers and elderly women who live alone, are at high risk. When the lens is widened, inequalities also mark women's and men's relative access to resources such as time and opportunities over the life course. The persistence of gender inequalities and differentials raises questions about the adequacy of the welfare state in securing women's welfare.

Following periods of retrenchment and the rolling back of the state across the eight countries, a new set of themes is beginning to emerge in welfare policy. One can, in fact, talk of attempts to forge a new contract between the welfare state and individuals, in which the latter are encouraged or forced to take on greater responsibility for their own welfare as well as that of their family members. Individualization and privatization are trends that are going hand in hand. Pensions policy is particularly marked by these trends. The gender implications of this emerging contract are fourfold. First, as beneficiaries of state redistribution, women will suffer disproportionately from any diminution in the role of the state. Second, the place of the family and the protection of relationships of familial interdependence are difficult to incorporate within individualized modes of provision. Measures such as those discussed in the creation of a funded pension in Sweden, which aimed to encourage joint savings while protecting individual rights to joint property, remain a rarity. Third, individualization and privatization mean that risk, rather than being pooled by the welfare state, reverts to the individual. It is the poorest, among whom women are overrepresented, who are least able to bear such risk. They have neither sufficient resources to provide a buffer against the uncertainties of the market nor adequate insurance to protect against risks to income. Fourth, moves towards individualization threaten the elements of familial protection common to many social security systems. The ability to claim as a dependant is being foreclosed by policy reform (such as that occurring in Sweden and the UK), while limits are in force on the ability to combine claims as dependants with those made on the basis of individual entitlement (in Germany and the USA).

When welfare is being reformed, different groups have to jockey for position and press their claims on welfare state resources over those of others. Current social trends mean that women are increasingly having to make claims in their own right and on behalf of the households that they head. It is questionable whether women have access to the power resources necessary to press their claims successfully. Female representation in decision making remains limited, and power structures often act to exclude women. There is also the matter of the legitimacy accorded to women's claims. Normative expectations of female dependency and the continued privileging of paid over unpaid work act as major points of resistance. Hence it is common for debate about supporting lone mothers to focus not on their needs but on whether such support privileges lone mothers at the expense of other families.

The more private aspects of welfare and the balance of resources among members of households are too seldom the subject of policy reform. The issue has, however, been brought into the public arena through discussion of a citizen's income. Universal access to a guaranteed minimum income is the objective here. This would require the individualization of entitlement and direct payment of some state resources to all citizens regardless of need. From a gender perspective, however, a basic income might not significantly address gaps in income between women and men. Neither would it address the gender division of labour – indeed, it might act to reinforce it. The extent to which the basic income proposal addresses itself to social transformation is limited. There is, doubtless, a dilemma involved for policy, in both supporting individuals as individuals and in taking account of people's family circumstances. Recognizing interdependence is the challenge, and this may be undermined by moves towards individualization.

Whether policy is sufficiently responsive to new and emerging risks is also open to question. Family instability is to all intents and purposes not addressed by welfare policy reform, with, among other things, too few efforts to recognize divorce as a risk to income that needs to be protected against. Policy has been slow to respond to new family forms. Although caring could now be said to be firmly on the policy agenda, it is not yet fully recognized as a risk to income. Another emergent risk that has been insufficiently incorporated into the welfare state is that of falling male breadwinner incomes, which may result in rising numbers of the working poor.

In times of welfare state retrenchment, cash transfers are an obvious target for reform. No welfare state has been immune to the push towards increasing contributions while reducing the generosity of cash transfer payments. In addition, public service provision has been scaled down in those welfare states that followed a public service model, while the option of public service development as a trajectory of reform has been vetoed for other welfare states. A related development has been the changing mix of welfare provision, with an increased role for the market, the voluntary sector and the family. The heavy reliance of women on the state as a source of income and support through services means that women are among those most vulnerable to cutbacks. Neither are they well placed in relation to purchasing services or accessing income through the market.

Finally, the mechanisms of welfare state delivery are also in question. There is a move towards the fiscalization of welfare policy in some countries, in the form of tax credits for employment. Because this tightens the link between welfare state support and paid employment, it further narrows women's opportunity to access resources from a variety of roles. Fiscalization also tends to residualize the benefit system. Hence, those women and men who cannot be employed are reliant on a benefit system that is increasingly means-tested.

To summarize, let us draw together political dilemmas from across the spheres of care, work and welfare. A number of pressure points for reform (such as the ageing of the population and family instability) cut across these spheres, but in each sphere such pressures take a particular form and push policy in a distinct direction. For example, the ageing of the population increases the demand for state involvement in care at the same time as creating momentum for more mixed models of provision for pensions. What is certain, however, is that in each of the eight countries, the policy and normative content of the welfare state are subject to continuous renegotiation. The degree to which gender relations are central to such reforms is more questionable, though. Family change and increasing participation in the labour market mean that more and more women are in a direct relationship with the state and the market. Yet persistent gender inequalities in power and other resources continue to limit the extent to which women's claims are heard and met on their own terms. In addition, in some welfare states, polarization among women means that their interests are splintered, with the result that quite distinct demands are made on the welfare state. This can result in policy makers shying away from intervention for fear that any measure will be seen to privilege some groups of women at the expense of others. Although most welfare states are moving away from models of provision that assume a male breadwinner/female care giver divide, the solutions that have come in their place are still problematic for women's welfare. For example, replacing the breadwinner model with one of family policy in which the needs of children are the only ones with a clear articulation may have the effect of bypassing gender inequalities. Similarly, productivist models of welfare, in which all are expected to participate in the labour market, tend to hide inequalities in access to and conditions of female and male employment.

We should be cautious, nevertheless, about painting an overly-bleak picture of the future of gender relations and the welfare state. Gender is one of the most fundamental social divides, defining roles, power relations, norms and life chances. It is not surprising, then, that the pace of relevant change, especially in gender relations in the private sphere, seems rather slow. But, as the review above shows, there are considerable pressures for change. Women's involvement in public life is serving to increase their resources, financial and power-based, and to politicize issues, in particular care, that were erstwhile seen as private. There is also growing demand that opportunities to care should be opened up to men, and issues around their quality of life be taken into consideration in future policy. In so many ways, then, the success of future welfare states depends upon meeting the varied expectations and demands of women and men as they pursue a lifetime's worth of care, work and welfare.

Technical Appendix

To support the analysis presented in chapters 5 and 6, this appendix discusses issues of data sources and country coverage, definition of household type, the unit of analysis chosen to measure income, and the measurement of state transfers as a source of income.

A.1 Data Sources and Country Coverage

Our investigation draws on original analysis of the Luxembourg Income Study (LIS) combined with data extracted from Eurostat's published statistics, which are based on the European Community Household Panel (ECHP). Data did not exist across all measures for each country, with the result that the picture for some countries is rather partial. There was no suitable Irish data in the LIS data base, and the USA is, for obvious reasons, not included in the ECHP. For most countries, however, a complete set of measures exists. The most recent data available from LIS pertain to the mid-1990s, dating from 1994 for France, Germany and the Netherlands, 1995 for Italy, Sweden and the UK, and 1997 for the USA. For the ECHP, the most recent data available refer to either 1996 or 1997. Full details of the LIS data base (including sample frames and size, weighting procedures and possible sources of bias) can be found at *http://www. lisproject.org*; likewise, a full description of the work of Eurostat is to be found at *http://europa.eu.int/comm/eurostat.*

LIS and the ECHP take slightly different approaches to ensuring comparability of data (although there is some overlap, since in some cases the ECHP data set is also the LIS dataset). For LIS, national datasets that ask different questions of respondents are passed through a process of 'LISification', which involves the production of comparable, aggregated variables (such as market income) for each country. The ECHP, by contrast, utilizes data that is drawn from uniform surveys in each country.

A.2   The Definition of Head of Household, Lone Parent and Older Households

The LIS data operate with a particular definition of head of household. The LIS data do not record any heterosexual couple households in which the female is nominated as head. This method is chosen because it is the practice of many national statistical agencies to nominate a man as head of household. This practice may result in the mis-classification of the small number of couple households in which the woman, as main wage earner or owner of housing assets, may have a stronger claim to the headship.

It should be noted that, along with income and other resources, household characteristics themselves vary quite considerably. In the data we use from LIS, around 30 per cent of all households are headed by a woman in Sweden (with similar proportions in the USA and Germany), compared with around 25 per cent in the UK and France and just over 20 per cent in Italy and the Netherlands. Similarly, there is considerable variation in the proportion of households containing a dependent child (driven by cross-national differences in fertility rates, the timing of fertility, and broader family patterns). Hence, 22 per cent of Swedish households contain a dependent child, compared with 37 per cent in the USA (see table A.1 for details on all countries).

While the definition of head of household is fixed in the LIS data, a set of decisions had to be made about how to define lone parent and households of older persons.

Table A.1   Characteristics of households with dependent children

	With a dependent child (% of households)	With a dependent child under 5 (% of households)	Headed by lone mother (% of households)	Headed by lone mother with child under 5 (% of households)
France 1994	32.8	14.9	2.8	0.9
Germany 1994	29.0	11.8	3.0	1.0
Italy 1995	32.9	13.2	0.8	0.1
Netherlands 1994	29.0	13.1	2.2	0.5
Sweden 1995	22.4	10.8	4.8	2.1
UK 1995	33.2	15.7	6.3	2.9
USA 1997	37.1	17.0	5.4	2.2

Source: Luxembourg Income Study, authors' analysis
Columns do not sum to 100%, since categories are neither exhaustive nor mutually exclusive

A.2.1   Defining lone parent households

For the sake of comparison and of working within the confines of available data, we defined a lone parent household as consisting of a sole adult who co-resides with at least one dependent child. But this belies the complexity of household types in which lone parents find themselves. For example, lone parents are likely also to live in the parental home or to share a household with other adults. Further, a picture of lone parents at a particular point in time fails to reveal important variations in the duration of lone parenthood. Had data allowed, we would have preferred to take a longitudinal approach, in which different durations of lone parenthood could have been distinguished. A further limitation is that our analysis focuses on lone mothers only. The data revealed a small number of lone parent households headed by men, the greatest proportion (1.1 per cent) being found in the USA. However, even here the proportions were too low to allow a robust statistical analysis, so lone fathers were, regrettably, excluded from the analysis. The statistical problem of small numbers is not completely averted by focusing on lone mother households: the low numbers of such households in Italy (103) and the Netherlands (159) meant that it was not possible to disaggregate this category any further. The proportion of female-headed households headed by lone mothers also varied significantly cross-nationally. From LIS data we estimate that 24 per cent of female heads were lone mothers in the UK, 19 per cent in the USA, and 15 per cent in Sweden. At the other extreme, only 3 per cent of Italian female-headed households were headed by a lone mother. (Figure A.1 shows complete figures for the composition of female-headed households.)

A.2.2   Defining older households

For ease of operationalization and comparability with Eurostat-generated data, we chose to define later life in terms of age, and included all households in which a person aged over sixty-five years resides, either as head of household or as co-resident. We are, nevertheless, mindful of the limits of chronological definitions (the transition to later life has no simple chronological profile and is rarely clear-cut or easily identifiable). Furthermore, we look only at older households that take a simple form, limiting our comparisons to households consisting of a couple in which one or more is aged over sixty-five, or sole men and women in that age group heading their own households. The benefit of this is that it allows us to measure the impact of the pension system and other direct provision for the older population. Couple households accounted for between one-third and two-fifths of the older population across all countries. In Germany, the Netherlands and Sweden, sole female-headed households were the most common older household type, and also the largest group of female-headed households. Differential longevity means that sole male-headed households were a much smaller group, representing

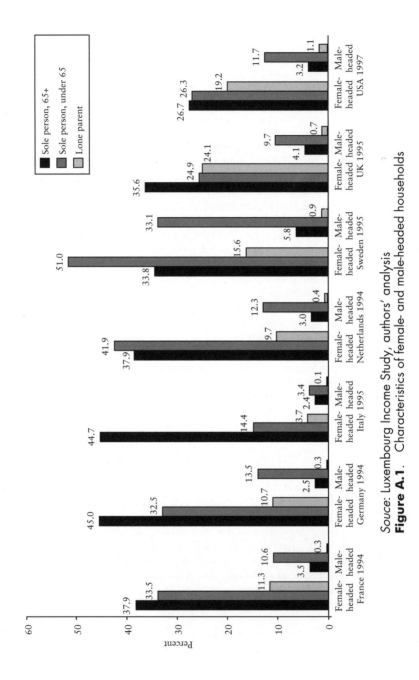

Souce: Luxembourg Income Study, authors' analysis

Figure A.1. Characteristics of female- and male-headed households

11 per cent or less of the older population in all countries bar Sweden. There is, however, a distinct outlier: Italy. There, a large proportion of households containing an older person were complex in form: multi-generational households (in which older people live with their children or even grandchildren) or older people co-residing with others (e.g. a pair of widowed sisters). Full details of each country are given in table A.2.

A.3 Measuring Income at the Household Level, Equivalizing Income, and Household Resource Balance

It is the convention to measure income at the household level, with adjustment made for household size. There is a limitation to this approach. Measuring household income and calculating poverty rates at the household level implies that incomes are shared equally within households. Where such sharing does not occur, it is women who are most likely to be affected, since they command lower incomes on average. Hence, this methodological practice tends to overstate women's access to income (and understate their poverty rates); for these reasons we also examine individual incomes. For the purpose of taking account of household size, we followed standard methodological practice and adjusted household income for the number of adults and children in the household. In the analysis of the LIS data base, we employed the OECD scale, adjusting household income by assigning a weight of 1 to the first adult, 0.7 to subsequent adults, and 0.5 to all children. Eurostat's statistics employ a slightly different scale (the modified OECD scale), which assigns a weight to additional household members according to their age (0.5 for all other household members aged 14 and over and 0.3 for those aged under 14). While standard, either approach may be criticized for being simplistic. The actual rates assigned may not reflect the economies of scale achieved by households of varying characteristics, and a more accurate adjustment might take account of factors such as age, disability and health status as well as income level.

Table A.2 Characteristics of households containing an older person (65 or over)

	Couple only	Sole female	Sole male	Other (complex) households
France 1994	41	34	9	16
Germany 1994	36	45	6	27
Italy 1995	27	27	5	41
Netherlands 1994	41	41	11	8
Sweden 1995	40	43	17	–
UK 1995	39	34	11	15
USA 1997	36	32	10	22

Source: Luxembourg Income Study, authors' analysis

A concern of chapter 6 is to link individual incomes with household incomes. This also imposed limitations. First, to conduct meaningful analysis of the household resource balance, we selected only households that contained two or more individuals between whom there was a partnership (marriage or cohabitation). For a number of households in each country, negative income was recorded. These cases may be 'genuine', in that they represent the operating losses of the self-employed or may result from reporting error or fraudulent or creative accountancy (most likely to occur in those datasets that are based on tax returns such as in Italy). Since it is difficult to determine how individual income (or debt) contributes to this income position, these cases were excluded. A further complication arose in the case of self-employment. Income from self-employment is recorded at the household level only, making it difficult to determine who earns and receives that income. These cases were therefore also excluded.

A.4   Measuring the Contribution of State Transfers to Family and Individual Income

It was important to identify the contribution of state transfers to the overall package of income. This was done on an equivalent basis – measuring both taxes and transfers – for all countries bar Italy (where the lack of gross income figures meant that the impact of the tax system was not discernible). Taxation was also an issue in measuring individual receipt of state transfers in chapter 6. In a great number of cases, tax liability is calculated for the household, so it is difficult to identify the tax paid by individuals. Hence, the analysis of the impact of the state on individual incomes is limited to cash transfers paid to women and men by the state. With regard to these transfers, we followed national rules governing the payment of particular benefits. To illustrate, in France we assumed that means-tested benefits are paid to the male head of household, and that women receive maternity and child benefit, child care allowances, and alimony in their own name. In reality, payment mechanisms are much less systematic in their targeting of individuals than this analysis implies. However, without access to the details of individual cases, this is the best we could do.

Notes

INTRODUCTION

1   See the Technical Appendix for full details of the Luxembourg Income Study.

CHAPTER 1   STUDYING THE WELFARE STATE AND GENDER: THE INSIGHTS OF EXISTING WORK

1   See Pierson 1991 and Daly 2000 for comprehensive reviews.
2   The work on poverty, for example, has revealed the many dimensions of poverty as a life experience, as well as developing a research methodology around poverty (Leibfried et al. 1995; Gordon and Townsend 2000).
3   See also Lister 1997 and Siim 2000.
4   Sociologically, one of the most interesting aspects of care is that it combines love and labour (Graham 1983). As labour, it invokes material circumstances, conditions of existence and a place where women and intimate relations are to be found (Finch and Groves 1983: 3). As love, caring draws upon consciousness, emotional bonds and social identity.
5   To call them 'sets of literature' may be to overstate the body of work and also its influence. It is probably more accurate to characterize them as emerging approaches.
6   See also the work of Drover and Kerans 1993.
7   While each is an avenue for establishing claims, the rationales on which claims making rests differ (although they do overlap, and within each realm many principles may operate simultaneously). In the family the principle of solidarity operates, in the economy it is contribution (in terms

of claims around work, capital or property), and in government it is the principles of the public interest (at the collective level) and citizenship (at the individual level).

8 Gender inequalities are seen as part of tacit social policy, which comprises the indirect or soft effects of policy. Leisering and Leibfried give three main examples of tacit social policy: the gender differentiations that inhere in pension policy, the threat of poverty that underlies the social risk management areas of policy, and the hidden curriculum of education. They offer no theoretical terms to understand these, however, and it is not immediately clear why they select these and not others.

9 Some words of caution are in order here. It is important to distinguish between the agency of the welfare state and the agent invoked. To talk of welfare state agency is not to imply that there is a singular or unitary agent involved. Rather, agency refers to the actions of a variety of agents that do not necessarily take a coherent form. As such, agency can refer to the actions of bureaucrats following a central mandate as well as to the actions of those (including the private and voluntary sectors) whose incentives to provide a particular service are altered by state provision.

10 Comprehensive reviews can be found in Shalev 1983, Uusitalo 1984, Wilensky et al. 1987, Amenta 1993.

11 See also the review in Gustafsson 1994.

12 An exception here is the work by Goodin et al. (1999) which, making use of longitudinal data on three countries, measures welfare state activity using broad-ranging indicators which draw upon more deep-seated phenomena such as the promotion of autonomy and efficiency.

CHAPTER 2 FRAMEWORK OF ANALYSIS

1 There have been recent attempts to open up these debates, however. See Lewis et al. 2000 and Cahill 1994 among others.

2 Women's political activity tends to take place in different spheres from that of men. See Lewis 1994.

3 For example, Niskanen's (1971) notion of budget-maximizing bureaucrats who exert an ever upward pressure on expenditure has been widely challenged (see e.g. Dunleavy 1991). A specific focus on welfare bureaucrats has revealed them as potential agents of social control and, in operating at 'street-level', uniquely placed to overturn the stated goals of policy (Lipsky 1980).

4 With the exception of Acker 1988 and Daly 2000.

5 Ragin (1987) provides one of the best expositions of the differences between these two approaches. Ragin and Zaret (1983) locate the two approaches in the classical literature.

CHAPTER 3   GENDER AND THE PROVISION OF CARE

1 A complexity reflected in the difficulty of finding an appropriate term within and across languages. The English term 'care' has tended to be imported into or imposed on other countries because of the difficulty of finding an indigenous term. However, the use of the term 'care' in English is not uncontroversial either.

2 It is important to emphasize that these rather general indicators miss some important aspects of variation within and across programmes. Among the factors not picked up here are the duration of child care (in terms of hours per day and up to what age the child is eligible to attend), the costs associated with it, the target group, the funders and providers, the ideological and historical origins of provision, as well as the operating conditions (such as staff–child ratios, the content of the care and so forth). See Kamerman 1991 for a good discussion of some of these factors from a comparative perspective. As regards maternity provision, what is not considered here is the contribution made by the employer and the legal setting within which the leaves and benefits are granted. Parental leave is also a highly variable entity.

3 France has a benefit-in-kind (*prestation spécifique dépendance*) which is granted for the payment of pre-defined expenses for dependent persons over the age of sixty-five.

4 The following proportion of care for the elderly was in co-resident households in 1995: the Netherlands, 30 per cent; Germany, 40 per cent; France, 46 per cent; the UK, 48 per cent; Italy, 50 per cent; Ireland, 60 per cent (Eurostat 2001a).

5 The participating countries in the former are Australia, Belgium, Czech Republic, Denmark, Finland, Italy, the Netherlands, Norway, Portugal, Sweden, the UK and the USA, and in the latter Austria, Finland, France, Germany, Italy, the Netherlands, Portugal and the UK.

6 For the part-time workers, the actual phrase used is 'housework and family commitments'.

7 The effect of three or more children for Germany is insignificant.

8 The poverty rates of lone mothers also compare very unfavourably with those of lone fathers, but these data are not reproduced here.

CHAPTER 4   GENDER AND WORK

1 For other gender-focused typologies see Siaroff 1994; Mósesdóttir 1995; and Daly 1996. For criticism of the breadwinner regimes' approach, see Hobson 1994 and Daly 2000.

2 In fact, these seven countries encompass more or less the extremes of variation in female employment rates in Europe.

3   In Sweden, for example, women's absences from work are considerable. Jonung and Persson show that, while the difference between male and female labour force participation rates in 1990 was 5 percentage points, the difference between their at work rates was more than double that (11 percentage points) (1994: 42). These authors are of the view that the most accurate measures of women's labour market pattern are either their at work rates (which measure the persons who are actually active in market work during an average week of the year as a percentage of the total population) or the market hours rate (which measures the total number of hours actually worked in the market per week for a given population group divided by the total size of that population group).

4   The main reason given by French women for why they work part-time is that they have not found another job. Italian women attribute the fact that they work part-time to 'other reasons', but do not elaborate (Eurostat 2000b: 3).

5   It is also something that is defined quite differently across countries. Hence the data in this fifth column of the table need to be treated with care.

6   These should be read with great care, though, because they are static and cannot indicate change.

7   The countries included in this study were Australia, Canada, France, Germany, Norway, the UK and the USA.

8   Note, however, that the wage ratios in the individual countries, together with the cross-national variation, are very sensitive to the base taken. That is, whether one takes hourly, monthly or annual earnings levels as one's base makes quite a big difference, as do whether the calculations pertain to full- or part-time employees.

9   Note that Ireland is not included in these analyses.

10   Given limited information, Europe here refers to the fifteen member states less Sweden and Finland.

11   The results reported in this section are from the 1996 wave of the European Community Household Panel. The study deals only with employees working at least 15 hours per week and the low-wage threshold is set at 60 per cent of the national median monthly wage (Eurostat 2000b).

12   And in eight member states of the EU as a whole. These are, along with France, Ireland, the Netherlands and the UK, Belgium, Greece, Luxembourg, Portugal and Spain.

13   Note that these figures pertain to 1999 and are gross – i.e. before the deduction of income tax and social security contribution.

CHAPTER 5   WELFARE, HOUSEHOLD RESOURCES AND GENDER RELATIONS

1   What is less clear is how such services should be valued. The multi-dimensional nature of services and the inability of recipients to exchange

them for other goods raise questions as to whether their value can be captured by a simple cash measure. For these reasons, and given that services are a key component of chapters 3 and 4, we do not cover the distributive effects of services here.

2   For example, women who have children within a cohabiting relationship may not be offered protection equivalent to that of their married peers, affecting their claims on an ex-partner's current income or their contribution to state or occupational pensions.

3   This is not to imply, however, that we view redistribution as a simple or linear process, in which state redistribution occurs 'after' the market has located its resources. Rather, no income can truly be considered as having been distributed 'prior' to the intervention of the welfare state, since the welfare state both critically affects the labour market opportunities of women and men, and, by regulating the labour and other markets, sets the very terms on which market distribution occurs.

4   Details of the data used and the methodology adopted can be found in the Technical Appendix.

5   As discussed earlier, the state's impact on the distribution of income is more complex, and complete, than that measured by the net effect of taxes and transfers. However, it is not possible to measure directly the role that the state plays in shaping the distribution of market income itself.

6   In the Swedish case, this inverse gender poverty ratio will be driven, at least in part, by high numbers of younger male-headed households with low incomes during the period of higher education.

7   The figures on the gender gap in poverty (and those on persistent poverty to follow) are likely to understate women's poverty rate. Poverty is here measured at the household level and estimates the numbers of women and men in poor and non-poor households. This method assumes that the income, and the risk of poverty, of women and men in multi-person households is shared equally. In order to compensate for this, we look in more detail at individual incomes in the following chapter, and explore how far women in couples have independent access to resources.

8   The full costs of children are difficult to estimate, since having children affects individual behaviour for a long time after (or indeed before) a child is born. A full assessment might need to take into account the lifetime effects (Rake 2000), but data limitations mean that we look only at economic costs, since they affect those whose children are currently dependent and co-resident.

9   In France and Sweden, for example, state sources account for at least nine-tenths of the incomes of the older population. In the UK and the USA, the state plays a diminished role in providing incomes to the older population, alerting us to the importance of private pension provision in these countries.

10 The one exception is the UK, where older single females receive slightly more income from the state (this is, nevertheless, in line with their lower

incomes overall, since male-headed households will be in receipt of more income from private pensions and other sources).

CHAPTER 6   INDIVIDUAL RESOURCES AND HOUSEHOLD REDISTRIBUTION

1   Note that these are the direct effects of the welfare state on individual entitlements, and, as we argued in chapters 3 and 4, service provision has an additional, albeit more indirect, effect on independent access to resources.
2   See Technical Appendix for further details.
3   Remember that these figures include only women with some personal income and would be much higher if we considered all women.
4   Patterns of partnership formation (which themselves may vary cross-nationally) affect inequality within the household in a way that cannot be predicted from the distribution of individual incomes alone. Where there is a high correlation between partners' incomes (such that high-income women partner high-income men), intra-familial inequality will be lower than where partners' incomes are not correlated.
5   We have chosen women aged under fifty years with children. This is a higher than usual cut-off point, but we chose it in the knowledge that with delayed fertility responsibility for child rearing reaches well into middle age.
6   Note that in this instance lack of access to micro data means that we are not able to look at balance within actual couples. Rather, the figures draw on averages calculated for all women and men.

CHAPTER 7   TOWARDS AN EXPLANATION OF NATIONAL CONFIGURATIONS AND CROSS-NATIONAL PATTERNS

1   As a crude measure, in 1995 social expenditure as a proportion of GDP was 30 per cent in France, 28 per cent in Germany and the Netherlands.

References

Acker, J. 1988: Class, gender and the relations of distribution. *Signs*, 13 (3), 473–97.

Agarwal, B. 1997: 'Bargaining' and gender relations: within and beyond the household. *Feminist Economics*, 3 (1), 1–51.

Alber, J., Esping-Andersen, G. and Rainwater, L. 1987: Studying the welfare state: issues and queries. In M. Dierkes, H. Weiler and A. Antal (eds), *Comparative Policy Research: Learning from Experience*, Aldershot: WZB/Gower, 458–69.

Amenta, E. 1993: The state of the art in welfare state research on social spending efforts in capitalist democracies since 1960. *American Journal of Sociology*, 99 (3), 750–63.

Arber, S. and Ginn, J. 1999: Gender differences in informal caring. In G. Allen (ed.), *The Sociology of the Family: A Reader*, Oxford: Blackwell, 321–39.

Atkinson, A. B. 1995: *Incomes and the Welfare State: Essays on Britain and Europe*. Cambridge: Cambridge University Press.

Atkinson, A. B. 1998: *Poverty in Europe*. Oxford: Blackwell.

Atkinson, A. B., Rainwater, L. and Smeeding, T. 1995: *Income Distribution in OECD Countries*. Paris: OECD.

Atkinson, A. B., Cantillon, B., Marlier, E. and Nolan, B. 2002: *Social Indicators: The EU and Social Inclusion*. Oxford: Oxford University Press.

Bacchi, C. L. 1999: *Women, Policy and Politics: The Construction of Social Problems*. London: Sage.

Beblo, M. 1998: How do German couples spend their time? A panel data analysis. *Vierteljahrshefte zur Wirtschaftsforschung*, 68 (2), 146–52.

Beck, U. and Beck-Gernsheim, E. 1995: *The Normal Chaos of Love*. Cambridge: Polity.

Bergqvist, C., Borchorst, A., Christensen, A-D., Ramstedt-Silén, V., Raaum, N. C. and Styrkársdóttir, A. 1999: *Equal Democracies?: Gender and Politics in the Nordic Countries*. Oslo: Scandinavian University Press.

Bettio, F. and Prechal, S. 1998: *Care in Europe*. Joint Report of the 'Gender and Employment' and the 'Gender and Law' Groups of Experts. Brussels: European Commission.

Bimbi, F. 1993: Gender, 'gift relationship' and welfare state cultures in Italy. In J. Lewis (ed.), *Women and Social Policies in Europe: Work, Family and the State*, Aldershot: Edward Elgar, 138–69.

Bittman, M. and Wacjman, J. 2000: The rush hour: the character of leisure time and gender equity. *Social Forces*, 79 (1), 165–89.

Blackburn, M. L. 1994: International comparisons of poverty. *American Economic Review*, 84 (2), 371–4.

Blank, R. M. 2000: Fighting poverty: lessons from recent US history. *Journal of Economic Perspectives*, 14, 3–19.

Boaz, R. and Muller, C. F. 1992: Paid work and unpaid help by care-givers of the disabled and frail elders. *Medical Care*, 30 (2), 149–58.

Boje, T. 1996: Welfare state models in comparative research: do the models describe the reality? In B. Greve (ed.), *Comparative Welfare Systems: The Scandinavian Model in a Period of Change*, Basingstoke: Macmillan, 13–27.

Bonnet, C. and Labbé, M. 2000: L'activité des femmes après la naissance du deuxième enfant: l'allocation parentale d'éducation a-t-elle un effet incitatif au retrait du marché du travail? *Recherches et Prévisions*, 59, 9–23.

Bonoli, G., George, V. and Taylor-Gooby, P. 2000: *European Welfare Futures: Towards a Theory of Retrenchment*. Cambridge: Polity.

Bosch, G. and Wagner, A. 2001: *Employment and Working Time in Europe*. Dublin: European Foundation for the Improvement of Living and Working Conditions.

Bourguignon, F. and Chiappori, P.-A. 1992: Collective models of household behaviour: an introduction. *European Economic Review*, 36, 355–64.

Brown, M. 1985: *Introduction to Social Administration in Britain*, 6th edn. London: Hutchinson.

Bureau of Labor Statistics 1998: Who's not working? In *Issues in Labour Statistics*, Washington, DC: US Department of Labor, 98–104.

Bureau of Labor Statistics 2001: *Highlights of Women's Earnings in 2000*. Report 952. Washington, DC: US Department of Labor.

Burgess, S., Gardiner, K. and Propper, C. 2001: *Why Rising Tides don't Lift All Boats: An Explanation of the Relationship between Poverty and Unemployment in Britain*. CASE Paper 46. London: Centre for Analysis of Social Exclusion, London School of Economics.

Bussemaker, J. and Van Kersbergen, K. 1994: Gender and welfare states: some theoretical reflections. In D. Sainsbury (ed.), *Gendering Welfare States*, London: Sage, 8–25.

Cahill, M. 1994: *The New Social Policy*. Oxford: Blackwell.

Cancedda, A. 2001: *Employment in Household Services*. Dublin: European Foundation for the Improvement of Living and Working Conditions.

Carers National Association 2000: *Caring on the Breadline: The Financial Implications of Caring*. London: Carers National Association.

Carmichael, F. and Charles, S. 1998: The labour market costs of community care. *Journal of Health Economics*, 17 (6), 747–65.

Castles, F. G. 1982: The impact of parties on public expenditure. In F. G. Castles (ed.), *The Impact of Parties: Politics and Policies in Democratic Capitalist States*, London and Beverly Hills: Sage, 21–96.

Castles, F. G. 1989: Introduction puzzles of political economy. In F. G. Castles (ed.), *The Comparative History of Public Policy*, Cambridge: Polity, 1–15.

Christopherson, S. 1997: *Childcare and Elderly Care: What Occupational Opportunities for Women?* Labour Market and Social Policy Occasional Paper no. 27. Paris: OECD.

Connell, R. W. 1987: *Gender and Power: Society, the Person and Sexual Politics*. Cambridge: Polity.

Cox, R. 1998: The consequences of welfare reform: how conceptions of social rights are changing. *Journal of Social Policy*, 27 (1), 1–16.

Curtis, R. F. 1986: Household and family in theory on inequality. *American Sociological Review*, 51 (April), 168–83.

Cutright, P. 1965: Political structure, economic development and national social security programs. *American Journal of Sociology*, 70, 537–50.

Daly, M. 1996: *Social Security, Gender and Equality in the European Union*. Brussels: Commission of the European Communities.

Daly, M. 1999: The functioning family: Catholicism and social policy in Germany and the Republic of Ireland. *Comparative Social Research*, 18, 105–33.

Daly, M. 2000: *The Gender Division of Welfare*. Cambridge: Cambridge University Press.

Daly, M. 2002: Care as a good for social policy. *Journal of Social Policy*, 31 (2), 1–20.

Daly, M. and Lewis, J. 2000: The concept of social care and the analysis of contemporary welfare states. *British Journal of Sociology*, 51 (2), 281–98.

Daly, M. and Yeates, N. 1999: Common origins, different paths: welfare state adaptation and change in Britain and Ireland. Paper presented to the European Sociological Association Conference, *Will Europe Work?*, Amsterdam, August 1999.

Davies, H. and Joshi, H. 1994: Sex, sharing and the distribution of income. *Journal of Social Policy*, 23 (3), 301–40.

Dingeldey, I. 2001: European tax systems and their impact on family employment patterns. *Journal of Social Policy*, 30 (4), 653–72.

Donnison, D., Chapman, V., Meacher, M., Sears, A. and Urwin, K. 1975: *Social Policy and Administration Revisited*, 2nd edn. London: George Allen and Unwin.

Drover, G. and Kerans, P. 1993: *New Approaches to Welfare Theory*. Aldershot: Edward Elgar.

Duncan, S. S. 1995: Theorising European gender systems. *Journal of European Social Policy*, 5 (4), 263–84.

Duncan, S. and Edwards, R. 1997: *Single Mothers in an International Context: Mothers or Workers?* London: UCL Press.

Dunleavy, P. 1991: *Democracy, Bureaucracy and Public Choice: Economic Explanations in Political Science*. London: Harvester.

Eisenstein, Z. R. 1981: *The Radical Future of Liberal Feminism*. New York: Longman.

Elshtain, J. B. 1981: *Public Man, Private Woman: Women in Social and Political Thought*. Oxford: Robertson.

Esping-Andersen, G. 1987: The comparison of policy regimes: an introduction. In M. Rein, L. Rainwater and G. Esping-Andersen (eds), *Stagnation and Renewal in Social Policy: The Rise and Fall of Policy Regimes*, Armonk, NY: M. E. Sharpe, 3–12.

Esping-Andersen, G. 1990: *The Three Worlds of Welfare Capitalism*. Cambridge: Polity.

Esping-Andersen, G. 1999: *Social Foundations of Post-Industrial Economies*. Oxford: Oxford University Press.

European Commission 1998: *Earnings Differentials between Women and Men*. Brussels: Directorate General for Employment and Social Affairs.

European Commission 1999: *Social Protection for Dependency in Old Age in the 15 EU Member States and Norway*. Brussels: European Commission.

European Commission 2001a: *Draft Joint Report on Social Inclusion: Communication from the Commission to the Council, the European Parliament, the Economic and Social Committee and the Committee of the Regions*. Brussels: European Commission.

European Commission 2001b: *Employment in Europe 2001*. Luxembourg: Office for Official Publications of the European Communities.

Eurostat 1998: *European Labour Force Survey 1997*. Luxembourg: Office for Official Publications of the European Communities.

Eurostat 1999a: *European Labour Force Survey 1998*. Luxembourg: Office for Official Publications of the European Communities.

Eurostat 1999b: Minimum wages in the European Union 1999. *Statistics in Focus*, *Population and Social Conditions*, 7/1999, Luxembourg: Office for Official Publications of the European Communities.

Eurostat 1999c: Women's earnings in the EU – 28% less than men's. *Statistics in Focus, Population and Social Conditions*, 6/1999, Luxembourg: Office for Official Publications of the European Communities.

Eurostat 2000a: *European Labour Force Survey 1999*. Luxembourg: Office for Official Publications of the European Communities.

Eurostat 2000b: Low wage employees in EU countries. *Statistics in Focus, Population and Social Conditions*, 11/2000. Luxembourg: Office for Official Publications of the European Communities.

Eurostat 2000c: Net earnings in the European Union 1998. *Statistics in Focus, Population and Social Conditions*, 7/2000. Luxembourg: Office for Official Publications of the European Communities.

Eurostat 2000d: Persistent income poverty and social exclusion in the European Union. *Statistics in Focus, Population and Social Conditions*, 13/2000. Luxembourg: Office for Official Publications of the European Communities.

Eurostat 2000e: *Table of Poverty Distribution According to Household Type and Sex, 1996.* Statistics commissioned by authors, January 2001.

Eurostat 2001a: *The Social Situation in the European Union 2000.* Luxembourg/Brussels: Eurostat/European Commission.

Eurostat 2001b: *The Social Situation in the European Union 2001.* Luxembourg/Brussels: Eurostat/European Commission.

Feder Kittay, E. 2001: From welfare to a public ethic of care. In N. Hirschmann and U. Liebert (eds), *Women and Welfare Theory and Practice in the United States and Europe,* New Brunswick, NJ: Rutgers University Press, 38–64.

Ferrera, M. 1996: The Southern model of welfare in social Europe. *Journal of European Social Policy,* 6 (1), 17–37.

Finch, J. and Groves, D. (eds) 1983: *A Labour of Love: Women, Work and Caring.* London: Routledge and Kegan Paul.

Folbre, N. 1994: Children as public goods. *American Economic Review,* 84 (2), 86–90.

Fraser, N. 1989: *Unruly Practices: Power, Discourse and Gender in Contemporary Social Theory.* Cambridge: Polity.

Fraser, N. 1997: After the family wage: a postindustrial thought experiment. In B. Hobson and A. M. Berggren (eds), *Crossing Borders: Gender and Citizenship in Transition,* Stockholm: Swedish Council for Planning and Coordination, 21–55.

Furniss, N. and Tilton, T. 1977: *The Case for the Welfare State: From Social Security to Social Equality.* Bloomington, IN, and London: Indiana University Press.

Gardiner, K. 1993: *A Survey of Income Inequality Over the Last Twenty Years – How Does the UK Compare?* Welfare State Programme Discussion Paper 100. London: London School of Economics.

Gershuny, J. 2000: *Changing Times: Work and Leisure in Post-industrial Society.* New York: Oxford University Press.

Giddens, A. 1992: *The Transformation of Intimacy: Sexuality, Love and Eroticism in Modern Societies.* Cambridge: Polity.

Ginn, J. and Arber, S. 1992: Towards women's independence: pension systems in three contrasting European welfare states. *Journal of European Social Policy,* 2 (4), 255–77.

Ginn, J., Street, D. and Arber, S. (eds) 2001: *Women, Work and Pensions.* Buckingham: Open University Press.

Ginsburg, N. 1979: *Class, Capital and Social Policy.* London: Macmillan.

Ginsburg, N. 1992: *Divisions of Welfare: A Critical Introduction to Comparative Social Policy.* London: Sage.

Glendinning, C. and McLaughlin, E. 1993: *Paying for Care – Lessons from Europe.* London: HMSO.

Glennerster, H. 1985: *Research Directions on the Future of the Welfare State: A View from Social Administration.* Welfare State Programme Discussion Paper 4. London: London School of Economics.

Glennerster, H. 1995: *British Social Policy since 1945.* Oxford: Blackwell.

Goode, J., Callender, C. and Lister, R. 1998: *Purse or Wallet? Gender Inequalities and Income Distribution within Families*. London: Policy Studies Institute.

Goodin, R., Headey, B., Muffels, R. and Dirven, H. J. 1999: *The Real Worlds of Welfare Capitalism*. Cambridge: Cambridge University Press.

Gordon, D. and Townsend, P. (eds) 2000: *Breadline Europe: The Measurement of Poverty*. Bristol: Policy Press.

Gordon, L. 1990: The new feminist scholarship on the welfare state. In L. Gordon (ed.), *Women, the State and Welfare*, London and Madison, WI: University of Wisconsin Press, 9–35.

Gordon, L. 1994: *Pitied but not Entitled: Single Mothers and the History of Welfare 1890–1935*. New York: Free Press.

Gornick, J. C. 1999: Gender equality in the labour market: women's employment and earnings. In D. Sainsbury (ed.), *Gender and Welfare State Regimes*, Oxford: Oxford University Press, 210–42.

Gornick, J. C., Myers, M. K. and Ross, K. E. 1997: Supporting the employment of mothers: policy variation across fourteen welfare states. *Journal of European Social Policy*, 7 (1), 45–70.

Gough, I. 1979: *The Political Economy of the Welfare State*. London: Macmillan.

Government Offices Sweden 2000: *Highlighting Pay Differentials between Women and Men*. Sweden: Government Offices.

Graham, H. 1983: Caring: a labour of love. In J. Finch and D. Groves (eds), *A Labour of Love: Women, Work and Caring*, London: Routledge and Kegan Paul, 13–30.

Gustafsson, B. 1994: Inter-country and interregional comparisons of inequality and poverty. *Review of Income and Wealth*, 40 (4), 461–4.

Haddad, L. and Kanbur, R. 1990: How serious is the neglect of intrahousehold inequality? *Economic Journal*, 100, 866–81.

Harkness, S. and Waldfogel, J. 1999: *The Family Gap in Pay: Evidence from Seven Industrialised Countries*. Luxembourg Income Study Working Paper no. 219. Luxembourg: LIS.

Hartsock, N. 1998: *The Feminist Standpoint Revisited and Other Essays*. Boulder, CO: Westview Press.

Hernes, H. 1987: Women and the welfare state: the transition from private to public dependence. In A. Showstack Sassoon (ed.), *Women and the State: The Shifting Boundaries of Public and Private*, London: Hutchinson, 72–92.

Hills, J. 1995: *Inquiry into Income and Wealth*; vol. 2: *A Summary of the Evidence*. York: Joseph Rowntree Foundation.

Hills, J. 1998: *Persistent Poverty and Lifetime Inequality: The Evidence*. CASE Report 5. London: Centre for Analysis of Social Exclusion, London School of Economics.

Hobson, B. 1990: No exit, no voice: women's economic dependency and the welfare state. *Acta Sociologica*, 33 (3), 235–50.

Hobson, B. 1994: Solo mothers, social policy regimes and the logics of gender. In D. Sainsbury (ed.), *Gendering Welfare States*, London: Sage, 170–87.

Hutton, S. 1994: Men's and women's incomes: evidence from survey data. *Journal of Social Policy*, 23 (1), 21–40.

Jarvis, S. and Jenkins, S. 1999: Marital splits and income changes: evidence from the British Household Panel Survey. *Population Studies*, 53 (2), 237–54.

Jenkins, S. 1990: Poverty measurement and the within household distribution: agenda for action. *Journal of Social Policy*, 20 (4), 457–83.

Jenson, J. 1997: Who cares? Gender and welfare regimes. *Social Politics*, 4 (2), 182–7.

Jenson, J. and Jacobzone, S. 2000: *Care Allowances for the Frail Elderly and their Impact on Women Care-givers*. Labour Market and Social Policy Occasional Papers no. 41. Paris: OECD.

Johnson, P. A. and Rake, K. 1998: Comparative social policy research in Europe. *Social Policy Review*, vol. 10, London: Social Policy Association, 257–78.

Jonung, C. and Persson, I. 1994: Combining market work and family. In T. Bengtsson (ed.), *Population, Economy and Welfare in Sweden*, Berlin: Springer Verlag, 37–64.

Joshi, H. 1998: The opportunity costs of childbearing: more than mothers' business. *Journal of Population Economics*, 11, 161–83.

Joshi, H. and Davies, H. 1996: The distribution of the costs of childrearing. Paper presented at conference *Il Costo dei Figli: Convegno Internazionale*, Bologna, Italy, September 1996.

Kamerman, S. B. 1991: Child care policies and programs: an international overview. *Journal of Social Issues*, 47 (2), 179–96.

Kangas, O. 1994: The politics of social security: regressions, qualitative comparisons and cluster analysis. In T. Janoski and A. Hicks (eds), *The Comparative Political Economy of the Welfare State*, Cambridge: Cambridge University Press, 346–64.

Korpi, W. 1989: Power, politics and state autonomy in the development of social citizenship: social rights during sickness in eighteen OECD countries since 1930. *American Sociological Review*, 54 (3), 309–28.

Korpi, W. 2000: Faces of inequality: gender, class, and patterns of inequalities in different types of welfare states. *Social Politics*, 7 (2), 127–91.

Korpi, W. and Palme, J. 1998: The paradox of redistribution and strategies of equality: welfare state institutions, inequality and poverty in Western countries. *American Sociological Review*, 63, 661–87.

Koven, S. and Michel, S. 1990: Womanly duties: maternalist policies and the origins of welfare states in France, Germany, Britain, and the United States, 1880–1920. *American Historical Review*, 95 (4), 1076–108.

Laclau, E. and Mouffe, C. 1985: *Hegemony and Socialist Strategy: Towards a Radical Democratic Politics*. London: Verso.

Land, H. 1978: Who cares for the family? *Journal of Social Policy*, 7 (3), 257–84.

Land, H. 1989: The construction of dependency. In M. Bulmer, J. Lewis and D. Piachaud (eds), *The Goals of Social Policy*, London: Unwin Hyman, 141–59.

Le Grand, J. 1982: *The Strategy of Equality*. London: Allen and Unwin.

Leibfried, S. 1990: Income transfers and poverty in EC perspective: on Europe's slipping into Anglo-American welfare models. Paper presented at EC seminar *Poverty, Marginalisation and Social Exclusion in the Europe of the '90s*, Alghero, Italy, 23–5 April.

Leibfried, S., Leisering, L., Buhr, P., Ludwig, M., Maedje, E., Olk, T., Voges, W. and Zwick, M. 1995: *Zeit der Armut: Lebensläufe im Sozialstaat*. Frankfurt am Main: Suhrkamp.

Leira, A. 1992: *Welfare States and Working Mothers*. Cambridge: Cambridge University Press.

Leira, A. 1993: Concepts of care: loving, thinking and doing. In J. Twigg (ed.), *Informal Care in Europe*, York: University of York, SPRU, 23–39.

Leisering, L. and Leibfried, S. 1999: *Time and Poverty in Western Welfare States*. Cambridge: Cambridge University Press.

Leisering, L. and Walker, R. (eds) 1998: *The Dynamics of Modern Society*. Bristol: Policy Press.

Lewis, G., Gewirtz, S. and Clarke, J. (eds) 2000: *Rethinking Social Policy*. Milton Keynes: Open University Press.

Lewis, J. 1992: Gender and the development of welfare regimes. *Journal of European Social Policy*, 2 (3), 159–73.

Lewis, J. 1994: Gender, the family and women's agency in the building of 'welfare states': the British case. *Social History*, 19 (1), 37–55.

Lewis, J. 1997a: Gender and welfare regimes: further thoughts. *Social Politics*, 4 (2), 160–77.

Lewis, J. (ed.) 1997b: *Lone Mothers in European Welfare Regimes: Shifting Policy Logics*. London and Philadelphia: J. Kingsley Publishers.

Lipsky, M. 1980: *Street-Level Bureaucracy: Dilemmas of the Individual in Public Services*. New York: Russell Sage Foundation.

Lister, R. 1992: *Women's Economic Dependency and Social Security*. Research Discussion Series, no. 2. Manchester: Equal Opportunities Commission.

Lister, R. 1994: 'She has other duties' – women, citizenship and social security. In S. Baldwin and J. Falkingham (eds), *Social Security and Social Change: New Challenges to the Beveridge Model*, Hemel Hempstead: Harvester Wheatsheaf, 31–44.

Lister, R. 1997: *Citizenship: Feminist Perspectives*. Basingstoke: Macmillan.

Lundberg, S., Pollack, R. A. and Wales, T. 1996: Do husbands and wives pool their resources? Evidence from the United Kingdom child benefit. *Journal of Human Resources*, 32 (3), 463–80.

Mabbett, D. and Bolderson, H. 1999: Theories and methods in comparative social policy. In J. Clasen (ed.), *Comparative Social Policy: Concepts, Theories and Methods*, Oxford: Blackwell, 34–57.

Marshall, T. H. 1950: *Citizenship and Social Class and Other Essays*. Cambridge: Cambridge University Press.

Marshall, T. H. 1964: *Class, Citizenship and Social Development*. Chicago and London: University of Chicago Press.

McIntosh, M. 1978: The state and the oppression of women. In A. Kuhn and R. M. Wolpe (eds), *Feminism and Materialism*, London: Routledge and Kegan Paul, 254–89.

McLaughlin, E. and Glendinning, C. 1994: Paying for care in Europe: is there a feminist approach? In L. Hantrais and S. Mangan (eds), *Family Policy and the Welfare of Women*, Loughborough: Cross-National Research Group, European Research Centre, Cross-National Research Papers, 3rd ser., 52–69.

Mink, G. 1995: *The Wages of Motherhood: Inequality in the Welfare State 1917–1942*. Ithaca, NY: Cornell University Press.

Mitchell, D. 1991: *Income Transfers in Ten Welfare States*. Aldershot: Avebury.

Mósesdóttir, L. 1995: The state and the egalitarian, ecclesiastical and liberal regimes of gender relations. *British Journal of Sociology*, 46 (4), 623–42.

Mósesdóttir, L. 2001: *The Interplay between Gender, Markets and the State in Sweden, Germany and the United States*. Aldershot: Ashgate.

Moss, P. 2001: Training of early childhood education and care staff. *International Journal of Educational Research*, 33 (1), 31–53.

Murray, C. 1984: *Losing Ground: American Social Policy, 1950–1980*. New York: Basic Books.

Murray, C. 1996: *Charles Murray and the Underclass: The Developing Debate*. London: Institute for Economic Affairs.

Nelson, B. 1990: The origins of the two-channel welfare state. In L. Gordon (ed.), *Women, the State and Welfare*, Madison, WI: University of Wisconsin Press, 123–51.

Niskanen, W. A. 1971: *Bureaucracy and Representative Government*. Chicago: Aldine.

O'Connor, J. 1973: *The Fiscal Crisis of the State*. New York: St Martin's Press.

O'Connor, J. S. 1988: Convergence or divergence? Change in welfare effort in OECD countries, 1960–1980. *European Journal of Political Research*, 16, 277–99.

O'Connor, J. S. 1992: Citizenship, class, gender and the labour market: issues of de-commodification and personal autonomy. Paper presented at conference *Comparative Studies of Welfare State Development: Quantitative and Qualitative Dimensions*, University of Bremen, 3–6 September.

O'Connor, J. S., Orloff, A. S. and Shaver, S. 1999: *States, Markets, Families: Gender, Liberalism and Social Policy in Australia, Canada, Great Britain and the United States*. Cambridge: Cambridge University Press.

O'Donnell, R. 1998: *Ireland's Economic Transformation: Industrial Policy, European Integration and Social Partnership*. Working Paper no. 2. University of Pittsburgh: Center for West European Studies.

OECD 1998: *The Future of Female-Dominated Occupations*. Paris: OECD.

OECD 2000: *Employment Outlook*. Paris: OECD.

OECD 2001a: *Employment Outlook*. Paris: OECD.

OECD 2001b: *OECD Public Management Service*. Paris: OECD.

OECD 2001c: *Starting Strong: Early Childhood Education and Care.* Paris: OECD.

Offe, C. 1984: *Contradictions of the Welfare State.* London: Hutchinson.

Offen, K. 1992: Defining feminism: a comparative historical approach. In G. Bock and S. James (eds), *Beyond Equality and Difference: Citizenship, Feminist Politics and Female Subjectivity,* London: Routledge, 69–88.

Okin, S. M. 1979: *Women in Western Political Thought.* Princeton, NJ: Princeton University Press.

Orloff, A. S. 1993: Gender and the social rights of citizenship: the comparative analysis of gender relations and welfare states. *American Sociological Review,* 58 (3), 303–28.

Orloff, A. S. 1997: Comment on Jane Lewis's 'Gender and welfare regimes: Further thoughts'. *Social Politics,* 4 (2), 188–202.

Palier, B. 1997: A 'liberal' dynamic in the transformation of the French welfare system. In J. Clasen (ed.), *Social Insurance in Europe,* Bristol: Policy Press, 84–106.

Pampel, F. C. and Williamson, J. B. 1988: Welfare spending in advanced industrial democracies, 1950–1980. *American Journal of Sociology,* 93 (6), 1424–56.

Pateman, C. 1988: The patriarchal welfare state. In A. Gutman (ed.), *Democracy and the Welfare State,* Princeton, NJ: Princeton University Press, 231–60.

Paugam, S. 1996: *A New Social Contract? Poverty and Social Exclusion: A Sociological View.* EUI Working Paper RSC No. 96/37. Florence: Robert Schuman Centre, European University Institute.

Peattie, L. and Rein, M. 1983: *Women's Claims: A Study in Political Economy.* Oxford: Oxford University Press.

Phillips, A. 1998: Democracy and representation; or, why should it matter who our representatives are? In A. Phillips (ed.), *Feminism and Politics,* Oxford: Oxford University Press, 224–40.

Phipps, S. and Burton, P. 1998: What's mine is yours? The influence of male and female incomes on patterns of household expenditure. *Economica,* 65, 599–615.

Pierson, C. 1991: *Beyond the Welfare State? The New Political Economy of Welfare.* Cambridge: Polity.

Pierson, P. 1994: *Dismantling the Welfare State? Reagan, Thatcher and the Politics of Retrenchment.* Cambridge: Cambridge University Press.

Piven, F. F. and Cloward, R. A. 1972: *Regulating the Poor: The Functions of Public Welfare.* London: Tavistock Publications.

Pringle, R. and Watson, S. 1992: Women's interests and the post-structuralist state. In M. Barrett and A. Phillips (eds), *Destabilising Theory,* Cambridge: Polity, 53–73.

Ragin, C. 1987: *The Comparative Method: Moving beyond Qualitative and Quantitative Strategies.* Berkeley: University of California Press.

Ragin, C. and Zaret, D. 1983: Theory and method in comparative research: two strategies. *Social Forces,* 61 (3), 731–49.

Rake, K. 1999: Accumulated disadvantage? Welfare state provision and the incomes of older women and men in Britain, France and Germany. In J. Clasen (ed.), *Comparative Social Policy: Concepts, Theories and Methods*, Oxford: Blackwell, 220–45.

Rake, K. (ed.) 2000: *Women's Incomes over the Lifetime: A Report to the Women's Unit, Cabinet Office*. London: The Stationery Office.

Rake, K. 2001: Gender and New Labour's Social policies. *Journal of Social Policy*, 30 (20), 209–31.

Rosanvallon, P. 1995: *La Nouvelle Question Sociale. Repenser L'État Providence*. Paris: Seuil.

Ruane, F. P. and Sutherland, J. M. 1999: *Women in the Labour Force*. Dublin: Employment Equality Agency.

Rubery, J., Smith, M., Fagan, C. and Grimshaw, D. 1999: *Women's Employment in Europe*. London: Routledge.

Ruspini, E. 1997: Gender differences in poverty and its duration: an analysis of Germany and Great Britain. *Vierteljahrshefte zur Wirtschaftsforschung*, 66 (1), 87–91.

Ruspini, E. 1999: *Lone Mothers and Poverty in Italy, Germany and Great Britain: Evidence from Panel Data*. Working Paper no. 99–10. Colchester: University of Essex.

Sainsbury, D. 1996: *Gender, Equality and Welfare States*. Cambridge: Cambridge University Press.

Sainsbury, D. (ed.) 1999: *Gender and Welfare State Regimes*. Oxford: Oxford University Press.

Scheiwe, K. 1993: *Männerzeiten und Frauenzeiten im Recht*. Berlin: Duncker und Humblot.

Sen, A. 1990: Gender and cooperative conflicts. In I. Tinker (ed.), *Persistent Inequalities*, New York: Oxford University Press, 123–49.

Sevenhuijsen, S. 2000: Caring in the third way: the relation between obligation, responsibility and care in *Third Way* discourse. *Critical Social Policy*, 20 (1), 5–37.

Shalev, M. 1983: The social democratic model and beyond: two 'generations' of comparative research. *Comparative Social Research*, 6, 315–51.

Shaver, S. 1991: Gender, class and the welfare state: the case of income security in Australia. In M. Adler, C. Bell and A. Sinfield (eds), *The Sociology of Social Security*, Edinburgh: Edinburgh University Press, 145–63.

Shaver, S. and Bradshaw, J. 1995: The recognition of wifely labour by welfare states. *Social Policy and Administration*, 29, 10–25.

Showstack Sassoon, A. 1987: Women's new social role: contradictions of the welfare state. In A. Showstack Sassoon (ed.), *Women and the State: The Shifting Boundaries of Public and Private*, London: Hutchinson, 158–88.

Siaroff, A. 1994: Work, welfare and gender equality: a new typology. In D. Sainsbury (ed.), *Gendering Welfare States*, London: Sage, 82–100.

Siim, B. 2000: *Gender and Citizenship: Politics and Agency in France, Britain and Denmark*. Cambridge: Cambridge University Press.

Skjeie, H. 1991: The rhetoric of difference: on women's inclusion into political elites. *Politics and Society*, 2, 233–63.

Skocpol, T. 1992: *Protecting Soldiers and Mothers: The Political Origins of Social Policy in the United States*. Cambridge, MA: The Belknap Press of Harvard University Press.

Smeeding, T., Ross, K., England, P., Christopher, K. and McLanahan, S. 1999: *Poverty and Parenthood across Modern Nations: Findings from the Luxembourg Income Study*. Luxembourg Income Study Working Paper no. 194. Luxembourg: LIS.

Sørensen, A. and McLanahan, S. 1987: Married women's economic dependency, 1940–1980. *American Journal of Sociology*, 93 (3), 659–87.

Sørensen, A. and McLanahan, S. 1989: Women's economic dependency and men's support obligations: economic relations within households. Paper presented at colloquium *Gender and Class*, University of Antwerp, Belgium, 18–20 September.

Stephens, J. 1979: *The Transition from Capitalism to Socialism*. London: Macmillan.

Stewart, K. 2002: *Measuring Well-Being and Exclusion in Europe's Regions*. CASE Paper 53. London: Centre for Analysis of Social Exclusion, London School of Economics.

Sutherland, H. 1997: Women, men and the redistribution of income. *Fiscal Studies*, 18 (1), 1–22.

Sykes, R., Palier, B. and Prior, P. M. (eds) 2001: *Globalization and European Welfare States: Challenges and Change*. Basingstoke: Palgrave.

Tawney, R. H. 1931: *Equality*, 2nd edn. London: Allen and Unwin.

Taylor-Gooby, P. 1996: Eurosclerosis in European welfare states: regime theory and the dynamics of change. *Policy and Politics*, 24 (2), 109–23.

Taylor-Gooby, P. and Svallfors, S. (eds) 1999: *The End of the Welfare State?: Responses to State Retrenchment*. New York: Routledge.

Therborn, G. 1993: Beyond the lonely nation-state. In F. Castles, (ed.), *Families of Nations*, Aldershot: Dartmouth Publishing Company, 329–40.

Thomas, D. 1990: Intra-household resource allocation: an inferential approach. *Journal of Human Resources*, 25 (4), 635–64.

Titmuss, R. 1974: *Social Policy: An Introduction*. London: Allen and Unwin.

Townsend, P. 1979: *Poverty in the United Kingdom*. Harmondsworth: Penguin.

Trifiletti, R. 1995: Family obligations in Italy. In J. Millar and A. Warman (eds), *Defining Family Obligations in Europe*, University of Bath Social Policy Paper no. 23, Bath: University of Bath, 177–205.

Trifiletti, R. 1998: Restructuring social care in Italy. In J. Lewis (ed.), *Gender and the Restructuring of Social Care in Europe*, Aldershot: Ashgate, 175–206.

Ungerson, C. 1995: Gender, cash and informal care: European perspectives and dilemmas. *Journal of Social Policy*, 24 (1), 31–52.

Uusitalo, H. 1984: Comparative research on the determinants of the welfare state: the state of the art. *European Journal of Political Research*, 12, 403–22.

Van Oorschot, W. 1998: From solidarity to selectivity: the reconstruction of the Dutch social security system 1980–2000. In E. Brunsdon, H. Dean and R. Woods (eds), *Social Policy Review 10*, London: Social Policy Association, 183–202.

Vleminckx, K. and Smeeding, T. (eds) 2000: *Child Well-Being, Child Poverty and Child Policy in Modern Nations: What Do We Know?* Bristol: Policy Press.

Whitebook, M., Howes, C. and Phillips, D. 1990: *The National Child Care Staffing Study: Who Cares? Child Care Teachers and the Quality of Childcare in America*. Oakland, CA: Child Care Employee Project.

Wilensky, H. 1975: *The Welfare State and Equality: Structural and Ideological Roots of Public Expenditures*. Berkeley: University of California Press.

Wilensky, H. 1982: Leftism, Catholicism and democratic corporatism: the role of parties in recent welfare state development. In P. Flora and A. J. Heidenheimer (eds), *The Development of Welfare States in Europe and America*, New Brunswick, NJ: Transaction Publishers, 345–82.

Wilensky, H. and Lebeaux, C. 1965: *Industrial Society and Social Welfare*. New York: Free Press.

Wilensky, H., Luebbert, G., Hahn, S. and Jamieson, A. 1987: Comparative social policy: theories, methods, findings. In M. Dierkes, H. Weiler and A. B. Antal (eds), *Comparative Policy Research: Learning from Experience*, Aldershot: WZB/Gower, 381–457.

Williams, F. 1989: *Social Policy: A Critical Introduction*. Cambridge: Polity.

Williams, F. 1995: Race/ethnicity, gender and class in welfare states: a framework for comparative analysis. *Social Politics*, 2 (2), 127–59.

Wilson, E. 1977: *Women and the Welfare State*. London: Tavistock.

Yeates, N. 2001: *Globalization and Social Policy*. London: Sage.

Index